DATE DUE

our children.—
our responsibilities

BLACK STUDIES
& critical thinking

Rochelle Brock and Richard Greggory Johnson III
Executive Editors

Vol. 13

The Black Studies and Critical Thinking series
is part of the Peter Lang Education list.
Every volume is peer reviewed and meets
the highest quality standards for content and production.

PETER LANG
New York • Washington, D.C./Baltimore • Bern
Frankfurt • Berlin • Brussels • Vienna • Oxford

CHRISTOPHER ANNE ROBINSON-EASLEY

our children.—
our respon,sibilities

Saving the Youth We Are Losing to Gangs

PETER LANG
New York • Washington, D.C./Baltimore • Bern
Frankfurt • Berlin • Brussels • Vienna • Oxford

Library of Congress Cataloging-in-Publication Data
Robinson-Easley, Christopher Anne.
Our children, our responsibilities: saving the youth we are losing to gangs /
Christopher Anne Robinson-Easley.
p. cm. — (Black studies and critical thinking; v. 13)
Includes bibliographical references and index.
1. Gangs—United States. 2. African American youth. I. Title.
HV6432.R62   364.106'60973—dc23   2011046962
ISBN 978-1-4331-1200-3 (hardcover)
ISBN 978-1-4331-1199-0 (paperback)
ISBN 978-1-4539-0265-3 (e-book)
ISSN 1947-5985

Bibliographic information published by **Die Deutsche Nationalbibliothek**.
Die Deutsche Nationalbibliothek lists this publication in the "Deutsche
Nationalbibliografie"; detailed bibliographic data is available
on the Internet at http://dnb.d-nb.de/.

The paper in this book meets the guidelines for permanence and durability
of the Committee on Production Guidelines for Book Longevity
of the Council of Library Resources.

© 2012 Peter Lang Publishing, Inc., New York
29 Broadway, 18th floor, New York, NY 10006
www.peterlang.com

Printed in the United States of America

CONTENTS

Acknowledgments   vii
Preface   ix

Introduction   1

Part One: The Context, Issues, and Mindset
Chapter 1. My Lens, Perspectives and Context: Yet a Collective Set
        of Challenges   11
Chapter 2. Owning the Problem: The Bigger Picture Beyond the
        Context of Our Personal Walls   33
Chapter 3. Linkages to Youth Violence: Twenty-First-Century
        Challenges in the African American Community   41
Chapter 4. Losing this Battle Is Not an Option: What the Real Loss
        of Our Children Means to the African
        American Community   67

Part Two: A Historical Look at My 1999 Results
Chapter 5. The Issues from the Lens of a Child   75
Chapter 6. Keeping It Real: If It Is Going to Change, and Our Youth
        Are to Be Saved, We Have to Do It   87

Chapter 7. Breaking the Chains of Our Spiritual, Mental and Physical
            Fatigue: The Role of Appreciative Inquiry in the
            Fight to Save Our Youth   101

Part Three: A 2011 Perspective
Chapter 8. The Role of Appreciative Inquiry in the Fight to Save
            Our Youth   123
Chapter 9. Critical Foundations and Constructs of Change   137
Chapter 10. The Model for Change   163

Part Four: Final Thoughts
Chapter 11. Celebrating Our Success: Appreciating Our Efforts,
            Youth, and Future   193
Chapter 12. The Global Application of This Model   197
Chapter 13. Reflections and Concluding Comments   201

Notes   207
Bibliography   209
Index   217

ACKNOWLEDGMENTS

First and foremost, I want to give thanks to God for carrying me as I have walked this journey. I began exploring the topic of youth gangs when I started my doctoral program in organization development. As I conducted my dissertation, I felt God's hand guiding me every step of the way. There was a story that needed to be told, but I also realized that my journey with respect to this topic was not over when I finished my doctoral program. So, here I sit, twelve years later, writing about what I learned during that time and over the last twelve years, which has taken my understanding of this topic to a very different level.

Spiritually inspired, I dedicate this book to my family: my late husband, Jodie, who never wavered in his support of any and all of my initiatives; my children, Caitlin and Jodie; and my late mother, Helen Robinson. From my two children, I have learned so much. It is quite inspiring when generations share and learn from one another, not just in the parent-child modality but as human beings teaching and sharing their truths. A child, in so many ways, is truly God's gift.

I will always be eternally grateful to the many people who have walked by my side, encouraged me, opened doors, read drafts, or just sat with me in dialogue as I traveled a road of challenge as well as opportunity while doing this work. Through God's grace and mercy, the list of people is very long. However, I want to give a special thank you to the faculties at Benedictine University in the doctoral program in organization development for their unwavering support during my doctoral program as I made the choice to write a dissertation that stepped outside the norm, and at Chicago Theological Seminary for challenging my paradigmatic perspectives as I grew in my theology and spirituality.

I also want to thank my home university, Governors State University, for granting me my sabbatical and requested leaves of absence to complete this project. And, I cannot leave out colleagues and friends, Drs. E. Renee Garrick and Sharon Latiker, and Ms. Valerie Washington (in concert with the staff at the National Black Catholic Congress), who opened both doors and their hearts, providing me with immeasurable resources, opportunity, and support during this journey. I also give thanks to my pastor, Reverend Dr. Ozzie E. Smith, at Covenant United Church of Christ. It never failed that when I had nagging doubts, God always inspired in Rev. Ozzie a sermon that illuminated the next steps of my path.

A very special thank you goes to Mrs. Dortha Brown for her support, encouragement, time and commitment to read as I wrote. When I had doubts, she was always a voice of encouragement.

Equally important, I want to thank Dr. Richard Greggory Johnson III for encouraging me to write the prospectus that enabled the publication of this book and for his unwavering support as my editor and colleague as we have collaborated on this and other projects that are critical to the African American community. Most people do not recognize the challenges faculties of color endure when we write about issues that are germane to our community. Richard has been a beacon of light for me as well as others as we step out on faith and address critical topics to the African American community with a fearless determination to speak and live our truth.

PREFACE

When I first began writing about youth gravitating to gangs while completing my doctoral degree in organization development, my focus was initially similar to those of other colleagues that have written about youth violence and gangs throughout the years. However, as I traveled my journey, I also began to understand and witness that we cannot look at the issues of youth gravitating to gangs and the resulting violence from a silo mentality. The issues are complex and they begin with us . . . the adults in the lives of our children, in concert with the complex problems we face within our communities.

After completing my degree, I began to work extensively in the African American community on projects that focused on driving change. I soon learned, however, that no matter how sophisticated a change design was, until we began to have conversations that addressed the hurt we, as African Americans, feel, there would be no sustaining change.

I also became more frustrated as I continued to read books and articles that addressed issues within the African American community. It seemed that they addressed only the issues and not solutions—solutions that would have well-defined roadmaps for evoking change. While some authors might begin a change-oriented conversation, the roadmap was typically very ambiguous and left you wanting more.

I understood that the frustration I felt was caused by my bias as a trained professional in change management. And I also understood the complexity of my experiences and resulting lessons were significantly "impacting" my viewpoints. Six years following the completion of my doctoral dissertation, I began seminary. My experiences working in the "field" helped me to understand that until I learned to touch and impact the hearts and souls of people who deal with oppression and hurt every day of their lives, the most sophisticated change design in the world would not make a difference in helping people envision the change they need and, most important, are entitled to.

The Structure of This Book

As you read, you will see the evidence of my journey from a very upfront and personal perspective. I intentionally insert myself into the conversation of how to evoke change in the African American community, a change that is focused on ameliorating the issues driving our youth to levels of gang violence that defies that which we have historically witnessed. My first-person perspectives are very pronounced in this book, and I don't shy away from my lens as a woman of color.

Yet, as a trained academic and scholar, I also utilized third person to provide an overview of context, history, and analysis that is designed to juxtapose that which we can become to that which we have endured for far too many years.

I also have taken the liberty of inserting into this conversation my seminary training and perspectives of theologians from a range of backgrounds. Our hearts and souls have to heal, and I have learned, via my work in the African American community, that grounding ourselves in a theological context not only provides us with a venue to gather where many of us already congregate but, most important, also provides us with a place that is healing and spiritually grounded. Consequently, my model for change begins in the Black church, which is designed to serve as our nexus: our place of healing, training, and teaching as we move through the model that is a starting point for our work.

The last chapters of this book posit a detailed model for evoking change in the African American community. I have grown tired of hearing about the issues. If our situation of dis-empowerment, disenfranchisement, and the loss of our most important gift—our children—is going to change, we have to begin the process for evoking that change. And when I say we, I truly mean it is time for our community to take ownership of our issues.

This model, however, might seem a bit prescriptive. In many respects it is because it represents my learning from my academic training and my work as a management professor in concert with my twenty plus years in the business sector, where I have had the opportunity to witness and understand why change processes fail. Consequently, the details I put into this model serve as safeguards for our success.

Last, in the final chapters I also posit the application of this model, the theories, and praxes discussed throughout the book to a global audience and context. Far too many people across the world hurt from the same or similar issues African Americans face in concert with the fact that there is not an inhabited continent in our world today that is not suffering or grappling with issues of youth violence and gang environments.

So as you read, I respectfully request your patience as well as attention to the multitude of propositions I insert into this book, which is a beginning conversation toward evoking change that we can no longer afford to wait on. Most important, mentally, spiritually, and physically walk with me as I urge our collective gathering to begin the change process. Our children, across the globe, are our future, and we must make a difference in their lives.

INTRODUCTION

"The Child that Fights"
Soul binding
mind cleansing
hold on to the fight . . .
and cry for the child that cries every night
for this child knows pain and can't take it anymore
this child needs a savior to open his door
the key to enlightenment awaits this child, but
the child won't stop crying until his savior comes,
so until then the child will have to hold on to life
but who will cry for that child that cries every night?
—Caitlin A. Easley[1]

Fifteen years ago, I began questioning why so many African American children were joining gangs. I was also puzzled by the level of violence that became second nature to the generation of youth I was investigating. The levels of violence that consumed our children significantly surpassed gang violence when I was growing up. Their views on community and their accountability to their community were also dramatically different: They saw no commitment to community or personal accountability. This disengagement seemed to be grounded in a variety of issues that affected the psychological stability of this particular generation. Over the course of three years, I studied youth in gangs, with a primary focus on African American youth.

After completing my doctoral studies, I continued to research this topic and, interestingly, found that problems of gang violence and the growing numbers of youth gravitating to gangs were not just relegated to the United States. There was not one inhabited continent that did not struggle with youth gangs. As I continued to work in urban African American communities, I found layers upon layers of issues impacting our youth. These issues had deep historical roots, which made isolating their etiology very hard. Yet, I continued to investigate, often finding myself in positions where I had to challenge my own guiding praxes, despite my believing that I had an inside track to the issues because of my race.

The complexities of our global environment strongly suggest that we can no longer rely upon the constancies of our beliefs, theological discourses, philosophies, interpretative schemas, policies, and procedures to govern the constantly changing dynamics of life. Inherent in the concept of change lies the necessity to challenge prevailing belief systems as to how we see the world and individuals situated in the world (Easley & Swain, 2003). The problem of youth gravitating to gang environments and being impacted by gang violence dramatically is not a problem that is situated in a silo concept. It is significantly tied to issues within the broader African American community, which are tied to issues within the global community.

Yet, far too many people continue to view issues and, equally important, outcomes of poverty, power, domination, race, and violence through lens and interpretative schemas that have not changed for years. However, I am drawn to ask how African Americans can look at these issues through a different lens. If we are to save our children, we must view the environment they live in from a very different paradigmatic perspective with change strategies designed and developed to awaken our people and help them envision options for changing the conditions of their lives.

My lens, and theoretical sensitivities and perspectives, emerge from a multidimensional interpretive schema. When understanding the rationale behind the questions and strategies posited in this book, I have continued to privilege my being an African American woman, who comes from a collective African consciousness, a consciousness that bespeaks of a spiritual connection to *all* life and a communal responsibility to the world at large that expands beyond the physical space in which one currently inhabits. Equally important, I believe that when we openly acknowledge our personal qualities and experiences, we concomitantly open space for another level of a consciousness of meaning to enter that can be subtle, yet of significant impact when deconstructing how we create and manage sense and meaning (Pettigrew, 1979). Consequently, when I view African American youth in gangs, I do not see them as subjects. They are children, our children, who for many reasons have lost their way. I also see that finding their way is challenging because of the mired issues that face the African American community.

Yet, I don't lose hope or find the problems overwhelming. As a PhD in organization development, my guiding praxis is to systemically assess and deconstruct situations and identify, develop, and design systemic change strategies that move those situations (e.g., organizations and systems) beyond conversation and toward a desired state. I must also factor in my being a seminarian. The combination of my experiences force me to question how we currently view our options with respect to helping our youth move past the issues that drive them to gangs, while concurrently understanding that overarching their issues is a bigger picture we must address. Are we drowning in a silent hopelessness? Are our spirits depleted to the point that the thought of taking on one more thing drains us? Or, are there options as a collective for ameliorating the conditions that are in reality draining us of our most precious resource, our youth?

We have to save our youth. The gang environment is not their answer, and the resulting violence cannot continue. But we cannot, whether it is in this country or in Australia, South Africa, or the Caribbean (to cite just a few examples), approach the problem from a silo mentality.

People want change, and they want to talk about and through their pain. Dialogue is the starting point for making a difference in our world. But we cannot afford to stop at dialogue, because eventually we only engage in episodic change with an overtone of complaining. Our actions have to be strategic and systemic, working to eradicate the root cause of the multiplicities of problems that give rise to the loss of our youth. It will take only one successful example where people work collectively to eradicate the many issues that face challenged communities across the world to ignite a fire that rapidly spreads across the globe.

The time for deep and systemic change is now. I am optimistic that the change will result in a positive, enriched environment where our youth will not want to gravitate to alternative environments. So I encourage your readership, irrespective of what part of the world you live. The issues of marginalization, dehumanization, dominance, and gang violence have no ethnic, race, or religious limitations. While I use my African American context to drive home critical points and frame our options for change, we have to remember that we are not alone in this world. As we engage in our challenges on a daily basis, we must remember that there are many parents across the globe losing their children to gang violence and gang involvement. This is a global problem in which we all have a critical stake. The children are our future, and without their ability to successfully navigate through the tumultuous water of life, our future will be quite dim.

Last, there is a story within the story. As I carry my own personal sensitivities and lens into the analysis of these issues, they are contextually framed by my own experiences—those that occurred while conducting the research and my experiences after I completed my doctoral degree. I suggest as you read this book to not be afraid to challenge your praxis and ways in which you think about change. This book brings into focus an integrated modality for invoking critical change to challenging issues. I have learned over the years that when we look to make a difference in our world, we have to use multiple lenses to see people on many different levels. But, equally important, the change must begin internally.

Through every step of the journey I have taken that has led me to write this book, I have had to come face-to-face with critical lessons. I have also had to make the choice as to whether or not I wanted to learn those lessons. Despite my having several initials behind my name, the place where I now sit has not been a direct result of just having matriculated through those degree programs. Life, if we choose to allow it, is out greatest teacher, as well as the dealer of very challenging hands. Yet it's a personal choice as to how we play this hand.

Yes, our children are dying at record rates due to violence that does not need to occur. And, yes, as parents, educators, and community leaders, we often sit in frustration. But have you ever looked into the eyes of a parent that lost a child? Violence in concert with loss of hope impact our youth to the point that far too many of them do not see a future in which they will be active participants.

The physical or spiritual death of a child is beyond the concept of overwhelming. Parents lose a major part of their souls when their children are lost. I have never lost a child to gang violence, but I had a close call. My son, while home from college one summer experienced a carjacking where fifteen or more members of a gang shot at him attempting to take my truck. It was only through God's grace and mercy that my son experienced minimal injuries and was able to get away with his life intact. The number of bullets in that vehicle brought my husband and I face-to-face with what could have been another outcome.

To this day I will never forget the call I received notifying us he had been shot. My husband, daughter, and I were waiting for him to pick us up at the airport. Ironically, we were returning from a short vacation before I had to leave for England a couple of days later to present my research on gang violence! Never in my life did I expect to conduct a presentation that had such a realistic perspective attached to what was a traditional academic paper.

When I received the call notifying us our son was shot, I started screaming at the top of my lungs. The reflections I had on that plane ride to London a few days later were more than I could even begin to write about. This situation brought me face-to-face with the realization that no one is safe from the violence that surrounds our communities. It does not matter if you live in an urban, suburban, or rural community. People's lives are being touched by gang violence at levels that have surpassed historical records.

The issues that impact the African American community also cause us to lose our children in other ways as well. As a result, when we address the loss of our children to gang violence, we must concurrently address the issues that reside within our community and, most important, address the concept of community.

At many levels, our children are facing voids in their lives that challenge parents. Parents need the support of their community. We talk about taking a village to raise a child, but I don't see many villages. Yet, collectively we need each other, particularly if you are a single parent raising a child or children.

My understanding the dark hopeless feelings that touch the depth of our souls when we begin to lose our children and the issues that go along with being a single parent began with the death of my husband several years after I finished my doctoral program. I will talk more about my own personal journey throughout the book as I try to tie together my experiences with the issues I see so that others can relate, but for now, I want to set the context of one of the more critical journeys I have embarked upon that impacts my lens.

My husband's death from a massive heart attack was sudden and was not precipitated by a history of illness or disorders. So, needless to say, the shock was more than intense. We had always worked as a team in parenting our two children. However, on the flip side we were only children, which in many ways caused us to cling to each other even more so than a family with siblings. While we had a strong extended family network, they had their own lives. My daughter was entering high school when he died. In fact, she was scheduled to begin a week after his funeral services. She was Daddy's little girl, and the loss of her father took her to levels of grief that I am sure few can relate to. That is not to say my son and I weren't experiencing our own intense pain, but the relationship between a daughter and her father is different—similar to the difference in relationship between a son and his mother.

I tried varying forms of counseling to help her: pastoral, psychological, and so forth. But after the death of her father, she embarked on a path that was nothing more than self-destructive to both of us. As she walked that path, it pushed me into a hell I never thought could exist. Yet, because of my work and reputation, I believed I could not allow the pain I felt day in and out to be seen. Three years into enduring this pain and watching my daughter die her spiritual death, she and I finally agreed for her to go to a boarding school where she would finish high school while going through daily counseling.

At this point, I want to say, I was one of the lucky ones. This school cost me close to $7,000 per month over and above my monthly bills, and that did not include her medical bills because there was no reciprocity between my insurance company and the state in which she resided for close to a year. At the "tender age" of 53, I would travel on weekends more than 1,000 miles to parent-teacher meetings, basketball games, and other school activities to give her support. The travel itself almost physically broke me, but again, I could not allow that vulnerability to be seen. Each time I traveled to her school, I cried all the way home, which consisted of a six-hour plane trip and a three-hour drive from her school just to get to the airport. I had no one to travel with me, since my son was completing his last year of college and no family or friends who really understood what I was experiencing. I was fortunate to have a friend that stayed in constant contact during my travels because of his fear for my safety, but beyond that I never felt more alone.

While this child did not experience a bullet, she was still facing a death just as bad—the spiritual death when life deals you a blow at a tender age that you psychologically cannot handle.

Over the course of years of working in African American communities I have heard many stories from young people where they too have experienced their own spiritual deaths, unfortunately without the support system needed to get them through their ordeals. But through all of this, I have learned one of life's most valuable lessons:

Never, ever give up on a child!

Seven years later, my daughter is moving forward positively with her life. And I survived this ordeal and am much wiser and stronger. However, I am also cognizant that because of my resources I had a way out that other parents may not have, which is why our moving back toward the era of community those in my age bracket surely remember is critical to the survival of our children. What a parent feels when they know they are losing a child and they do not know what to do is almost as painful a loss as it is when your child takes a bullet.

We have to work together in community in order to provide infrastructures of support to one another. We cannot continue to operate from a silo mentality. Our world is too complex for individuals to work through life alone.

Travel with me as I weave together the many issues we have to address. But please do not lose me as I walk through our options. We must move beyond simply talking about our issues. We can evoke change in our community and with our youth. We have to do this, and we must do it in community.

Our youth are too precious to lose!

PART ONE
THE CONTEXT, ISSUES, AND MINDSET

· 1 ·

MY LENS, PERSPECTIVES, AND CONTEXT: YET A COLLECTIVE SET OF CHALLENGES

I have written the introductory paragraphs to this book more times than I care to admit and was never happy with the results. I was trying to be politically correct with my wording, yet my reality check is that there is no polite way to say that the African American community is in a state of crisis—a crisis that continues to grow at exponential levels. Center stage in this crisis is the disproportionate number of African American children dying due to gang violence. Yet the question remains what are we doing to ameliorate the death toll of our children?

As I have worked in various African American communities, I have learned that we cannot look at our issues from a silo perspective—a point I will continue to emphasis throughout this book. The loss of a child is a great loss to our community. However, the reasons we lose our children to many forms of violence, which includes gang violence, evolve from reasons beyond a silo focus. Our community has been in crisis for years, and we severely lack strong leadership. Our vision for change is fragmented, and oftentimes we don't claim our rightful place in the country that we helped build. Our children do not have consistent examples of positive role models to follow, and our lives are so busy, we do not have the time to give them what they need.

Yet each of these issues systemically is tied to a bigger overarching problem that we have to acknowledge. We will never be able to change the lives of our youth, until we take on the responsibility to deeply change our own lives and the status of our communities. The stakes are too high for us to choose to continue in either fragmented or no activity. A child is precious and a gift God has given to us. Gang violence is not new; neither are the issues that historically birthed gang activity ours to claim. Simply stated, the first gangs in this country did not originate in our communities. However, similar to many other dysfunctional institutions, we have absorbed the negativities associated with this one and have successfully taken them to a new level.

I am not attempting to explain away or identify strategies focused on eradicating gangs. That is not the focus of this book. I address the reasons why our youth feel the need to gravitate to gangs, which inevitably results in negative outcomes. Most important, my focus is to begin the conversation as to how we can holistically begin ameliorating the death tolls of our youth.

Our youth must have role models, mentors, and family as well as community members who are committed to spending time with them in order to help them change their lives. To effectively do this, however, requires our immediately ceasing and desisting activities that continue the demise of community. We have to move toward effectively caring for one another coupled with actions oriented toward accountability. In doing so, we must concomitantly reclaim our heritage, culture, and theology. I intentionally am not using the word *religion* because religion is an individual preference. But to know our strength means we must understand our strong cosmology and theological roots.

Because I am a change-oriented person, I am not going to simply write a book that reiterates our problems. I do, however, frame the problems so that we can begin to understand how to weave our present social context from a new lens that will help us understand how to view the loss of our children from a perspective where the issues tie together. I also suggest a model for change. But we will have to make a conscious decision to invoke the model, which requires coordination, hard work, accountability, and a bias for action with concrete measurable results.

We do not have a choice but to engage in this higher level of integrated thought and action. The central topic at hand—the loss of our youth to gang violence—has reached levels that make it impossible for us to walk away from a plausible solution. I will never suggest my model cannot use refinement or modification. It serves as a beginning praxis for starting a concerted whole systems action plan that is aimed toward strategic and systemic change. And, as we are taught in management theory, particularly from a quality focus, one should always be willing to evaluate, refine, implement, and keep on refining until the process yields the desired results.

The Beginning

I began researching youth gangs in 1996, research that resulted in my doctoral dissertation titled *The Role of Appreciative Inquiry in the Fight to Save Our Youth*. The major focus of my research at that time was the examination of an alternative strategy for helping youth who had gravitated to gangs. Consequently, the focus of my research centered on examining the effectiveness of an organization development strategy called Appreciative Inquiry.[1]

During the course of that research, and the subsequent research and work I did examining the growth of youth gangs on an international level, I continued to ask why we engage in the same strategies to address a problem that continues to grow exponentially. We consistently examine the growth of youth gangs as a situation rooted in the plight and despair of joblessness, economic challenges, and so forth. However, I do not believe that these are the appropriate answers for the African American community. Yes, we face significant economic issues, and yes, we continue to be presented with trials that challenge even the strongest human spirit. We have to move past acknowledging those challenges and delve deep into our consciousness as to why WE have not stopped the bleeding.

> When people lack a critical understanding of their reality, apprehending it in fragments which do not perceive as interacting constituent elements of the whole, they cannot truly know that reality. To truly know it, they would have to reverse their starting point: they would need to have a total vision of the context in order subsequently to separate and isolate its constituent elements and by means of this analysis achieve a clearer perception of the whole. (Freire, 2006, p. 104)

While the results of my research suggested that Appreciative Inquiry could be a very viable alternative for removing youth from gang environments, I have also learned over the course of the years since I completed my doctoral degree that deep strategic and systemic change within the African American community has to result from a deep, reflective, and reflexive understanding of what is really going on in the community and how these actions are driving our youth to gravitate to gangs. We have to move past our propensity to react when there is a current crisis. And we have to have a plan that addresses all of the intricate issues that give rise to youth consciously walking into alternative environments.

Since completing my doctoral research in 1999, I have worked in African American communities designing and leading whole systems change processes. One of my biggest challenges was helping people understand what comprises systemic and strategic change and how it differs from episodic strategies and the listing of tactical steps—actions that are very comfortable for us. We talk about what we should be doing, we sometimes march, and our religious leaders often hold well-intentioned vigils. If the death toll becomes severe enough, for a moment we will engage activists who then engage or confront city or state officials. Yet, long term, the problem does not change, and after a while we go back to business as usual.

Over the years, I have also learned that youth in gangs are affected by many external influences that are typically out of their control. As the adults in their lives, we have to be real about how broken the systems are that they look to for support. In most urban environments, the school systems are in deplorable condition due to overcrowding, extensive budget cuts, teachers who are ill-trained to deal with multiple learning styles, and all the classic "isms." As a community we fail to connect with our neighbors. Yet I can distinctly remember when I was growing up that if a child in the neighborhood acted out, that child had to contend not only with the parents but also with the neighbors. When my children were growing up, my neighbor's mother, "Ma Dear," never missed a day sitting in front of the window watching my children get off the bus and safely into the house.

Yet during my research, one student extensively asked me why neighbors no longer engaged with youth in their community. He related the stories his mother shared during the years she was growing up. She told him about how the neighbors would get a switch to spank you if they saw you doing something wrong, and then when you returned home, you typically received another whipping. I had no answers for why communally we seem to be in a disjunctive state.

Let's reexamine what I just conveyed: In conversation with me was this gangbanger asking me why his neighbors no longer cared about the youth in the community. One can argue that perhaps their behaviors are so extreme that people are too afraid to care, but is that a realistic approach when our children face indifference from multiple sources? While we may be afraid to pull out the "switch," however metaphorically we choose to identify that switch in today's environment, we should be asking if our failure to act is a significant contributor to youth violence in our communities.

One of the most significant lessons I learned during my research was that efforts to work with youth gangs alone is not going to improve our challenges. One proposition I concluded in 1999 was that a micro-approach to current intervention strategies may be a contributing factor as to why many of those strategies do not sustain change. While we need to work constantly with youth in gangs on a microlevel, we also have to address change on a macrolevel in order to sustain the change. The data the young people in my study generated clearly spoke to how youth in gangs are affected by many external influences over and beyond their families, such as peers, their school, community constituents, and images and language they hear and see in the media. Consequently, simply working with the youth in gangs without the active engagement of the stakeholders and support systems that directly influence and impact their lives will yield marginal results, which we have historically witnessed since the beginning of gang de-activation strategies.

As we fast forward from 1999 to 2011, in concert with the exponential growth of African American youth gravitating to gangs is the fact that the African American community continues to face some of the most critical challenges we have had since slavery, challenges that defy logic. Yet, these challenges are the results of much more complex problems.

Unfortunately, the complexity of the problems that impact our communities also impact our youth. When people who are critical to the lives and progress of our children are fighting what appears to be losing battles on a daily basis, their spirits and souls are so depleted that there is no way they have much support to provide to a child. They are barely holding up. When the soul and spirit is depleted it is hard to think our way out of situations that seem impenetrable. Consequently, far too many people give in with the attitude that there is not much more I can do. And the unfortunate truth is, from an individualist perspective, there may not be much more one person can do. But if there ever is a concept I want to drive home, it is the fact that strength is in numbers, and unfortunately we have lost the power of our numbers. We have also collectively lost the power of our theology and cosmology. Now, I am not challenging those that believe themselves to be spiritually grounded are indeed grounded, but if we were to reexamine our historical roots, one of the major reasons we survived the atrocities of slavery is that we prayed together, even if it had to be in the wee hours of the night, and in concert with prayer, we worked collectively to develop strategies to deal with the system. In other words, we worked and prayed in community.

Shortly after writing my dissertation, I went to South Carolina because I wanted to further research what helped people get through the roughest period in our history. During the time in which I conducted doctoral research, it appeared to me that, as an African American society at large, we had lost something. I wanted to find that "something," yet returned home with even more disappointment in what I saw.

It was not until I began matriculating through seminary that I understood what that "something" really was. Our ancestors understood who they were and knew the strength of their historical, religious, and cosmological roots. Somewhere down the path as we have walked through our history, we have lost that perspective from a holistic orientation. Yet, in order to move past the "isms" and losses that we encounter, we must regain this strength, which is why the change model I propose will begin in the church.

We have to commit to understand the complexities of our issues and maintain a willingness to engage head-on in change, despite the discomfort of engaging in a reality check. To do so will require an intense support system where we can encourage one another without fear of reprisal. We no longer can, or should, count on others to remediate our situations. Until we identify, understand, and deconstruct the many layers of brokenness we have to work through, which attack the mind, body and spirit, our change efforts will continue to yield minimal results. Our children will continue to kill one another and our race will continue in a downward spiral.

The complexity of issues in the African American community calls for strategies that involve many agents of change from many different socio-economic backgrounds and perspectives. This is not a job just for the elite. An engaged African American community is the only way we will stop the genocide that continues to manifest. It is the only way we can save our children and help them move toward a much more productive path in life that will change the history of Black people in this country. However, we have to understand that change strategies call for our total engagement when we analyze, design, and implement processes necessary to make these strategies work effectively. We have to continue to reiterate that change calls for collective action and not the continuation of fragmented efforts that has been our propensity for far too many years. Equally critical, we have to reexamine our concept of what constitutes effective leadership—a topic I address in this book—and how we cannot allow individuals to assume leadership roles who really do not possess the intellectual capital, heart, or personal vision to make a difference.

In 2009, in the city of Chicago, parents, school officials, community members and leaders, and police officials were shocked at the brutal death of Derrien Albert, an innocent child caught in the middle of a gang fight at Fenger High School. On September 22, 2009, the *Huffington Post* reported that from 2006 to 2009, Chicago experienced a sharp rise in violent student deaths. While the average was 10–15 students before 2006, in 2006 that number rose to 24 fatal shootings. In the 2007–2008 academic year, the numbers were 23 deaths and 211 shootings. By 2008–2009, the numbers had grown to 34 deaths and 290 shootings.

Exacerbating the issue in 2010 was the report (by a lesser mainstream news publication, hiphopwired.com) that two government officials were requesting backup from the National Guard in Chicago due to the continued increase in gang violence, a reaction to the shooting that claimed the life of a 2-year-old girl who was shot in the head after the assailant attempted to shoot her father. And in August 2010, a meeting called by Superintendent of the Chicago Police Department Jody Weis was held with other local and federal law enforcement officials and a few reputed gang members. At this meeting, it was reported that gang members were told to either stop the violence or they would be locked up. Yet the gang leaders questioned the logic of ultimatums versus viable options, such as jobs for people in impoverished neighborhoods (Main, 2010).

Police officials have been delivering ultimatums for years. Gang intervention tactics have not historically changed. In this book, I provide you with an overview of this history and a synopsis of the context in which it lies in order to understand that which we can no longer tolerate. Now you might wonder why I take the time to walk through this history. The answer is simple. We have to understand the history in order to not repeat the past, a past that does not work for us. Others will continue to repeat the past simply because the stakes are not as high for them. As African Americans, we do not have that luxury because the stakes are far too critical for us. We lose the most valuable resources we have: our children.

So, why did I write this book now, years after completing my dissertation? Why in the face of reports that suggest strategies, such as ultimatums provided by law officials, have "worked" in other cities for about 15 years, bringing down homicides in Cincinnati, Boston, and other metropolises do I challenge these guiding praxes by offering a different view and strategy for change (Main, 2010)? Equally important, why did I choose to write this book in a format that does not address just the academy, but is written to address multiple venues and educational levels of an audience?

Stirring the Pot with a Call for Action

I have felt compelled for a while to stir the pot by promoting a conversation within the African American community via my challenging prior praxes and assumptions that have emerged from more than 80 years of research that still yield questionable results. And I have written this book in first-person, where I take comfort in inserting myself into the conversation, from multiple perspectives: that of a researcher, scholar, participant, but equally critical, as a member of the community for whom this book primarily addresses. The continued growth and stability of youth gravitating to gangs, on an international as well as a domestic front, should evoke questions as to why we continue to utilize the same strategies that have historical evidence of neither working nor sustaining change. Inclusively, we have no choice but to incorporate into our understanding of youth violence in the African American community the issues that collectively plague our community as a whole.

We cannot afford to work toward addressing one issue without understanding how the challenges we face work as a system to support the dysfunctional behaviors we have learned to live with. Yet, too many times we do not understand, engage in, or work toward changing systemic problems. Equally devastating, as researchers, we fear coming to grips with understanding that those propositions and theories we have posited in the past no longer work. Over the years I have spent in academia, I have had the opportunity to hear two major international figures whose work spans decades as to where their research is housed, say with humility that they were challenging now all that they once thought. There is nothing wrong with that. What we posited and implemented in the past may not in fact work in an environment that is constantly changing. But are we strong enough in our beliefs to open the door to challenge while concomitantly looking for new answers that fit the current context? Many people will not take that step for fear of losing "respect," while not understanding that their failure to do so promotes more disrespect because of the reticence to change with the times.

I have been blessed since completing my doctoral work to travel a journey that has forced me to come face-to-face and challenge that which I was taught in the academy and those propositions I thought were applicable across cultures. This has not been an easy journey, but it is clearly one that has helped me understand change as it pertains to my community from a very different lens, which I will share throughout this book. As you read, you will also hear me say that to evoke deep change within our community we must be willing and able to examine our issues from a holistic perspective. Systems theory is very important to our survival because it is the integration of destructive systems that we have to work through.

Equally important, we have to stop talking about the need for change and engage in a collective change process that is by us and for us. Or, as one parent said after the Fenger tragedy, "It is our problem. We have to take control of our children" (Main, 2010). I will take her statement one step further: It's our problem and we have to take back our community and the lives of our children.

Since the time has come for me to move my writing on this topic beyond the parameters of academic journals, I have also discovered that many of my views may not always come across as politically correct—but I am okay with that. As I said earlier, the stakes are too high to continue to sugarcoat these issues. Our children continue to either migrate to or be negatively impacted by gang violence, which results in an ongoing loss of our most precious resource— the children who represent our future.

My Lens, Perspectives, Learning, and Journey toward This Book

So, who am I and why should you even want to read this book? My lens and background definitely impact what I write. Very simply, I am an African American woman who professionally is a college professor in the management discipline and who also consults to public- and private-sector organizations. My education credentials include three academic degrees: a bachelor's degree in psychology, a master's degree in industrial relations, and a doctoral degree in organization development; and I am working on my fourth degree, which is a master's in divinity. My publication and presentation lists are extensive, and my research and consulting endeavors span both domestic and international boundaries. I have served in executive and management roles in higher education, and before my academic career, I spent more than 20 years in management and directorship positions in the corporate business sector. My work has primarily addressed social issues that focus on at-risk youth, diversity, leadership development, and community and organizational strategy and culture, and I have been blessed to be invited to lead these change processes versus having to seek work. In other words, God has blessed me with a sound professional reputation.

Yet, none of my background is germane to my writing this book. I simply state my credentials in order to make it a little more difficult for others to discredit my work. I am not an angry Black woman talking "stuff" or a pseudo-academic who wants to gain acclaim for writing a provocative book. I have already accomplished my goal of being provocative.

The most important credential I carry when relating to the issues discussed in this book is my personal relationship with those issues. First and foremost, I am an African American woman who daily deals with the dualities that emerge from being Black and a female in a racist and male-oriented society. Through my walk in seminary, I have learned to embrace the heritage of my collective African consciousness. I grew up in the inner city of Chicago, and my early childhood years were spent in the Woodlawn community, where the Blackstone Rangers originated. Consequently growing up in a gang environment was something I experienced on a daily basis. I was never "recruited" into a gang because I had the protection of a cousin who was a close friend of Jeff Fort, co-founder of the Black P. Stone Nation. While violence was a part of the gang culture, during those years, the gang was viewed very differently by the community. Equally important, there was a very different definition of community. Our communities were protected by our own, thus making it much more difficult to tear it apart with random violence. This historical backdrop led me to ask when I began this research, what caused a change in the African American community?

I have seen and experienced racism throughout my life, despite my credentials, which simply means that it does not matter how many degrees you have. Racism and glass ceilings are alive and well. I have seen hopelessness in my communities to a point that the anger would just rise like bile in my throat. I had been working on a project in New Orleans for close to a year, and days before Katrina hit in 2005 I left to give my report to the organization sponsoring this work. It was by God's grace and mercy I got out in time. Unfortunately, the events in my life had not allowed me to return until October 2010. I can't begin to describe the anger at the disparities I saw relative to reconstruction initiatives. The same mess we were dealing with before I left continued in the aftermath of reconstruction.

Despite my being in an environment where only a small percentage of people ever get to the "academy," colleagues like me, who are of color, are not devoid of extensively experiencing what it means to be locked out and marginalized in our work communities, even with PhD behind our names. So when I speak to issues of "isms," it is not from a voice of privilege.

Similar to many American institutions, racism in the academy is alive and prospering. Yet, I have learned to move past that drama—it's not "clothing" I intend to wear. Years ago, one of my seminary professors and I had a discussion about how difficult it is sometimes to write for the academy when you are Black and feeling marginalized. But what stuck with me was his simple question: "You are tenured, right?" To which I replied, "Yes." At that point he said, "Well, you can basically write what you want." We are often chastised in the academy for investigating, researching, and publishing on issues that pertain to us. However, if we are researching and publishing within the contexts and constraints of appropriate academic rigor, why should we be apologetic for studying our own issues (Easley, 2011)? Therefore, in my analysis of a situation that continues to impact my community—the loss of our most precious resource, our children—I have chosen to authentically addresses these issues, irrespective of who might be offended. While I insert my own perspectives, as an academic I am trained to provide you with supporting or, where appropriate, challenging references. Yet, I think it is important to weave our personal perspectives to bind us to one another. My stories I share are in many ways stories shared by other African Americans across this country. It is critical that when we ground ourselves in action, we do it with a critical lens that juxtaposes theory to practice, yet humanizes our issues in order to better relate.

Change will not easily occur, as all change is painful, until we make concerted efforts to strategically and systemically design intervention strategies that can concomitantly begin a healing process for all of us, as well as remove unwarranted barriers. We must be equally critical when choosing the change strategies we employ. Since entering seminary, my guiding praxis toward understanding change and change theories has been more focused on critically examining the epistemology, ontology, hermeneutics, and root metaphors of a change strategy juxtaposed against the environments in which we work in order to be far more comfortable with whether or not they will holistically address the critical issues that permeate our communities. A one-size-fits-all strategy will not work in our community (Easley, 2010).

When I wrote my doctoral dissertation, my intent then, as it is now, was not to address gangs from an organizational context, or import a value perspective on the existence of gangs. As I previously said, I am concerned with understanding why our youth gravitate to these alternative environments and how we can effectively turn around their need to migrate to gangs in order to diminish how many children we lose to senseless violence. In other words, we need to understand what continues to break down within the constructs of their lives and environments that makes them want to walk into an alternative environment where they clearly understand the consequences of membership. Yet we cannot continue to address this issue from an isolated perspective. We have to understand the relational issues that reside within the African American community and how they impact the loss of our youth to gang violence. But by training and work experience, I am a change agent. So, while I will explore the connectivity between issues that plague the African American community and its impact upon youth gravitating to gangs, I am more focused on assessing how we can emerge as our own change agents.

I have also asked myself, what is compelling me to write this book now, versus in 1999 when I completed my doctoral degree? I did not have a complete picture relative to the interrelatedness of the issues we face. It was not the time for me to write "the" book. I see now that my dissertation was the beginning of my journey. We each have our journeys that are designed to teach valuable lessons—if we are willing to embrace the challenges of the journey and the resulting lessons. As I have moved through these eleven years, my learning, which emerged from profound experiences in concert with my spiritual walk through seminary, has enlightened and enlarged my understanding and perspectives of the African American context.

The Lessons

So, what have I learned? First, I had to understand, at a deep level, the severity of our social fabric and context. More specifically, as a society and, most important, as a people, we are in crisis. Violence is a part of our guiding praxis that invades far too many components of our lives and negatively impacts the healthy growth and development of our children. Poverty continues to run rampant due to ongoing socioeconomic imbalances that are perpetrated by those that have in contrast to those that have not. "Those that have" perpetrate racism and sexism in order to keep populations of people disempowered. As a society, but most important as African Americans, we have not been successful in challenging and changing these imbalances.

Historically, we are rooted in the myth of redemptive violence that originates from ancient Babylonian mythology that now impacts foreign policy, nationalism, the cold war, militarism, the media, and even children's comics and cartoon shows; and it invades our communities (Wink, 1992). Real democracy in a global world appears to be another unresolved problem of modernity (Hardt & Negri, 2005) and equally important an unresolved problem in the African American community. Far too many people continue to view issues and, equally important, outcomes of poverty, power, and domination through a lens and interpretative schemas that have not changed for years.

However, I am drawn to ask how can African Americans look at these issues through a different lens? The strategies of domination and control continue to work, and there is no reason for those in power and control to change. Those paradigms and strategies continue to serve them. Therefore, those that are subjected to poverty and other issues of "isms" must learn to alter their perspectives in order to effectively topple these imbalances. A new movement that awakens the masses of people who live in abject poverty and moves them to vision options for changing the conditions of their lives is long past due. Yet through vulnerability comes great strength. So, while we have been subjected to these injustices that have resulted in far too many inequities, we have thus far survived and must learn to acknowledge the positive attributes within ourselves that have rendered us strong.

I have publicly wrestled with hopelessness in African American communities, the meltdown of our family structures, which tends to result in the loss of our children to gang violence, and issues relative to the struggle of African American women. The restlessness I struggle with has caused me to write more critically. In 2005 I began to explore issues of identity through the work I was doing in inner-city areas and across the country. However, my most significant learning resulted from the work I did in New Orleans. Days before Hurricane Katrina, I addressed close to 2,000 people across four church services, where we examined their perception of entitlement to a better life through their connection to God. Despite the struggles I saw African Americans endure in New Orleans before Hurricane Katrina, there was evidence of a divide between classes of African Americans; a reluctance on the part of far too many people to vision their rights to equal treatment, access, and resources; and an inability to envision how strategic change could go beyond the boundaries of building new buildings or engaging in other types of structural "rehabbing" and how it could look in their community. There was also an inability to envision their rights to a better life, an inability I have witnessed nationally when I worked in African American communities. While this problem is not unique to the African American race, nevertheless it is our problem, uniquely defined by the characteristics of our history and social context, which in and of itself is quite complex. Unfortunately, post-Katrina, these issues still exist.

While toward the end of the book I will address the connectivity of these issues across multiple cultures, I want to point out one example from the late Gloria Anzaldúa, who addressed similar issues within the Mestiza culture. Her points help contextually frame the mindset that is critical for all people who daily live with domination, poverty, and a need to develop a mindset of liberation. Her points contextually frame why a journey toward change is so critical.

> The dominant white culture is killing us slowly with its ignorance. By taking away our self-determination, it has made us weak and empty. As a people we have resisted, and we have taken expedient positions, but we have never been allowed to develop unencumbered—we have never been allowed to be fully ourselves. The whites in power want us people of color to barricade ourselves behind our separate tribal walls so they can pick us off one at a time with their hidden weapons; so they can whitewash and distort history. Ignorance splits people, creates prejudices. A miss-informed people is a subjugated people. (2007, p. 108)

What are the lessons we can draw from Anzaldúa's experiences and analysis that are germane to African Americans? Anzaldúa closely examined issues of walking a borderland of consciousness, which she saw as being marked by a plurality of personality that possesses psychic restlessness. Juxtaposed against this psychic restlessness was a conflict she observed between perceiving oneself as visible and concomitantly invisible because one has been forced to walk outside the boundaries of that which was originally your culture, a culture that was taken over, rendering you as the "other" (Anzaldúa, 2007; Anzaldúa & Keating, 2002). In liberation theology, we often find the concept of *othering* addressed. The term *othering* is often used to connote difference and, when speaking of people who have different characteristics from those considered to be "mainstream," will incorporate the demonization and dehumanization of groups, which further justifies attempts to civilize and exploit these "inferior" others ("Other," Wikipedia).

However, because the Mestiza endures and is able to cross over these invisible (and physical) barriers, Anzaldúa posits that the Mestiza evolves from this othering experience and emerges a stronger and a more malleable species, forced to embrace hybridity and flexibility, attributes which strengthen the character and will to survive (Anzaldúa, 2007).

African Americans possess that same hybridity and flexibility and display it on a daily basis, as do our youth. However, I believe because we have engaged in wearing a mask for so long, we don't recognize it for its strength and utility. Equally critical, throughout our communities we do not actively engage in deconstructing what the othering processes really entail. Our children are othered every day they walk into a school, yet we do not empower them to see this process for what it really is. Yet Anzaldúa wanted to make sure her community understood its existence as well as utility.

Within the context of her discussions of this Mestiza, she also addressed added layers; for her the layer equally profound was that of a lesbian woman who had to work through the internal trauma of going against the grain of her culture relative to the role and responsibilities of a traditional Mexican woman (Anzaldúa, 2007). We have those layers as well, and they can and will impact our perception of strength. But similar to her proposition, as we understand and deconstruct those layers, we cannot allow them to become impediments to the need for us to collaborate as we work to invoke change within our communities.

Anzaldúa also saw the counterstance that the Mestiza assumes as a step toward liberation (Anzaldúa, 2007; Anzaldúa & Keating, 2002). When we take on a defiant "Hell no, I am not buying your attempts to marginalize me" attitude, I believe we are forced to come to grips with who we are and look internally to our strengths. If we don't, we risk perishing, either mentally or physically. Yet, when one examines the commentary about Anzaldúa, she is labeled as angry.

People of color who face oppression have every right to be angry. Labeling represents unsophisticated, yet far too often, bought-into defense mechanisms. However, the beauty of what Anzaldúa brings to this contextual conversation, which parallels so many of our own experiences, is that out of our anger we can emerge far more actualized than we were when we initially embarked upon crossing our own borders. Inherent in this emergence is also the flexibility that we develop because of our counterstance to the rigidity of definition and superimposed attempts to place us where the dominant culture prefers for us to reside.

Yet, while African Americans walk the "in-betweens" of our borders, we still must claim our right to the country in which we live. It is our home, despite attempts to keep us on the fringes, and we helped build it. Consequently, we have every right to critically examine the systems that bind us in order to change that which is killing us. Far too many African Americans have difficulty navigating through the psychological traumas that keep us imprisoned. Our answers are not in textbooks, nor are they in the traditional paradigms of social service and social work. Those paradigms typically address the desire to act *upon* a situation versus inspiring people to take control of their lives.

Learning through a Different Lens: The Walk through Seminary

To complete an overview of who I am, I think it is also important to share my walk that I continue to take through seminary. A theological and cosmo-logical perspective is a critical component to that which I see germane to our change processes, and I want to share why I hold that perspective.

In 2005, I began my walk through seminary. It has been a slow walk and is not yet complete. I have chosen not to burden myself with a large number of classes each term but balance my studies with my work. While it has been a slow walk, it has been critical to my professional and spiritual growth and has facilitated my asking questions that are far deeper than those I asked during my doctoral program. Moving beyond a descriptive analysis of our struggles has positioned me to examine our story from a deeper intrapersonal perspective.

While I have never felt my calling to be that of a preacher leading a con-gregation, I strongly believe that we have to envision the role of change as a distinct ministry that moves the pulpit outside the domains of the traditional church in order to better understand what entitlement to a better life means. Yet all of my years of academic study never prepared me for the level of hope-lessness and despair that plagues so many of our communities. Those years of doctoral training, which focused on my learning and mastering change man-agement strategies taught by many of the masters in our field, did not prepare me to deal with the overwhelming unwillingness of many to change the issues that were prevalent in our communities. But those years of training did help me understand how to differentiate between what I call "blue smoke and mir-ror" strategies that are designed to look like they will authentically work, but in reality will barely make a dent relative to solving the problems that perme-ate through dis-empowered communities.

Ironically, in the change management literature, researchers looked for strategies that would build hopeful organizations and find spirituality. I don't believe, however, when looking to understand how we can become strong enough to defy the challenges that we daily face, we can find those answers in traditional management texts. The starting point for us is through understand-ing our spirituality from an individual context and from the larger context of our African heritage. This is not a new concept for African Americans. The spiritual autobiographies of Harriet Tubman and Sojourner Truth revealed a radical use of traditional forms of spirituality that led them to intently question what they perceived to be illegitimate authority and to not allow fear to stop them from engaging a sexist and slaveholding society (Townes, 2005). In other words they walked past the descriptions of angry Black women.

So, similar to the tortoise, I have walked slowly through seminary juxtaposing my learning to the work I continue to do in the field, and as I have walked, I have challenged many of my prior theological praxes. Seminary has also taught me to integrate the literatures of liberation, Black, and womanist theologies in concert with staying connected to my organization development background in order to fill my voids. Those literatures speak to the souls of African Americans. As I have studied and worked, I have also aimed to better understand the meaning behind this statement:

A profound piece of surgery has to take place in the very psyche of the disinherited before the great claim of the religion of Jesus can be presented. The great stretches of barren places in the soul must be revitalized, brought to life before they can be challenged. (Thurman, 1976, p. 9 in the 1996 forward by Vincent Harding)

There are many who claim to understand what it means for people who have been disenfranchised to rise up against oppression. However, does the global context of this new millennium call for different strategies? Should, perhaps, the first stage of the surgery Rev. Dr. Howard Thurman referenced incorporate a critical examination of our African religious and cosmological heritage that largely informed our slave ancestors and was deemed to be instrumental to their survival? A major criticism that surfaces in African American communities is that we rarely explore our history and prior social contexts beyond surface levels.

When we fail to understand our past, critically examining where we are going can be difficult for a variety of reasons. It has been suggested that African Americans have always been America's wilderness in search of a promised land (West, 1993), a statement that coins the double-consciousness and issues of duality that I have continued to see in the African American community, dualities that each of us experience daily. We have to be willing to engage in conversations as to what that duality means and how it may stand in conflict with our ability to conceptualize our rights to a better life in this society, which also translates to a better life for our children devoid of the violence that is exponentially taking their lives.

In concert with issues of duality is the proposition that to be Black in White America is to suffer. As a theologian in training, I continue to struggle with how we so holistically embrace the concept of suffering and reconcile issues of theodicy. It has been suggested that African Americans suffer by existentially questioning our value and worth within this society, in concert with our suffering physically from hunger, homelessness, unemployment, ill health, drug abuse, and countless other issues (Townes, 2005), which fosters an identity crisis. We also cannot discount how we suffer because of our feelings of hopelessness and helplessness. When we cannot get our arms around the exponential loss of our children and the growing violence that permeates not only our large cities, but also our rural environments, rendering few if any safe havens for our youth, we feel dis-empowerment at levels that defy explanation.

Many also feel dissonance because on Sundays we will articulate a belief that God loves us, yet our actions infer a rooted self-hate, which suggests the need to deeply reconnect to our inner strength and spirit. To instill change in our communities, we have to walk with the knowledge, faith, and understanding that through our connection to the Divine, we are our instrument in the deliverance of our people. We have to critically examine the "isms" we have internalized. Is this the fruit we bear as suggested in Genesis 3, or is our God (however we personally internalize our concept of God) simply waiting for us to learn a different subset of lessons? As we continue to move through these post-modern times, I continue to ask whether or not there is a different outcome that God is looking for? Could He simply be waiting for us to redefine the concept of change?

> Always there is some voice that rises up against what is destructive, calling attention to an alternative, another way. It is a matter of more than passing significance that the racial memory as embodied in the myths of creation, as well as in the dream of prophet and seer, points ever to the intent to community as the purpose of life. (Thurman, 1963, p. 94)

We must challenge the institutionalized and mutating systems of systemic racism that continues to decimate our community and emerge with a different concept of community that drives our purpose of life. True change also does not incorporate undermining or criticizing the work of others in this arena. We have to understand what they did and strategies they used as we move past that historical context. It is in the shadows of our intimate relationships with self and those that we live with in community that we must connect with and deeply examine the pain that plagues our community. But it is through this same communal connect that we must also find ourselves loving one another again to a point that our connectivity cannot be broken. At this point in our existence it is a moot point what others did not do for us because it is within our own personal shadows that our answers to very critical questions and resulting change strategies emerge. The questions we must ask are difficult questions. The engagement in this type of dialogue calls for communal strength and support.

To effectively evoke change, we must also deconstruct and understand how we have formed our identity. It has been suggested that the role of African American identity formation, in and of itself, is a distinctive and multilayered process within American life, which must be de-layered in order to move beyond resulting blockages (Butler, 2006). I believe this de-layering must also be done within the context of community in order to carve open a sacred space for us to share our deepest feelings regarding how we really feel about our layers, while at the same time forming a *community* of sacred space and support. It is interesting to me how many different churches I visit still feel compelled through either sermons or other activities to address the need to ameliorate the divide that exists even within the walls of church.

The forces of racism, color consciousness, sexism, genderism, and American religiosity have impacted the formative experiences of persons of descent, and have perverted self-esteem, challenged or changed the social stability, and significantly threatened existential security (Butler, 2006). Consequently, when we examine the root cause of why our youth gravitate to gang environments, we must honestly examine our issues as the adults in their lives, as they pertain to our self-esteem, our subconscious reasons for allowing others to take care of the business of our communities, and how we envision our ability to evoke change despite barriers—change that is needed to save our children. Equally important we must challenge how we treat one another even in the sanctuary of church.

As the actors in our own storyline, we cannot take a dispassionate role in critically examining how we internalize our environment and our perception of our place within this society. These processes won't be comfortable for us, but they are needed. I am reminded of the first time I read Dr. Na'im Akbar's book, *Breaking the Chains of Psychological Slavery*. It made me very uncomfortable, and even though I had met him ten years prior and highly respected him as an academic, I immediately went to my White colleague's texts for validation of his propositions. I had to come face-to-face with why I challenged him and went to the literature written by my Caucasian colleagues to question the validity of Dr. Akbar's propositions. Why did I immediately go to those that historically have othered us to validate that which I knew, in the deepest recesses of my soul, to be true?

Coming face-to face with my own inability to internalize the dissonance caused by one of my academic brothers helped me grow. My challenging why I went to White scholars for validation of what my esteemed African American scholar wrote also humbled me and made me feel shameful of my actions, a humbling I obviously needed, and a humbling I think many others need when we engage in othering our own, including our youth.

It is my goal to evoke that same cognitive dissonance within those that read this book. We must move out of our comfort zones, destabilize our current mindset by actively engaging in the examination of all of our issues in order to open space for internalizing what a new reality, constructed by us, can look like. A new reality is vital for our children. They are fighting daily for their survival in a world they really do not understand. They need us, and as the adults in their lives, we cannot walk away from the premise that we need each other to effectively move forward as we take on what could be the biggest challenge of our lifetime. As we engage in what will be an uncomfortable destabilizing change process, we must also draw upon the foundational strength that has permeated our race for centuries.

Our Cosmology, Our Strength

The foundations of our African heritage were the glue that held us together during slavery. In the European culture, religious experiences were perceived to be beyond the natural order of things. In contrast, in an African context, there was no difference between the sacred and the secular. African cosmology signified that man and woman live in religious harmony with all of God's creation (Mbiti, 1990). Therefore, people also had a relationship with nature and the physical world surrounding them, which grounded them spiritually and psychologically. Issues of self-esteem will not prevail when people understand their relationship with God. Inherent in the African ontological experience and expression of religion were oral traditions, rituals, ceremonies, and festivals that gave honor and order to a *communal* life (Mbiti, 1990), again bringing us back to Howard Thurman's concept of community. Living and working collectively in community is our heritage. It is how we survived in the homeland, and it was how we survived the atrocities of slavery. Yet we must question if in today's modern society we have lost our sense of community. If we answer honestly, the resounding answer is yes. But that does not mean we can't recapture that which we have lost.

We must bring forth the values that may be buried within the historical context of our heritage because they are germane to our survival. The critical principles that grounded us as a people for centuries have been either mutated or lost. The recovering of those principles, even if it is within a twenty-first-century context and interpretation, will be critical to our ability to overcome the issues that plague both our communities and children.

Equally important, as we walk through our journey of self, community, and societal examinations, we must inspire our youth to walk that journey with us. I believe as they concurrently embark upon a critical analysis of our current situations, while examining the richness of our heritage, a change will be sparked within them that will help them sustain any psychological attacks that can occur.

> If our children are to overcome the troubles of this world, they must learn to incorporate the valuable lessons of the past into their vision for the future. (Butler, 2000, p. 91)

Encouraging our children to work side-by-side in our movement toward change will strengthen our bonds with them. Throughout this book, I share my experiences with the youth who participated in my research. These were young people who had no problems articulating their desires to have active adults in their lives. Incorporating our youth into our critical examination of our lives, reexamination of our historical, theological, and cosmological contexts will make them stronger in their own pursuits for liberation throughout the rest of their lives. They will know, beyond a shadow of a doubt, that they are resting on a foundation of strength.

· 2 ·

OWNING THE PROBLEM: THE BIGGER PICTURE BEYOND THE CONTEXT OF OUR PERSONAL WALLS

Gangs are not new, nor do African Americans make up the majority of the gang population. Across most urban environments, African Americans comprise, on the average, one-third of the gang population, with the majority held by Hispanic gangs. The population of Caucasian gangs in the country continues to rise and in smaller city and suburban communities have outpaced the African American gang population (*Race/Ethnicity*, 1999). In other words, *we* did not begin this mess nor do we make up a majority of its membership. In 2002, I presented in England my research that addressed the issue of gangs from an international context. The literature on the international rise of youth gangs was expansive, and the growth of youth gangs and the resulting youth violence was a problem in all of the inhabited continents.

I first took a 2000 view of the issue as it pertained to growth patterns in the United States. In 2001, it was reported that over the past twenty years, the United States had reported a tenfold increase in the number of cities that experienced gang problems. Gang migration patterns extended to smaller cities, towns, and villages in the United States; the average size of the city population containing gangs fell from 182,000 to 34,000 (Miller. 2001). Yet the United States was not alone.

Many Cambodian Americans, who left Cambodia to escape violence, fell into the violent culture of American street gangs (Isett, 1994). Within Cambodia, violent crime had outpaced all other forms of homicide and the number of youth gangs participating in these violent crimes had significantly increased (Sivaraman, 1998). But Cambodia was not alone. In Brazil, poverty, domestic violence, and abandonment confronted many children, who were sent to the streets to make money for family support, often being recruited as foot soldiers for gangs, placing these children at heightened risk for AIDS and acts of violence (Jeffery, 1993; "When Death Squads," 1993). In 2001, it was reported that gangs had been an ongoing issue in parts of South Africa for the past 40 years and had rapidly become well-organized criminal units that set up drug, extortion, and international smuggling rings, building networks in neighborhoods, prisons, and schools—similar to the gang profiles and their respective activities in the United States (Itano, 2001). Late 1990s police in New Zealand reported approximately 70 major gangs in the country with about 4,000 hardcore gang members and another 7,000 categorized as associates and prospective wanna-be members (Macko, 1996). New Zealand officials were concerned that these gangs were forming links with Asian triads, thus moving up the ranks of organized crime. In 2009, I was contacted by a New Zealand researcher who wanted to draw upon my work to structure her study because the problem in New Zealand continued to grow.

In 2001, Paris officials reported that their youth gang violence was moving beyond poorer neighborhoods and into the elite communities (Jeffries, 2001). The number of 13–18 year old youths jailed in Paris and its suburbs between 1993 and 1999 doubled from 2,247 to 4,326, and in 1998, 3,825 teenagers were jailed for committing violent crimes, compared with 1,379 in 1994 (Jeffries). In Finland, Norway, and Sweden, researchers investigated the rise of racial violence, believed to be attributable to youth gangs associating themselves with Skinheads. Russia also experienced increased racial violence, which was directed toward minority students studying in Russia, by youth gangs also believed to be associated with the Skinheads (MacWilliams, 2002; Virtanen, 2001; Graff, 2002). In Australia, an intensive study was conducted by the Australian Multicultural Foundation to develop a better profile of growing ethnic youth gangs (White, Santina, Carmel, & Rosario, 1999), and, as a final example, in 2001, the BBC reported on the activities of the youth gang Haika in Spain, which was believed to be the training organization for the violent separatist group ETA, from which important terrorists are alleged to emerge (Botsford, 2001).

While these are older statistics, the growth trend has not reversed, domestically or internationally. The *Chicago Tribune* reported in the first quarter of 2009 that Police Superintendent Weis released the final crime statistics for 2008 in Chicago, which showed that both violent and property crime rose from 2007. Weiss pointed to continued gang crime as a major source of the violence, saying that 92% of murder suspects and 72% of murder victims had criminal records (Rosas, 2009). In 2007, a survey conducted by the National Youth Gang Center (NYGC), which is operated by the Office of Juvenile Justice and Delinquency Prevention (OJJDP), revealed there has been a steady increase of gang problems since 2000. The survey questioned law enforcement agencies across the United States specifically about youth gangs. The results estimated that 788,000 gang members and 27,000 gangs were active in the United States in 2007 (Jacinto, 2009). Similar to the 2001 statistics on U.S. gang patterns, while large cities and suburban counties continued to be the primary location for 60% of gangs and 80% of gang members, there was an increase in gangs and gang members in rural counties between 2002 and 2007. One in five larger cities reported an increase in gang homicides in 2007 compared to the previous year, and two in five reported an increase in gang-related violence (Jacinto).

On the international front, the increase in gang activity also does not seem to be diminishing. In 2007, the *New York Times* reported in 2007 that two gangs that originated on the streets in Los Angeles, California, have grown so large in El Salvador that there are two prisons in that country devoted exclusively to their members, one for each gang, according to officials who traveled there recently to meet with the local authorities (Cathcart, 2007). And, in 2007, the BBC ran an article on how Antonio Villaraigosa, the mayor of Los Angeles, called for international efforts to deal with gang crime because his city had become the "ground zero" for Latino gangs that were now impacting North and Central America ("Plea for Gang Violence Crackdown," 2007).

A call for collaboration between El Salvador, Guatemala, Honduras, Mexico, and the United States was deemed to be a beginning strategy ("Plea for Gang Violence Crackdown," 2007). Yet a 2006 report stated that the most dangerous gang, which was now intently infiltrating the United States, did not begin in the United States, but originated in El Salvador. The Mara Salvatrucha 13 had begun to develop as one of the most organized and deadliest gangs to hit the United States and was expanding into other countries. Mexico was taking steps to fight back against this gang by dealing with them from the perspective of their being a threat to national security. What was most interesting in this report was that although this gang primarily recruits members from Central America, African Americans are also members of this gang, which has members between the ages of 11 and 40 (Domash, 2010). This begs the question: Why are our youth gravitating to violent gangs with whom they do not even share a common ethnic heritage?

Our understanding these statistics is very important. When people believe they are the central cause of a problem, their spirits become very heavy. For too many years, African Americans have been led to believe that the gang phenomenon is ours. Clearly it is not. Unfortunately, the loss of youth to gang violence is an international epidemic impacting countries all over the world. The prevailing ways for intervening with gangs—diversion, detention, alternative schools, and so forth, the systems discussed in this book—are breaking down on an international level.

When we look at the glass half full versus half empty, we have an opportunity to set international benchmarks as we creatively and effectively work to design, develop, and implement strategies that will work to save our youth in a twenty-first-century context.

The loss of youth on an international level is a loss to the world. As much as our children are our future, children across the globe are the future of the world. Yet people are often afraid to try new strategies despite our continuing to get the same results with the old ones. We cannot allow ourselves to succumb to or be impacted by naysayers because the stakes are clearly too high.

Recently, I had the opportunity to research a reform process in another sector. The people who put down this process were clearly the biggest perpetrators as to why reform is needed. Yet they were the loudest complainers as to why the new processes would not work. The energies they put behind working to thwart efforts were amazing. They spent monies to hire a "hired gun," figuratively speaking, to communicate his version of propaganda as to why these new processes would not work, monies that could have been used more effectively. Yet, as I continued to research, the new process was definitely on the right track as I examined other nations that had implemented similarly designed change strategies.

We have to understand, however, that the naysayers' actions were not unusual. People are always going to be reluctant to do something different, particularly those that will be forced to engage in significant change relative to their behaviors and psychological contracts, despite how dysfunctional both may be. Consequently, we cannot allow their dissent to impede our processes when developing change strategies, because as we will see in the next section, more than 80 years of the same cannot be a viable option.

Eighty after Thrasher: Why?

While the current status of gangs suggests that they continue to develop into complex international organizations, we also have a strong historical context for gang-intervention strategies. Gangs have existed as we experience them today for more than 100 years, and in many respects have become institutionalized components of our communities. Delinquent gangs in twentieth-century United States did not just emerge, but grew from a long and varied tradition of group violence. As a result, street gangs have been the objects of study within the behavioral science field for many years.

This research has roots going back to the 1920s, beginning with the prominent sociologist Frederic M. Thrasher whose 1927 study, *The Gang*, of 1,313 gangs in Chicago is considered the first serious academic treatment of gangs (Decker & Van Winkle, 1996). Thrasher's studies convinced him that juvenile delinquency was extremely difficult to control and that the control of gang behavior along with the *redirection* of gangs was of primary importance to the problem. He chastised conventional institutions for their failure to provide socializing experiences consistent with the needs of gang members. Thrasher was also not naive enough to believe that "wholesome recreation" was the solution to the problem, for such programs would have to compete with the structure and excitement of gang life. His study, which offered original insights and dimensions of concern that remain key topics in the discussions on gangs and their behavior became the foundation for subsequent gang research (Goldstein, 1991). Thrasher's work also gave gangs a cultural and ecological context. Using the concepts of culture and neighborhood ecology, he sought to explain gang transmission as part of a process of collective behavior. Gangs in Chicago were found primarily in interstitial areas, characterized by deteriorating neighborhoods, shifting populations, and mobility and disorganization of the slum (Decker & Van Winkle, 1996).

Additional work that followed (which included examining the complexity of the roots of gang formation, ganging as a process, situational gang leadership, the influence of community forces on gang organization and behavior, and the role of what came to be called *groupthink* in gang functioning) were each anticipated by Thrasher (Bolitho, 1930; Landesco, 1932; Tannenbaum, 1938). Other early members of the University of Chicago's School of Sociology built significantly upon Thrasher's work and provided further description of the organization and functioning of Chicago's delinquent gangs, furthering several of Thrasher's central conclusions (Goldstein, 1991).

During the Depression years, sociologists focused on explaining the gang phenomenon in terms of social causation. Landesco (1932, pp. 238–48) emphasized the effects of conflicting immigrant and American cultures. Shaw and McKay (1942) stressed a more complex combination of slum area deterioration, poverty, family dissolution, and organized crime. Tannenbaum (1938) analogously proposed that the gang forms not because of its attractiveness per se, but because positive sociocultural forces such as family, school, and church, which have the potential to train a youth into more socially acceptable behaviors, are weak or unavailable. Others also stressed socioeconomically substandard neighborhoods and lax parental supervision (Wattenberg & Balistrieri, 1950).

We must take a critical look at an issue that warrants analysis. If social scientists and other change agents knew in 1938 that declining sociocultural forces, particularly our educational institutions, contributed to youth gravitating to gangs, why, in 2011, are we still dealing with the same issues, particularly the deplorable conditions of inner-city schools and the gang violence within the confines of those schools?

Academicians are still attempting to explain, from psychological and sociological perspectives, why youth form gangs. The reemergence of gangs in cities in the 1950s facilitated a new generation of gang research, theory, and policy. For example, studies emerged that focused on developing theories on status frustration (Decker & Van Winkle, 1996). Conditions basic to the social order have been consistently evaluated in attempt to understand the gang phenomenon. Yet, for African Americans, the social order continues to deteriorate; conditions, which include a division of labor between the family and the peer group, in the socialization of adolescents have not successfully been addressed.

Researchers also examined and emphasized issues of masculinity and collective action in the male subculture; a stress on excitement, congregation, and mating in the adolescent subculture; the importance of toughness and smartness in the subcultures of lower-status populations; and the density conditions and territoriality patterns affecting the subcultures of urban and urbanized locals (Goldstein, 1991). Offering a different perspective, Egerton (1988) posited that the major factors contributing to gang formation included residential segregation in low-income areas, poverty, poor school performance, little parental supervision, discrimination, and distrust of law enforcement. He also viewed these factors as being key to young people spending much of their lives together on the streets. The gang, therefore, was seen as serving as the surrogate family, providing friendship, pride, prestige, belonging, identity, self-esteem, and a desire to emulate family members who were in gangs (Egerton, 1988).

When we examine the resulting gang intervention strategies that emerged from historical research, they represent thematically similar forms. Some have been oriented toward changing, primarily on an individual basis, the behavior, attitudes, or values of youth either through such court dispositions as diversion, probation, parole, or diverse therapeutic interventions (Goldstein, 1991)—strategies that continue to prevail. Others have been directed toward the gang as a group, as in the youth outreach or street gang work approaches popular in the 1950s and 1960s. A third intervention strategy, most evident during the 1960s and 1970s, has been the provision of social and economic opportunities via employment, educational, recreational, family, or other community interventions (Goldstein, 1991). Yet, when the economy shifts, youth feel the impact of the downward spiral of a job market.

The most popular gang intervention strategy in the 1980s was arresting youth in gangs and incarceration (Goldstein, 1991), strategies such as the 2010 threat by Chicago police superintendent Jody Weis (Main, 2010). However, one must seriously question what happens to youth after their release from incarceration. Typically when our youth enter the prison system, they already lack educational skills, competencies, pro-social behaviors, and an ability to envision an alternative life. Consequently, when they exit the prison system, they will be just as unqualified and therefore prone to repeat the cycle of dysfunctional behavior. The prison system in this country has far too many of our males already. This is a cycle that must be conquered.

In the early 1990s, the *Economist* reported gangs to be strong and thriving institutions in a part of the world where every other institution had broken down ("When Death Squads," 1993). Teenage nihilism was a deadly issue. In 1988, *Ebony* magazine reported the effects on these children with respect to drugs, gang violence, parental neglect and abuse, poverty, and an ineffective educational system. They stated that the jobless rate for black teenagers was down 40% that year and that Black college enrollment was down—downward trends that still prevail—with the road to the middle class less accessible than ever for poor young people ("Save the Children," 1988). In my doctoral dissertation, my research supported the proposition and prevailing statistics at that time that murder by other African Americans was still the leading cause of death for Black men from ages 15 to 44.

In 1996, the Department of Justice published its survey results with respect to what were the critical factors contributing to the growth of gangs.

Of significance were the answers to the question: *What do you believe is the biggest contributor to the street gang problem in California?* (California Department of Justice, 1993). Respondents cited several issues: poverty; lack of education and job training; breakdown of the family unit; lack of parental control, supervision, and family values, resulting in the gang family replacing the traditional family; lack of positive role models; lack of community involvement; community apathy; perception that there is a lack of economic opportunity combined with the increased economic problems; and a lack of employment opportunities and adequate jobs to earn a living. Inclusively, the lack of prevention programs for teaching youth alternatives to gangs was seen as a major issue (California Department of Justice, 1993). Why do we continue to feel disempowered? Most important, how do we turn this disempowerment into empowerment? These are the psychological issues we must understand simply because until we deconstruct the psychological issues that continue to plague our community, we cannot successfully evoke change.

But, first, let's continue looking at our history and context in order to better understand the linkages that must be deconstructed.

· 3 ·

LINKAGES TO YOUTH VIOLENCE:
TWENTY-FIRST-CENTURY
CHALLENGES IN THE AFRICAN
AMERICAN COMMUNITY

While there are some variations on the theme, the overarching theory as to why youth gravitate to gangs is predicated upon environmental issues that reside in and impact a community toward disempowerment. We also can attest to the fact that there have been far too few results relative to changing the socioeconomic issues that are alleged to give rise to the growth of gangs. If African Americans are to make their own necessary corrections, we must understand how our problems are layered and how they affect our youth.

Inclusively, we cannot walk away from a reality that is rooted in our present-day African American culture. Gang involvement is generational. Concomitantly, the gang has often served as the alternative environment to a society where African Americans feel locked out. Therefore, if we are to change the pattern of our children gravitating to gangs, we have a much bigger pattern to change—the pattern of far too many people of color's disenfranchisement from mainstream society, which makes this a collective problem that the African American community must pull together to address. The issues that the African American community face are complex, layered, and span the multiple dimensions of abject poverty and racism, combined forces that attack the mind, body, and spirit and obviously are going to impact youth gravitating to gangs.

Prior to this more recent economic decline, we had one of the longest-running economic expansions in the U.S. history, according to many indicators of social and economic well-being, yet our situation was getting worse. We continued to face issues of decline in economic growth, with the rise of health issues at epidemic rates. African Americans continue to die in epidemic proportions from a few particular illnesses and health-related conditions (Ashby, 2003). We continue to endure unemployment rates that rise above those of our White counterparts even in periods where unemployment has been at its lowest. We face issues of no insurance or working with inadequate insurance, which systemically places our health conditions at higher risks. Homicide and HIV/AIDS are the two leading causes of death among Blacks aged 15 to 34, and AIDs is the number 1 cause of death among African American men and women between the ages of 24 and 44 (Ashby, 2003)—pandemics that negatively impact our growth as a race.

When we investigate issues of stagnation or reversal in African American communities, we have to factor in our issues of self-esteem and the absence of a clear articulation of a vision for the future (Ashby, 2003). Black-on-Black crime is a form of internalized oppression within the cycle of racial conditioning (Ashby, 2003). The African American family structure is deteriorating, and the most precious resource in the African American community—our children—is being sacrificed at record rates due to gang violence, drugs, absentee parents, and a disconnect from society. However, we understand and talk about the impact on our youth and men with respect to the principally funded intervention strategy, suppression, yet that cycle of oppression, despair, hopelessness, and incarceration continues.

Consistent feedback and data collected during the years that I spent investigating the issue of youth gravitating to gangs suggested that our children articulated that they were missing critical role models in their lives. They ached for the adults in their lives to spend time with them, support them, and help them to realize that they could succeed. Linked to the disconnection felt by our youth is the state of affairs of African American families. Our marriages are breaking up at record rates. Although historically we have been a matriarchal-focused race, it has become more "chic" for African American families to join the ranks of the cordial but divorced groups, which continues to decimate our family structures. We continue to face controversial and troubling questions that must be addressed relative to the link between declining numbers of marriageable males and drugs, incarceration, and Black-on-Black crime, which if we make the circular and systemic connection, starts with the youth we are losing.

The Challenges to the Nurturers of Our Family: The African American Woman

Women are a critical foundation within our community. We nurture our families, and, in more ways than one, we are the foundation for our children. Yet African American women face multiple issues that tear at our psyche, often rendering us disabled when having to deal with the additional complexities that emerge on the home front.

Having worked in the corporate sector for more than twenty years, I know from firsthand experience that the glass ceilings for women are alive and well, and the disparities with respect to opportunities between women of color and majority women are also wide. In an eight-year study comparing the lives and career struggles of successful Black and White women in corporate America, Bell and Nkoma (2001) found that women come to their workplaces not just from separate directions but also separate definitions, which are created out of individual junctures of family background, educational experiences, and community values.

African American women continue to remain in the shadows and are essentially invisible with colleagues who do not understand or relate to the realities we face in a workplace. Uniquely positioned in this dualistic state, our ability to find and live as our true self remains elusive to many. Yet the role women play in our family structure is critical. It is hard to come home and be there for your family after you have daily dealt with "isms" centered on the dual identity of race *and* gender (Terhune, 2005–2006). Those "isms" manifest into an internalized dissonance that emanates from the struggles we experience working within a social context that does not appropriately represent or want us as actively engaged participants. But when we come home to our children and families, we have to psychologically put aside these issues.

African American women have to understand the struggles we internalize. It has been suggested that within the story of African people in this country, there is also a history specific to African American women that we ignore, a history that is essential to understanding African American women's perspectives on life in America (Watkins Ali, 1999). It is also suggested that African American women belong to a unique subculture that is not shared entirely with Black men or White women (Watkins Ali, 1999), a perspective that is critical if we are to begin to heal the issues that plague our families—a perspective that must be noted if we are to be a critical part of the team that works to evoke change within our communities.

Although African American women endured the same physical and psychological trauma during slavery as did our men, the rape and separation from their families as well as the physical labor they had to endure while pregnant added more layers of trauma. In far too many instances, African American women suffered even more at the hands of the White slave mistresses, whose homes and children they cared for (Watkins Ali, 1999). Consequently, the current issues articulated by Bell and Nkomo should not be a surprise because they are shaped by and emerge from a callously designed history, a history that still haunts us (Easley, 2010).

Adding insult to injury are the current issues we face that are just as draining. Professional African American women still see gender disparity in education, business professions, and professional careers, which also impacts our relationships with our men. During the past 50 years, the percentage of African American women between the ages of 25 and 54 who have never been married has doubled from 20% to 40% (compared to just 16% of White women who have never been married) ("African American Women and Where They Stand," 2007). Consequently, there are major impacts upon our family structure that do not emerge from poverty.

Mortality rates for African American women are higher than any other racial or ethnic group for nearly every major cause of death, including breast cancer. African American women with breast cancer are nearly 30% more likely to die from it than White women. African American women are 85% more likely to get diabetes, a major complication for heart disease, and, like breast cancer, more Black women die from heart disease than White women ("African American Women and Where They Stand," 2007). Inclusively, African American women are working through issues of a deteriorating African American family.

There are controversial and troubling questions that must be addressed relative to the link between declining numbers of marriageable males and drugs, incarceration, and Black-on-Black crime, which is a circular and systemic connection. Adding to the woes of the decline in the family structure, Bell and Nkoma (2001) found a significant percentage of professional African American women they interviewed reporting how they felt stressed by the lack of significant personal relationships with men. Climbing the corporate ladder often means going home at night facing a nonexistent personal life and recognizing that the prospects of finding a mate similar in background and stature may be quite slim. If you engage in conversation with professional women today, it becomes clear that the situation has not changed. Yet, more often than not, we carry these burdens by ourselves versus engaging in strategic and supportive actions that can provide networking and support.

When our psyche is wounded, it is hard to be supportive to our children. Children have very accurate radar when it comes to understanding what is going on with their parents. They grieve for us as much as they grieve for themselves. Despite those challenges, despite a breakdown in our communal relationships and shared responsibilities, despite a lack of partners in our community, African American women do not give up, which is an encouraging outcome for our children to see. Our not giving up is miraculous. I can't help but wonder, when so much is depleting our spirits, when we feel we have nothing left to give, how do we move beyond our challenges, which despite our resilience, silently signals hopelessness to our youth? And if so, do strategies for our own healing have to become a significant part of the dialogue for change?

The Circular Patterns that Just Won't Stop

The blanket racism that fails to level the playing fields with respect to opportunities for African American men is also alive and well. It has been suggested that African American fathers are under siege. Historically, the enormous expansion of this country's welfare system, and the resulting systems that have been put into place to provide assistance for economically disadvantaged families, have also made it impossible for the father to reside in the home, resulting in men being pushed out of the nest (West, 1999). There are many linked issues to the fact that far too few of our African American fathers are bonding with their children. When the parent-child bond is weakened, we are only contributing to growing evidence that connects the absence of a father in the home to child poverty, juvenile crime, and teen suicide (West, 1999).

However, a rhetorical question I have to posit is why we fail to recognize circular patterns of systemic behavior that separates our families, drives our youth away from us, and puts us at odds with one another. It becomes easy to point the blame at "them," whoever "they" are, at the moment. It becomes harder to face our own issues and develop a proactive and strategic stance to change these conditions, where we lead the charge. If we know the welfare systems are designed to disintegrate our family structure, if the need for federal or state assistance is a priority, then the concomitant priority of the family should be finding a way to make sure that the family bonds are still in place versus playing into the hands of the "system." Our children feel alienated, walking through this world without support:

> I am in a house full of dope fiends. I don't care. It's a life style. It is hard for us to change 16 years of brain washing. My mother said, with tears in her eyes that if I die she is going to walk over me. That's why I told her (meaning me), one week is not going to do it. Everyone at _____ school thought I was a disturbed child. All they had to do was live my life. If you are in my shoes, what are you going to do? I am going to stay at home. I love my mother to the fullest. If I get a job, all I have to do is give my mother her cut and I'm not in the house that much. I raised my little sisters. I ain't going to make it. Every time I take one step forward, there are two steps backwards happening. The only cycle I broke in my family was not getting pregnant. (Easley, 1999)

Adding to our woes are the serious dilemmas we are challenged to endure in our educational systems. These dilemmas impact our ability to compete in this continually changing and global environment, which also results in popular terms such as *digital divide*. Complicating the disadvantages we face in the educational system is another well-kept secret. You see, at least 30% of the population in this country is economically categorized as working poor or at the poverty level, a statistic I have encountered continuously during the last 17 years that I have taught compensation management. People have jobs, but they are effectively underemployed and do not make a wage significant enough to maintain a decent standard of living. This reality forces people to live in communities where lack is common. However, this is not just an issue relative to the poor. Across all economic strata, in far too many African American communities, our educational systems are despicably failing youth of color throughout major metropolises in this country.

We must move past describing and discussing the issues and strategically understand their relationships. So, if I were to summarize the key points I have made, is it fair to assume that there is accuracy and relational ties within the constructs of these propositions?

1. Proposition 1: Gangs have historically existed for many years in communities that expand beyond the African American community, as well as context.
2. Proposition 2: The social context that historically was said to give rise to the growth and continuation of gangs continues to exist in socioeconomic communities where there is a huge lack of resources.
3. Proposition 3: Strategies that were designed years ago against a backdrop of declining communal resources continue to prevail despite

their failure to historically delimit those problems. So, if gangs are said to thrive in environments where there is lack, why aren't there more attempts and action aimed to equalize the divide?

4. Proposition 4: Gangs and the resulting youth violence is an international problem that continues to span and grow across every habited continent. The social and economic conditions that exist within the communities where gangs are growing fastest are the same as they were in the earlier years when gangs were studied in this country, which leads to the question posited in proposition 3: Why are we to believe the situation will get better if the social and economic context does not change and the same strategies are being used?

5. Proposition 5: If African Americans critically understand the meaning behind the prior propositions, is it now safe to assume that, unless we evoke the required change, it will not happen? And the change that we evoke must be dramatically different from previous strategies.

Our landscape of African American communities is complex and riddled with social decline. If in 1928 it was suggested that declining social and economic conditions were the impetus for the manifestation and growth of gangs, and these conditions within a significant number of our communities have not changed, why should we believe that prevailing intervention strategies will work? Historically, they have not, despite the many variations that have been added to the initial design. What we are now witnessing is the growth and manifestation of a problem that is significantly contributing to an exponential loss of Black youth that social scientists began studying more than 80 years ago. When we examine the major constructs embedded within my propositions, movement beyond the confines of these barriers is within our reach. The history of gangs and the lackluster results of strategies aimed to address the gang problem cannot be changed. It is history; yet embedded in that history are lessons we can learn to move forward.

Over the years, I have heard in the theological community that it's hard for a child to be what that child cannot see. Albeit our children witnessing our resilience, in order to help them build their own survival mechanisms, we must help them understand how to move past barriers and to develop the capability to knock them down as they move toward patterns of success. Modeling this behavior is critical for their survival as well as for our own in a global context. The beauty of our living in a global context is that the world can be our playground. We do not have to relegate ourselves to the dynamics that oppress us. I have felt more personal liberty within my own soul by virtue of my traveling to different cultures and countries. The freedom to know that I can and do control my destiny is powerful, and the lessons I have learned from others in different cultural environments have been uplifting to my soul. Our youth have to have that same feeling of power and we have to be their teachers.

To invoke this type of change requires major paradigm shifts. Shortly after receiving my doctoral degree, I was working in a community of 35,000 people. The majority of the community—more than 90%—was African American and Hispanic. I had been asked to work with the police department on a project funded by the Department of Justice. The major scope of the project was to address the exponential increase of youth dying in this community as a result of gang violence. Yet there were many systemic and systems related issues that were contributing to the death toll of youth in this small community.

A major gridlock on change was the fact that this community had been led by the same person for more than 30 years. Under his leadership, major and entrepreneurial business rapidly moved out of the community, leaving two major employers: the city and the drug dealers. Hopelessness was rampant in concert with a rising death toll of youth due to gang violence.

Utilizing organization development intervention strategies, we were able to mobilize more than 25 churches in a call to action. We also discovered that this city was eligible for a significant number of seven figure grants and empowerment zone monies that had been relegated by the federal government to this community. Yet what was interesting was that the only "grants" that people in this community had ever been aware of were the $2,000 or $3,000 "grants" by the city for "minor" reform. The empowerment zone monies alone totaled more than $10 million and the profile of this community met every major grantor's profile for economic reform dollars. The people in this community had been "hoodwinked," as we used to say, into believing that they did not have viable resources other than the city government. People wanted change, but for reasons to this day I don't understand, they were afraid to challenge or even at minimum question the person they kept electing into office.

When it looked as if we were going to be able to garner the economic support to make a difference, and put forth the processes that would address the systemic issues, suddenly the project was called to a halt by the same man who drove fear in the hearts of the people in this community. I will never forget the meeting where those working with me announced the discontinuation of the project, citing that they were sorry that I would not be able to continue. I responded by asking them: who were really the victims? When I asked them about the children, all they could do was drop their heads. It was apparent to me that these people were terrified, but at that stage of my career, I did not know how to help a room full of adults terrified of one man! To me, the solution seemed simple: stop supporting his candidacy and bring in viable candidates to run against him.

What I did see and understood was their immense fear of this man they elected. The dichotomy here clearly did not make sense. They kept putting a man in office who for more than 30 years oppressed them and continued to drive the conditions of their environment to a point to which they were forced (at least in their mindset) to rely upon him. This was a classic case where the oppressed assumed the values and veneer of the oppressor. Yet the people who resided in this community, at large, could not see the deterioration of their own personal power. In essence, years ago, they gave away that power and continued to suffer at his, as well as their own, hands. Ignorance is no longer an excuse in this century. The complexity of our global environment really does call for our engaging in a massive wakeup call. Our failure to do so has significant consequences. Already the United States is being challenged on multiple fronts relative to our global positioning economically, educationally, socially, and politically. Simply stated, we don't have the same "juice" we used to possess. As I have traveled to many countries, I find ourselves being the laughing stock of our international colleagues because they do not understand our reticence for deep systemic change and our propensity to go toward the easy answers. In other words, our insularity and silo foci have precipitated our losing the respect of our international peers. Now some might ask: why does that matter, when I am focused on daily survival?

It clearly does matter because the venues in which we operate no longer have localized walls, which forces the need for us to be beyond the mindset of daily survival. If we continue to give away our personal power when it is needed to drive the change that will enable us to stand toe-to-toe with our international colleagues, we risk losing more jobs, economic status, and credibility in concert with even more precious resources such as our children. You see, there truly is a systems issue here. When community financial resources leave, such as the tax base that is provided by businesses and institutions, critical resources are lost. Consequently, the retention of a mayor who historically drove out those viable resources impacted the quality of education for our children, the ability to bring in quality teachers and other public officials because of low wages and benefits, and the continued perpetration of a declining housing and job market, which spirals more hopelessness within a community. Therefore, when we critically examine the systemic impact of poor decisions in concert with the global impact, our standing up for change moves beyond the dimensions of "nice to do," into the arena of "we had better get moving if we want to survive."

Many human beings are resistant to change at multiple levels. Change is perceived to involve too much personal or institutional risk, yet the failure to study and personally integrate issues of social justice and the unconscious or conscious inaction on the part of those who have the ability to invoke change continues the blockage of change efforts and the perpetuation of a sinful societal status quo (Townes, 2005). Social injustice and the perpetuation of socially unjust structures as occurred in this city are made possible by the unspoken cooperation of the oppressor as well as the oppressed (Townes, 2005). We must remember our history. The process of mental liberation is quite unique. Freedom from our mental captivity must be taken, not passively requested. As our great Ancestral Saints, Harriet Tubman, Nat Turner, Ida B. Wells, Frederick Douglass, Medgar Evers, Rev. Dr. Martin Luther King, Malcolm X, and many others found, taking one's freedom can be dangerous. When one moves past singing songs of freedom to dreams and from dreams to action, you have to be prepared for the onslaught of resistance from the oppressors (Akbar, 1996). Resistance from the onslaught of oppressors is very possible. However, we must be real when we begin concerted strategic change by building in contingencies for the onslaught of activity that we know will occur. If I were to incorporate the learning I gleaned from this project today, it clearly means incorporating strategies to deconstruct and analyze the internal lessons of oppression that had a gridlock on this community, points that are addressed in later chapters in this book.

While it took five years, the people in this community finally did break free of the oppression that held them down for more than 30 years. A new mayor was elected and a new life began for many. I don't know if our work sparked fires in the hearts of the brave few; I certainly hope so. But this experience helped me to better understand the real concept of fear of change and why it is so critical to have strong leadership helping to herald the way for our liberation.

Does Our Lens "Color" Our Results?

Where we start is typically the first question one will ask. The first place where we must make a commitment to engage in processes designed to help our youth is within ourselves. Let me give an example. I remember in the early 2000s standing at the bank of the Thames River becoming very agitated about something that was occurring at my home university. It was as if Spirit took a two-by-four and hit me on the head because the first question I heard in my internal dialogue was, "Where are you?" To that internal dialogue I replied, "At the bank of the Thames River." The next question I heard Spirit posit was simply, "So why are you worrying about something you have no control over when the world can and is your playground?" I never forgot that internal dialogue.

From that point on, my worldview toward change began to dramatically shift. I first worked hard to change my internal dialogue as to what I could or could not do and where my real barriers lie.

Change is a process that moves beyond the domains of descriptive analysis. The process of moving toward change begins with one's ability to understand the situation from a holistic perspective in concert with understanding how we internally respond to challenge. I believe if the people in the community I described had possessed a different internal dialogue, the oppressor that ruled their community—and the operative words are "their community"—would not have lasted beyond one mayoral term.

Yet I wonder how often we challenge our internal dialogue and closely examine where we self-impose our barriers. My daughter recently decided to return to college. This became her decision and she set her sight on the school she wanted to attend. Despite the many challenges this young lady incurred during the past seven years as she struggled with the loss of her father, her internal dialogue simply said, "I want to attend this school and failure is not a possibility." Well, she will attend that school and it was the only school to which she applied. The power of her will made her believe that failure was not an option. As a result, doors opened that under normal circumstances would have been closed.

The power of one's will is awesome. Yet our internal dialogue is constantly bombarded with words that signal failure, issues related to self-esteem and perceptions of lack. Juxtaposed against the propensity to engage in internal (and external) conversations that provide descriptive analyses of our situations utilizing verbiage that connotes lack are post-modern organizational theorists' propositions that the manner in which people perceive their future reality can be permeable, emergent, and open to the mind's casual influence, which is created through our anticipatory images, values, plans, intentions, and beliefs (Cooperrider, 1986).

If, however, the prevailing dialogue is always negatively oriented, and the resulting intervention strategies (individual and whole systems) are primarily focused on suppressive techniques that also emerge from negative deficient orientations, ensconced in deficient-oriented linguistic representations, one can conclude that the anticipatory images, values, plans, intentions, and beliefs will follow in a similar deficient pattern, thus squelching one's ability to vision options. In other words, if you keep engaging in an internal and external dialogue as to how bad something is, and throwing up reasons to reinforce the "badness," you will soon internalize that worldview, which immanently blocks your ability to envision anything positive. Failure does become the option. Our internal dialogue reflects a lot of information as to how we see the world. But what African Americans often do not deconstruct is how our worldviews are formed. We are exposed to many intentional and unintentional methods of programming for failure.

When I began my work in 1996, I questioned how gangs constructed their existential life in vivo. What I did not see in the literature was an approach by the more "mainstream" (if there is such a category) researchers that closely examined how youth gravitating to gangs internalized societal myths, which could also become their teachers for learned behavior, thereby impacting their internal dialogues. The imagery and metaphors that youth in gangs have been historically exposed to will drive their choices and understanding of associated meaning (Barrett & Srivastva, 1991).

These metaphors must be understood as ways of seeing an object as if it were something else. Metaphors act as a way of organizing one's perceptions and work as a framework for selecting, naming, and framing characteristics of an object or experience by asserting similarity with a different, seemingly unrelated, object or experience. Metaphors transfer meaning from one domain onto another and can either enrich or enhance meaning or make sense out of something in a new and different way (Srivastva & Barrett, 1988). When we engage in sense making, we concomitantly impact our language. Interesting, the intersection between metaphors and language is quite complex. Metaphors are more capable of capturing the continuing flow of experience than literal language and can transfer more meaning that impacts our internal dialogue than that which one can say in literal translation (Srivastva & Barrett, 1988). Post-modern organization development professionals also posit that metaphors can be clues to the underlying paradigms of a given social system and indicators of changes and development in that system's vision of its reality. Metaphors can also be seen as frame expanding, a facilitator of radically new knowledge (Srivastva & Barrett, 1988). Yet the African American community at large is not surrounded by images or metaphors that suggest we can either control or change our environment, life conditions, or future. For example, the images and metaphors that inner-city housing has provided have to be examined. Before the Chicago projects were torn down, when walking through those projects that were largely populated by African Americans, you would see cages surrounding each floor, which hypothetically were designed to prevent children from falling over the railings.

The negative messages these cages projected were voluminous and should have been deconstructed by the African American community long before they began to send images of hopelessness and lockdown. We needed to understand the meaning one derived from living in brick rooms, so typical of Chicago inner-city projects. We needed to understand how our youth associated learning with policemen daily patrolling their schools, as they walked through metal detectors before entering class. How could we have helped them change their interpretations of these artifacts that were (and still are for many) a part of their daily surroundings? During my research, I asked one youth what he associated with the projects in Chicago. While this young man had never lived in a project, he responded that bad people live in those projects. I pushed the button a little further by asking him what he would think of himself if he lived in the projects. His answer: he would then *be* a bad person.

The Lens of Researchers of Color

Researchers of color who investigated gang behaviors provided a very different perspective on the historical context and dynamics of gangs, which suggested youth in gangs possessing competencies beyond their ability to just evoke violence. For example, Martin Sanchez-Jankowski (1991) from the University of California at Berkeley conducted a 10-year study of 37 gangs of varying ethnic backgrounds in three major cities: New York, Boston, and Los Angeles. The research centered in low-income areas, where gangs had been an institution for years. The ethnic groups studied included Mexican Americans, African Americans, Salvadorans, Nicaraguans, Puerto Ricans, Dominican Jamaicans, and Irish gangs. Sanchez-Jankowski reported these gangs to be an organizational response to inequality and poverty that act in an *entrepreneurial* manner (Lockwood, 1993).

While gangs did at that time frequently engage in criminal activity, Sanchez-Jankowski (1991) reported that crime was not the central issue. He challenged the majority of gang studies that sought to explain gang behavior and crime as an outgrowth of the persistent and pervasive poverty, which afflicts certain black and Latino communities.

Sanchez-Jankowski's study (1991) focused on the organizational traits of gangs, which included the nature, dynamic, and impact of the gang's organizational qualities. He reported that one of the reasons that society does not understand gangs or the gang phenomenon very well was due to there not being enough systematic studies undertaken as to how the gang works as an organization. Sanchez-Jankowski theorized that the gang emerges not as a result of disorganization or the desire to find order and safety, but as a consequence of a particular type of social order. He identified this social order as one that is associated with low-income neighborhoods in American society that are organized around an intense competition for and conflict over the scarce resources that exist in their areas (1991). Therefore, the structure, methodology, and projected theory of Sanchez-Jankowski's work investigated the gang phenomenon and gang behavior by analyzing the dynamics between individuals in gangs, gang organizations, and their relationship to the institutions outside the world, issues grounded in socioeconomic survival (1991).

During the ten years Sanchez-Jankowski studied gangs he found many characteristics of the gang as an organization to be similar to those characteristics of corporate America. Organizational characteristics reported included the gang possessing a selective membership process, similar to corporate recruiting, and selection practices complete with applications and interviews (1991). Padilla (1992) and Hagedorn (1988) concurred with Sanchez-Jankowski's findings that gangs do not allow in every individual who wants to join the gang.

Decisions were made concerning membership, predicated on organizational needs. The observed criteria for membership included the optimal number of members needed to maintain the goals of the organization, the prestige of the gang, the efficiency of its operations, and the adequacy of services to its members (Sanchez-Jankowski, 1991). Similar to corporations, Sanchez-Jankowski also observed that the gang's ability to hold its members was dependent on its capacity to provide services and benefits, including entertainment, protection, financial assets, and material possessions (1991).

During Sanchez-Jankowski's study, informants confirmed that they joined the gang for financial security, viewing the gang as an organization that could provide gang members and their families with money in times of emergency. The gang represented a combination of a bank and a social security system, similar to the security blanket the political machine represented to many immigrants in the 1920s and 1930s (1991). He also recorded observations about how the gang engaged in strategic planning, mobilizing resources (including human resources), creating new resources, and assessing the effectiveness of how plans were being implemented, while also observing that the gang's ability to be an efficient organization was contingent upon its capacity to establish legitimacy in its authority structure (1991).

Sanchez-Jankowski also recorded three basic forms of organizational structure and leadership styles within the gang: the vertical-hierarchical structure, similar to the hierarchy of many organizations where the central leader delegates responsibilities and the authority to execute those responsibilities to gang members in designated ranks; the horizontal-commission type where leadership is a shared process (similar to participative management); and the influential structure where the leadership is assumed by the most charismatic authority figure or figures (in cases where shared leadership exists) and executed in a manner that does not invite participative decision making (1991). During my research, when the topics would move toward the organizational context of the gang, my respondents reported similar information.

Felix Padilla from DePaul University focused on the entrepreneurial traits of gang organizations and interpreted the experiences of the Chicago Puerto Rican gang he studied as extending beyond the conventional "deviant social scene" paradigm. He viewed the gang's behavior as a response to the only course of action still available to them, one with which they could challenge the existing constraints dominated by mainstream society (1992).

Padilla reported that the gang clearly saw their criminal behaviors as their most logical answer to the "vision" that they perceived mainstream society to be delivering, a vision that offered limited amounts of resources and opportunities available for ethnic and racial minorities in the United States. The young men he studied viewed joining a gang as their opportunity to pursue economic advantages through entrepreneurial enterprises, a perspective corroborated by my own research (1992).

Both Sanchez-Jankowski (1991) and Padilla (1992) observed the entrepreneurial side of the gang and noted their patterns of risk taking in business activities. Although these reports represented the feedback by gang members who were primarily in their late teens to early twenties, there were frequent discussions regarding investment of time, money, and resources.

Sanchez-Jankowski (1991) reported instances where gangs ran mom-and-pop stores that sold groceries, candy, and soft drinks; took over abandoned apartment buildings, renovated them, and rented them cheaply for the community members; and provided free accommodations for those in the community that had no place to go. This behavior was consistent with antidotal information I heard when interviewing my subjects who readily talked about how, in the 1960s and 1970s in Chicago, gang members would own entire blocks within communities that consisted of store and apartment buildings. I also witnessed these entrepreneurial enterprises growing up in Chicago's inner city.

What interested me then, as it does now, is the difference between the lens of researchers of color versus those that have had no ethnic or racial ties to the subjects. If we accept the premise that knowledge is linguistically and relationally constructed, then it becomes difficult to ignore the role of the researcher. Not only do researchers play a role in constructing what they discover as reality, their theoretical sensitivities also impact how data is collected as well as analyzed (Barrett, Thomas, & Hocevar, 1995). The researcher's individual identity, culture, and diversity attributes do impact perception of the situation, design of the intervention strategy, or their interpretive schemas, which can impact results. I have often wondered if these perspectives had been incorporated into whole systems change strategies during the time in which all three of us were conducting our work, would we be having a different conversation at this time regarding the loss of youth to gang violence?

African American people in this country have a history of working outside the system. We often hear from our elders stories of the policy wheels (our version of the lottery before it became legal) that sparked economic reform in the African American community and helped make many African American families rise above an average income. I remember those stories, although the peak of those days existed before I was born. I remember the stories about communities in Chicago where African Americans lived, had entrepreneurial enterprises, and successfully conducted their nonmainstream activities. I remember hearing reminiscences about culture in the African American community, accountability, and visions of prosperity. Yet, in today's environment, those same communities (at least those that have not undergone regentrification) are ghettos, riddled with violence, drugs, ill-kept housing, and poor-performing schools supporting the youth that now live there.

Often when conducting and analyzing inquiry, our attempts to be value neutral are actually conducted within a field of values (Allen & Hardin, 2001),which begs the question as to how researchers who studied youth in gangs viewed them prior to engaging in their research. Could it be that those researchers who studied gang subjects from their own ethnic backgrounds openly acknowledged their personal qualities and experiences, thereby opening space for another level of a consciousness of meaning to enter that can be subtle yet of significant impact when deconstructing how we create and manage sense and meaning (Pettigrew, 1979)?

When you set forth expectations of success, people will rise to the occasion. Yet, when researching gangs and proposing solutions, we have to consider the premise of post-modern organization behavioral theorists who believe that our knowledge of social phenomena is fundamentally shaped by the subjective worldviews through which we perceive events (Tenkasi, Thatchenkery, Barrett, & Manning, 1994).

Albeit, more than 20 years ago, this point was interestingly reinforced via a study of gangs in their natural environment. Hagedorn, a researcher from the University of Wisconsin at Milwaukee, asserted a problem with current gang research, citing issues appeared to have an intense focus on gangs from the perspective of law enforcement agencies. He posited that the media images of gangs were not to be trusted as true pictures of gang behavior and suggested that the media forms and reinforces a law-enforcement focus on gangs that may not be the only lens through which to look at today's gang members (1988).

The original Pygmalion research and a subsequent study that investigated the Pygmalion Effect with youth in gangs provided empirical data that suggested the relational pathways of the positive image–positive action dynamic and of the transactional basis of the human self (Rosenthal & Jacobson, 1968; Garcia, 1981). Although this is a concept that will be explored throughout the book, it is critical to note it at this point.

Social construction theorists also suggest that an individual's future reality is also permeable, emergent, and open to the mind's causal influence; that is, reality is conditioned, reconstructed, and often profoundly created through our anticipatory images, values, plans, intentions, and beliefs (Cooperrider, 1986). Yet, due to researcher's existing paradigms and language, individuals may already hold beliefs of what is to be *perceived*, thus disabling our ability to see the beauty in these young people. Consequently, our theories and cognitive schema may determine what will count (Tenkasi et al., 1994).

Therefore, as researchers, we must be careful in avoiding phenomena where the questions we pose to gang members may in fact be contributors to the guiding praxis for the sophisticated or violent development of gangs. Moore (1978), when evaluating the institutions that gave rise to the barrios of California, succinctly stated that "the professional opinions of institutional officials were increasingly challenged as ultimate judgments of effectiveness in minority areas. Some of this challenge is part of a general and radical critique of society, but much of it is quite specific" (p. 23). She further stated that there are three fundamental themes that belonged to institutional researchers at that time: "internal colonialism"; "blaming the victim"; and "programming for failure."

Comprehensively understanding our world is said to emanate from our activity, which produces a social context that defines who we are. Yet, when researching, we tend to play multiple roles: that of subjectively coherent participants in jointly produced storylines, or that of an objective participant (Davies, 1991). The questions asked by Sanchez-Jankowski, Padilla, myself, and others of similar circumstances, as well as the results we have generated, have stemmed from a lifetime of having lived, albeit not in all, but in many of the social constructions of the actors we described. Reflexive research in the organizational literature has emphasized the inclusion of the researcher in the subject matter he or she is trying to understand (Hardy, Phillips, & Clegg, 2001). Over time, many social scientists have concluded that the quest for objectivity in research is hopeless (Gouldner, 1970) and have posited that our knowledge, relationship to self, others, activity, and to our world is constituted and mediated by our engagements in our world, our resulting discourse as well as our social practices (Ricoeur, 1992; Cobb, 1994; Piaget, 1972; Steffe & Gale, 1995; Tobin, 1993; Von Glasersfeld, 1993; Packer & Goicoechea, 2000).

Our lens toward understanding the situations and people that reside in those circumstances is not to put them down but to offer alternative views for their existence. But oftentimes our work is overshadowed by the more mainstream research that can and will grab the attention of the media. Which means a different story will emerge . . . a story that has historically been grounded in a negative discourse relative to the multiplicity of lack that is found in our communities. These are the perspectives and stories our children hear, which continues to ground them in hopelessness.

Unfortunately, when African Americans try to understand themselves and the issues that reside within their communities from traditional streams of research, study, and change, we typically face Eurocentric psychologies that have historically been replete with bias, making it extremely difficult to understand who we truly are in order to systemically cope with our realities, realities that are plagued with layers of challenge (Mitchem, 2002; Akbar, 2003; Easley, 2010). As African Americans, we are first rooted in a culture very different from our European counterparts, and second, the quality of our environment is systematically different from the environment in which Western writers use as a point of reference for relating to and understanding our condition (Akbar, 2003). Therefore, if the cultural environment is different from the perspective that is used for relating to and understanding our condition, is it fair to say that change-management strategies may have similar limitations (Easley, 2010)?

These are differences we cannot ignore. They drive the question as to whether we should intentionally utilize more *culturally* appropriate points of reference for developing an attitude of liberation that results in new paradigms that also allow us to reach the fullest potential of our minds and bodies (Hopkins, 2005). And they drive the proposition that as researchers we have to be willing to help our subjects understand the paradigmatic perspectives of all the results that impact decisions with respect to evoking "change." We have to be willing to help our people become discerners of "truth" and not be afraid to challenge the results that are set forth as ultimate reality. I wonder what would have happened if, years ago, we challenged researchers to conduct their research from a different mindset?

All human systems are conditioned by their internal dialogue, and our minds are influenced by any number of cognitive environments, such as the family, school, church, play, and even the environments created by our research methods and problem-solving technologies. Yet, in 2010, our children still face challenges to their psychological existence via inappropriate value-laden insinuations and propositions emanating from research that is supposed to be designed to remediate the situation. The promulgated results and recommended strategies from this research typically serve to challenge our youth's competencies and self-worth. Metaphorically, they are told via the lack of resources within multiple venues in our community that they are not worthy. Therefore, to effectively understand our structural issues is to also understand the bigger picture of power and domination and how it works to subjugate people across the world.

Deconstructing Our Situations from a Different Paradigmatic View

When I began my dissertation work in 1996, gang members were also concerned as to why the younger gang members were engaging in such brutal levels of violence. Consequently, while I was given access to interview and work with the younger gang members, I was very clear in understanding the limits relative to the age groups I could work with. During my research, I met an older man who mentored me through this process. I never once, however, believed our meeting was by chance. I have always intuitively felt that he was "assigned" to me. He was quite intriguing—in his sixties at the time, a resident of Cabrini-Green, educated (albeit did not complete his degree) at Dartmouth, and one of the most intelligent men I had ever met who taught me significant life lessons. He had been involved in gangs for the majority of his life, having at one time served in a leadership role with one of the first Chicago gangs.

The very first conversation he and I had as I was interviewing two other people began to challenge my initial assumptions.

Mentor:	What you are doing, how are these two brothers going to benefit? 'Cause, I can understand what you are doing, it is a behavioral study. How are these two individuals directly benefiting? Hypothetically?
Mentor:	I don't want to sound like I am directing a personal attack.
Interviewer:	Go ahead.
Mentor:	But, I have been through what you are doing thirty some years, and to just sit and discuss only for the sake of you doing a dissertation. (Easley, 1999)

This man was fully aware that sociologists, criminologists, and psychologists had been researching gang behavior for many years in concert with little to no history of successful and sustaining work toward changing the socioeconomics of these communities.

Mentor:	They found the answers.
Interviewer:	Sure they did, Thrasher did, Foote did, all of them found the answers. And that is the step beyond that I want to go. Now that they have put their dissertations on the shelf and made money, I am not interested in doing what they have done, because I could make it a lot easier for me. That is what I'm at. So, it is not a personal attack. I understand where you are coming from. There is a lot of legitimacy in your question.

Mentor: I was just curious, 'cause I have been listening to things like that for thirty years. Somebody coming in, doing a thesis and talking about some social dynamic about gangs and it ends right there. Creates these expectations with brothers like me. Two years down the line, that is why they get discouraged and wind up gravitating back to these corners and buildings. (Easley, 1999)

However, what was critical with our working together were our conversations that focused on exploring, through dialogue, what could happen if the African American community, through a deep discursive analysis of our bondage coupled with a willingness to dislodge the metaphorical meanings we have internalized via strategic engagement, began to formulate a new reality for ourselves and our children. The simplicity of his challenging my initial assumptions helped me to expand my thinking of possibilities—an intentional dialogue that began to dislodge my initial unrealistic guiding praxes.

> Liberation is thus a child birth, and a painful one. The man or woman who emerges is a new person, viable only as the oppressor-oppressed contradiction is superseded by the humanization of all people. Or to put it another way, the solution of this contradiction is born in the labor which brings into the world this new being: no longer oppressor no longer oppressed, but human in the process of achieving freedom. (Freire, 2006)

The negativity that we are bombarded with in concert with more salient issues that contribute to the destabilization of the African American community impact how we internalize self-worth and envision our ability to question collectively that which is placed in front of us as "truth." Our knowledge of social phenomena is fundamentally shaped by the subjective worldviews through which we perceive events (Tenkasi et al., 1994). Yet, as a collective, do we critically examine the etiology and sustainability of those worldviews?

> The peasant begins to get courage to overcome his dependence when he realizes that he is dependent. Until then, he goes along with the boss and says "What can I do? I'm only a peasant." (Freire, 2006, p. 61)

Our youth must learn from the adults in their lives how to deconstruct and analyze negative messages that can result in internalized negative behaviors. But this awareness must reside first with parents and community members. For example, many parents struggle with school systems labeling their children.

Drugs have become the typical answers to address children who are said to have ADD or other various learning challenges. Unfortunately, many of our youth wind up in behavioral disorder classes, when in reality the options to challenge and engage our children are not being fully explored.

My daughter was diagnosed with ADD in first grade. What brought the situation to the attention of my husband and I were the notes that began to come home from the first-grade teacher shortly after my daughter entered her class. The language she began to use to describe not only the behavior but also my child was totally unacceptable in our eyes, so we engaged and challenged her labeling.

What many parents do not understand is that young people have rights under the law, and those rights do not entail the ability of a school system to automatically engage in warehousing a child. My husband and I strongly suggested that the school conduct an evaluation to identify resources my daughter needed in concert with our garnering help from her physician. The interesting outcome was her requiring minimum help. But helping my child manage through those years took effort in order to ensure that other teachers did not engage in labeling once they knew she had been diagnosed with ADD. Each year at the beginning of the academic term, I required a sit-down with her teachers and principal throughout all of her primary and junior high years. During those sit-down sessions, I explained to them that language can and does mediate our reality. In other words, they had to have their academic training in Appreciative Inquiry and a revisit of Pygmalion research.

They had to learn, as had I, that instead of saying to a child you are ADD, when you change the dialogue to "You have ADD," the perception of internal locus of control dramatically changes as does the child's internal dialogue. So, each year we had our appreciative conversation that identified my expectations relative to teacher-student interactions and outcomes. The outcomes were appropriate, and I can only hope that what they learned was passed on to other children. Was this time consuming? Absolutely. Was I unhappy that I had to do it? Yes. Frankly, because they were experienced educators, I was very unhappy with having to go through an education process before the term began. Would I have altered my interactions? Unequivocally no!

You see more than just the teachers learned lessons. My daughter internalized many lessons from the support she received from her father and me, lessons, I believe, that were foundational to her eventually moving past the blockages she experienced with the death of her father. While we may not always see the results of our actions in real time, the lessons and support we provide a child, I am convinced, never get lost.

What has always amazed me is that there is significant research that suggests the existence of multiple learning styles with children. Even when teaching traditional-aged students and older adults returning to school, I always have to utilize multiple strategies to ensure that the information is being effectively processed simply because people learn via different styles and at different rates. It does not make them bad people; it simply is life. I am a visual learner, but my husband was just the opposite. Consequently, when we had to do things that required learning new tasks, we learned to accommodate our differences.

But as I have talked with K–12 educators over the years, especially those that work in inner-city schools where so many of our youth reside, I always get pushback on their utilizing multiple strategies to engage the multiple learning styles because the classrooms are too full. Quite frankly, I find that to be a poor excuse for inappropriately educating and challenging our youth. Equally so, I find our willingness to accept these excuses without a community engagement as to investigating and demanding options to be equally, if not more, inappropriate.

However, I want to be clear. These types of inappropriate and negative dialogues are abundant in many educational environments that impact our youth, not just inner-city schools. As I will continue to posit throughout this book, our children are attacked on multiple fronts and if we are not actively engaged in their lives, we won't always understand or know the parameters of and damage caused by those attacks. The dismissal of African American students as viable contenders in our global society is more widespread that we can even imagine. Consequently, the ability to lose a child via he or she assuming and internalizing a dialogue of hopelessness can occur at points in their lives that we may not recognize if we are not on top of our own game, which means our own internal dialogue as well as community support systems have to be strong to provide the protection our youth need.

So, bear with me as I provide one more personal example outside the boundaries of inner-city schools. My son attended a state high school whose mission was to select and educate the top talent in our state. Because there was an element of experimenting with this concept, this school brought in the best and brightest educators available, many with doctoral degrees (to teach at the high school level) and many being recipients of very prestigious awards in their field, including Nobel prizes.

The first day he and the few other African American children selected arrived on that campus, they encountered a very pronounced derogatory dialogue by some of the instructors who were bold in their assertions that the only reason these kids were attending this school was to meet the affirmative action guidelines imposed by the state. Not once did those perpetrators of doubt open my son's academic file to see that his IQ was at genius level. He did not "look" like a gifted child according to their standards, so they initially did what they could to challenge his right to be there.

But you see my son was well equipped with his own internal dialogue that did not allow him to succumb to their perceptions. Nor did he desire to look like them during his entire tenure at the school. He maintained who he was and "whose" he was (and is) with the attitude of success that surprised many. He graduated from the school, still being himself and went on to attend the college of his choice, not the state school he was "expected" to attend because he graduated from this program. Because his internal dialogue that impacted his self-esteem was strong, I only had to go to the school twice during the years he attended to have a conversation with a couple of instructors. And trust me, after our conversation he had no more encounters.

If a mother and father do not understand the dynamics of their child's experiences, they cannot effectively address those dynamics within the home or school, thereby effectively not equipping the child with the appropriate defense mechanisms to fight onslaughts to their self-esteem. The same proposition holds true for African American adults. We have to deconstruct the dynamics impacting our ability to envision ourselves from a different lens, a lens that suggests our ability to stand in our own personal power. Most times the mere presence of a parent in the school is enough to put educators on guard that they do not have the right to arbitrarily and capriciously dismiss a child. But far too often I hear my fellow colleagues who educate at the K–12 levels talk about how few parents even come to open houses or report card-pickup sessions in order to dialogue with their schools and teachers. This lack of support for our youth is not a function of the system; it is a direct result of our own inability to manage critical processes that impact the growth and development of our youth.

While community will be addressed in other areas of this book, I want to make another point regarding community. Many might say, because you are an educator and possess a doctorate degree, you knew what to do. Yes, I did know what to do, but that does not mean I have not and am not willing to share my knowledge with others. Everyone does not know what to do, and in many situations I do not. But we all need someone to call upon to provide guidance. That is what standing in community is all about. I also believe that this is what it means to be a supportive African American community to one another, particularly when it comes to our youth. Strength is and always will be in numbers. However, we have to have a strategy for ensuring that we always function in community, which is why a strategic and systemic plan is critical to our moving past survival mode.

· 4 ·

LOSING THIS BATTLE IS NOT AN OPTION: WHAT THE REAL LOSS OF OUR CHILDREN MEANS TO THE AFRICAN AMERICAN COMMUNITY

If we reexamine my propositions, one conclusion is that the social order has not and does not appear to be changing. Until there is a change in how African Americans understand and respond to the prevailing socioeconomic landscape of this country that either directly or indirectly gives rise to the continuation of gangs and their resulting violence growing at exponential levels, we will not be able to save our youth. We cannot continue to passively engage in or episodically address these issues.

We must understand the composition of the oppression in which we reside. Some say there is a duality in oppressed people. On one level, they are themselves, and on another level, they represent the image of the oppressor, which they have internalized—an issue that African Americans have been unofficially addressing in our communities for years. It is not until the oppressed concretely discover their oppressor and, in turn, their own consciousness that they can move past a fatalistic attitude toward their situation (Freire, 2006).

What has continued to intrigue me as I walk through seminary and examine various literatures is that power and domination are common themes across far too many cultures. It is also quite interesting to examine how people in these varying cultures grapple with their status in life and their relationship to God. Now, why am I bringing this issue into the picture? For far too long, African Americans have been told that they are less than their White counterparts. Even in the midst of the abolishment of laws that eliminated the inability of African Americans to equally participate in the various institutions of life, we still get messages that we are not equals in this society. However, if we closely examine what kept our slave ancestors alive—their refusal to believe that God had left them—was for many the rock that fortified their survival. So a belief in something higher than ourselves is critical to our ability to move past the barriers we daily endure. This same belief is also critical for our youth. If you closely examine many of those cultures and ethnicities that are moving beyond survival, what continues to keep them surviving is a grounded faith in something or someone bigger than themselves.

Issues of poverty and domination extend not only to the inner cities of the United States but also across the world. Third World poverty and domination has been the subject of many researchers, particularly theologians. The intersection of our acceptance of poverty and domination juxtaposed against our theological beliefs is something African Americans should critically analyze in order to mentally shift our worldview. The two states are in conflict with one another. Yet we have allowed them to exist in our own minds side by side.

The practice of subjecting people has deep historical roots. So does our theology and cosmology. If we are one with God there is no justifying our accepting the conditions we have lived in, particularly post slavery, because we have had opportunities to turn this situation around. Yet we tend to lose sight of our real power. Oppression and the resulting poverty still are unequal geographical distributions along the lines of race, ethnicity, and gender. South Asia and Sub-Saharan African account for about 70% of the global population of people living on less than a dollar a day, up from about 60% a few years ago (Hardt, & Negri, 2005). However:

> When it becomes a program, hopelessness paralyzes us, immobilizes us. We succumb to fatalism, and then it becomes impossible to muster the strength we absolutely need for a fierce struggle that will re-create the world. I am hopeful, not out of mere stubbornness, but out of an existential concrete imperative. (Freire, 1997)

What can this existential concreteness mean in the African American community? Belief in something or someone greater than ourselves who has made us in one's own image is one of the most powerful beliefs one can have. This belief moves us beyond objectification and our resignation to living in a dualistic society. It facilitates our embracing a right to move past hopelessness and immobilization and claim that which is, and has been, ours for a lifetime. However, before we can seamlessly move into a new mindset, we must understand why we continue to wallow in objectification and allow domination to impact the one resource we cannot afford to lose—our children.

Dr. Na'im Akbar (1996), who sits center stage as one of our own preeminent psychologists, evaluates our history of slavery and its impact upon our current state from a perspective that views many of our worldviews and relationship issues to emanate from our being in an ongoing crisis of posttraumatic stress syndrome, which began with slavery:

> The slavery that captures the mind and imprisons the motivation, perception, aspiration and identity in a web of anti-self images, generating a personal and collective self-destruction is more cruel than the shackles on the wrists and ankle. (pp. v–vi)

Slavery is therefore seen as the beginning point for understanding our psyche. I have no argument with Akbar's propositions that our views, relationships with, and habits toward critical areas of our lives, such as our interactions with one another, how we view work, property, leadership, our view of and relationship with God, as well as how we engage in mockery toward one another are grounded in the roots of slavery. Equally critical is his proposition that the most serious effect emanating from slavery has been the destruction of the African American family, which under normal circumstances is the very foundation of healthy, constructive, personal, and community life (1996).

In the absence of a strong family, individual life and community can become very unstable (Akbar, 1996). Historically our ancestors weathered storms that one can only imagine. The trek through the Middle Passages alone would have psychologically and mentally broke most people. Yet a vast majority of our people survived. We cannot, however, deny the mark of this terror on our present-day psyche. While many will say get over it because slavery is a thing of the past, there are others that point to the continuation of our suffering on a daily basis. Far too many of us are treated daily as if we were invisible; and our fears often impact our relationship with one another. We wallow in fear of being vulnerable to one another, resulting in a lack of trust, authentic love, and true community (Butler, 2000).

These stress-related circumstances that surround our lives have to be analyzed for what they truly are. Losing our children cannot become a fatalistic reality just because we cannot get our arms around the problem in order to effectively envision viable solutions:

If we understand the historical origin of these roles and patterns, then perhaps we will
refuse to play them any longer. (Akbar, 1996, p. 22)

Throughout this book, I have continued to posit that spiritual death, a
death without hope, is just as destructive as physical death. Our conquer-
ing spiritual death must begin with an internalization that we are special—
human beings who operate based upon our self-consciousness, which means
our limitations rest only in our ignorance. Therefore, it is critical that we
acquire a consciousness of who we are and what we have been in order to
operate to our full human capacity (Akbar, 1996). A movement toward new
perspectives requires we shed the identity crisis with which we have become
comfortable, while realizing that it is not our legacy to suffer all our lives. Our
ultimate human power is our mental power, our consciousness, and our awareness (Akbar, 1996), which means that we must never lose our understanding
of our spirituality.

As I have researched our communities, I continue to ponder an issue originally posited by Rev. Dr. Howard Thurman (1976). Why is it so difficult for
us to believe that in a core analysis of our theology lies the truism that we are
children of God, the God of life that sustains all of nature and guarantees all
the intricacies of the life process itself? Even when we examine those that rose
up against slavery, can we effectively posit that perhaps a common denominator in their understanding of their relationship with God was in their belief
that God does indeed guarantee all the intricacies of the life process itself,
which was not a far stretch from their cosmological and theological belief that
emanated from Africa? Why have we lost that grounding? And, equally important, how do we regain it? Our African roots were grounded in the belief that
held all life as sacred and singular, not a world split into multiple parts with
irreconcilable opposing parts (Butler, 2000). If we fast-forward this worldview
into today's context, what happens to our children is the problem of every
African American in this country—in other words we go back to the basic
concept of community.

The deconstruction of our present reality cannot be left to happenstance
because the problems are too deeply rooted. It has to be a nationwide conversation among African Americans if we are to redirect the path of our youth.
Within the framework of that conversation we begin to holistically understand and address our issues, which is foundational for a multidimensional
approach that will involve many working to ameliorate the issues of youth
gravitating to gangs and the ensuing violence.

The risk of not addressing the issues that plague our communities as well as our children guarantees a continuation of strategies that yield limited-to-no results. For example, in 2008, the University of Chicago's Crime Lab posted a report online. They reported that a total of 510 people were murdered in Chicago during 2008, with 80% of these victims killed by gunfire. Half were between the ages of 10 and 25, with the vast majority of these youth being male (Ander, Cook, Ludwig, & Pollack, 2009).

They found that the dramatic overrepresentation of both young males and firearms in homicide is not unique to Chicago, nor are these new patterns. Over the past 55 years they reported that, while the age-adjusted death rate in the United States declined by nearly 45%, from 1,446 to 799 deaths per 100,000 people, in contrast, despite some cyclical ups and downs, the murder rate during that same time span remained about 20% higher than its 1950 value (Ander et al., 2009).

These are alarming statistics, but what were more alarming were the stories they reported by the parents of a youth who had died:

> In 1999, my son was killed by these two guys. I had to go to the hospital and see my son's lifeless body lying on a slab. Then I had to go to the morgue to see where they cut his head open for an autopsy. . . . Within a month . . . my other brother got killed. And it needs to stop. People [are] just taking people's kids' lives for no apparent reason. They have no value on life. They don't know what the parents go through, how they feel. (Ander et al., 2009, p. 4)

By now we should understand that programs will not work. A new vision that embodies an entitlement to that which is afforded mainstream society is the beginning of our making a difference in the lives of our children. Our children need us to vision hope for a better future. The children I worked with had little to no hope.

> I ain't going to make it. Every time I take one step forward, there are two steps backwards happening. (Easley, 1999)

Within the context of hope lie the content qualities of relationship such as love, joy, peace, goodness, beauty, and freedom (Marcel, 1963). However, when we examine the lives of our youth who gravitate to gangs, many have been stripped of those content qualities of relationships. Therefore, they gravitate to the gang environment searching for that which is missing in their lives. When the lives of African Americans, and especially African American children, are continually stripped of quality relationships, it stands to reason that they will turn to any type of relationship that appears to offer security. We often fail to acknowledge that the gang itself is seen as a family, with their own set of family values. Consequently, when our children enter the gang environment, they are engaging in a set of relationships where the survival of gang members at any cost becomes a primary focus. Therefore, when a "family member" is lost, the gang's bond is strengthened rather than weakened, which typically leads to destructive behaviors in order to cope with their feeling vulnerable (Butler, 2000).

Yet there is hope. However, in order to successfully understand how a new reality can be constructed, we must first understand how our current reality paralyzes us as well as how we are historically, systemically, and strategically placed into location and roles that do not address our realities, thereby providing limiting answers to looming questions (Mitchem, 2002). We have to understand how our current patterns of interacting with one another, especially our children, are patterns that were formed as early as the Middle Passages.

> Our relationships are governed by power differentials and power plays. U.S. slavery set up a racial caste system, which continues to influence our relationships. Our interactions tend to be controlled externally by negative images and forces dictated by a dominant hierarchical culture. While a high degree of mutuality has fostered our survival in the U.S., we have been inclined to live according to superior/inferior roles. We have imitated the dominant culture's norms for relationship rather than clinging to the ideas that brought us through our hardships. (Butler, 2000, p. 25)

To continue in the manner we have without effecting appropriate support systems, in concert with a dialogical process that works to emerge deep-change strategies, is counterproductive to ourselves, our families, and our future. How do we heal the pain we feel on a daily basis and do we even understand how deeply rooted that pain is in our children?

PART TWO

A HISTORICAL LOOK AT MY
1999 RESULTS

· 5 ·

THE ISSUES FROM THE LENS
OF A CHILD

When I began my doctoral work, I will never forget sitting in a committee session where Dr. David Cooperrider warned me that I would have to defend what there was to value about youth in gangs. While each of us sitting in that room clearly understood the value of this work, David was preparing me for what surely did occur as I proceeded through the process. I learned that I would and did have to be prepared to deal with public scrutiny. Yet the answer to this question seemed so simple.

The children I worked with, as well as some of the college students I mentored who were former gang members, helped me to understand that when we stripped away the publicized concept of the gang, the images we would see in the media and movies and the descriptions we read in the newspapers, the answer was very clear—they are *our* youth. And in many cases they could be children each of us knew or they could be our own children. Unfortunately, they are and continue to be a critical part of our population that we are losing to the death tolls that result from gang violence. If we are serious about stopping gang violence, we have to look within the hearts of these young people and beyond the hardness they attempt to project and help them to find their inner beauty.

When we examine youth in gangs and their behaviors, it is easy to assume that, because of their gang affiliations, they may not share mainstream values.

However, when I asked, they were very willing to talk about their hopes and dreams, which were no different from those that you or I would have shared, or those of our own children. I learned during the three years I listened to youth in gangs that when stripped of all the bravado, many of them were young teens attempting to cope with their perceptions of reality, which was very painful to them.

A child is a gift from God that should be nurtured. And in our community, our children are our future, our hope, as well as our blessings. During the course of my interviewing many of these young people, it was hard for me to believe all that they endured within their lives, which were a very short span of years. Many of the interviewees were not much older than my son, who was 15 at that time. The strife these young people were exposed to was overwhelming. I could not begin to conceptualize my own child having to work through so many issues, hardships, and assaults on his sense of self and worth. Listening to their pain was an overwhelming experience.

In 1999, the *Chicago Tribune* published an article that talked about the biggest enemy of children at that time, a perspective that the children I interviewed corroborated. Children have an enemy that can be as potentially fatal as child abuse. That enemy is indifference. Whether by social workers, teachers, police officers, judges, or the public, to turn our backs on a child in pain is to guarantee the pain will continue (Green, 1999). Throughout my research, I heard the pain of young people involved in gangs. At every level of their lives they were told that they had no future, that they were less than other young people, and that adults had no time for them. They articulated a belief that they would not be able to succeed in reaching their dreams. Yet their dreams were quite interesting.

When asked what future they envisioned, these young people were quite clear in their need to turn their lives around, move away from the gang environment, and continue their education process. A number of the young people I interviewed were already in college and had successfully disengaged from the gang life. Yet, they fully understood how easy it would be to return to that life if they did not continue along the path of matriculating through a more "mainstream society."

What I have often also found interesting, as I conducted this work, is the underlying attitudes youth had toward the gang environment. They saw the gang as an alternative environment to their ability to move through a more traditional society that was closed to them. Yet their visions of what their lives should be were no different from any other youth. They saw education as critical to their successful matriculation through life. They had many creative and interesting variations on the theme of making something out of themselves.

Equally interesting were their responses when asked why they joined a gang. Their comments communicated feelings of isolation juxtaposed against a need to belong to something. In far too many cases, these young people felt abandoned by the same institutions they needed to make it in life. Yet their challenge was how to reopen the doors of those institutions and the people within them that they needed. Consistently, they talked about the need to reconnect to family, community, and school. A majority of them consistently communicated how they did not like the gang environment but saw that environment as the only viable source for connecting on a physical- and mental-bonding level. Many discussed feeling isolated and needing someone to help them navigate through life's challenges. And they consistently talked about how spending time with them was so important. The failure to spend time with a child appeared to be central to their needs and desire to find alternative solutions to joining a gang. Spending time emerged as the primary theme within the coding structure when I analyzed their data.

It is so easy to say what young people must do to turn around their lives, but we have to understand that at the bottom levels of their actions that cause us discontent are emotional voids that we must work hard to understand. Similar to them, I was reticent to open up and talk about my real feelings. It was not until I felt I was in a safe environment that could I talk about the emotional pain of loneliness, which begs the question of where and when do our youth have "safe" space. As parents, they are constantly facing the frustration we feel because of their actions, which leads to nothing more than a vicious circle. They act, we become frustrated, and that frustration causes more isolation, which ignites more bad behavior. At some point the circle has to break in order to allow a more constructive emotional dialogue.

I also began to understand that before discounting if there was anything to appreciate about youth in gangs, I needed to understand and help others understand why they felt so much was missing in their lives. These young people were quite open and willing to share their beliefs that the adults in their world had written them off. And they understood how and why the adults in their lives reacted to and felt about gangs. Unfortunately, it became a vicious circle. The more the adults in their lives disconnected from them, the more attractive the gang environment became because of the loneliness they felt.

The more I interacted with these young people, the more I felt that we had an obligation to help them begin to look within themselves and see their positive attributes. Like a butterfly embedded in a cocoon, when given just half a chance, these young people had and desired the ability to emerge as a beautiful butterfly and capture one's heart.

A Story within the Story

My doctoral research was the beginning of my own personal transformation that is still ongoing. I believe God places us in situations that provide opportunities for us to truly understand our life's work. I found that there was no way possible that the researcher who attempts to understand and listen to the hearts and souls of youth will not change. Although I strongly believed that prior researchers had not given credence to young people's ability to appreciate themselves and their skills, I quickly found when I first began decoding data that I looked at it from the same perspective as those researchers I had so vehemently criticized. I could not finish the process, but had to return to the field.

Although my self-appointed assistant continued to communicate how alternative value systems and structures were playing out in the gang situation, I was so busy expounding my views at first that I did not listen to him. At the same time, I asked a friend who was also conducting gang research to read what I had thus far written. She criticized my views and cautioned me relative to my initial assumptions that youth in gangs might not have a vision. We had long conversations on how they could be developing alternative systems, language, and structures. Her research had led to her examining the role of rap music as a form of formal, but coded communication. Through a new lenses, I revisited the data. The relational patterns became much clearer to me. This new information also led me to be interested in a different type of literature. I had read the rehashed issues from sociological and psychological views on gangs and their origins. However, as my friend pointed out, this information is old history. She challenged me by saying that if I am truly building grounded theory, my interpretative schema must change.

When I visited the literature on narrative analysis and ethnography, I also had to realize that integrated into the analysis of data were my experiences and observations over the three years I was in the field. It was then that I had my "ah ha" moment.

I began my work in Cabrini-Green, which was one of the most notorious projects in the country. Initially, I spent time as a passive observer. However, as the months passed and as I began to interact with my "self-appointed" assistant, I slowly found myself changing as to how I viewed issues in that community.

Cabrini-Green was one of the most widely publicized housing projects in the country. Housing projects in Chicago historically sent the most negative messages of failure, hopelessness, and containment to our children. The buildings had dark passages, small squared-off rooms, and apartment walls made of brick. On top of living in structures that depicted no way out, Taylor (1986) reported that gang rivalry had made Cabrini-Green one of the most notorious and dangerous places in America. Cabrini-Green, originally intended as a temporary way station for working-class families when the first building went up in 1943, had become the permanent home of poor blacks, predominantly single mothers and their children. It was not uncommon for innocent children to be caught in the crossfire between the predominant gangs, which were the Gangster Disciples, Vice-Lords, and King Cobras (Taylor, 1986).

When I started the research, I was invited to come to a new alternative school in Cabrini-Green. I drove five blocks in the opposite direction of Cabrini-Green, and came face-to-face with buildings coming down and the city working toward moving upper-income people into the area. As I heard community members articulate feelings of powerlessness and fear, I became angry, angrier than I had been in a very long time. Residents were redeployed into areas where many felt their safety would be at risk because of a rival gang or issues with not being welcome. I also wondered what would happen to the self-esteem of children in that community as they went to school with other youth who were in higher economic brackets. Would our children actually be allowed to go to the same schools?

The high school where I initially conducted observations housed children from the Cabrini-Green community, who came from an intense gang and crime environment and had basically been written off as undesirable and unable to be taught. The traditional high school for that area had a 51% dropout rate, with no remediation plan to bring these students back into the school system. However, in 1996, the Chicago Board of Education, in concert with one of the private Chicago universities, piloted an alternative high school project within the Cabrini-Green community. The alternative school opened in September 1996, headed by a former professor of mine. However, in the midst of learning, conflict ensued. During the last week of February 1997, and the first week of March 1997, the Cabrini-Green community had intense altercations with the Chicago Police Department and the Chicago Housing

Authority Police Department. People from the community began protesting the city of Chicago's plans to tear down buildings within the Cabrini-Green housing projects. The alternative plans for relocation proposed by the city were not perceived by the inhabitants of that community as viable because of the basic questions postulated above.

People within this community were hurt and the children (i.e., gang members) were positioned to engage in violence. On Sunday, March 9, 1997, I met with community activists. We explored how organization development strategies (e.g., using skills such as facilitative leadership to organize thoughts and processes for identifying and articulating concerns to the city versus verbal altercations with the police) could assist in redirecting the energies of the youth. It was at this meeting that my former professor gave an account of some of the stories she had been told from the children in her school. There were several cases when, prior to the incidents, children had come to school crying (yes, these were "hardcore gang members") because their families were being evicted from the projects due to their inability to pay the rent. Three days later, I met with some of the community and gang leaders. The community leaders wanted to know my motives for being there. In other words, they needed to know why a middle-class Black woman would be interested in conducting research designed to help kids that were not a part of my community.

The community leaders fully agreed on the objectives of the study, the plan of implementation, and the proposition that the community must learn to revert to communal living and start to take control of the economics of their community. They, however, continued to question my motives. First and foremost, I was seen as being an outsider. Rooted in our culture in this country has been a propensity to see many layers of difference between us, when we can least afford to entertain difference. And we cannot discount that one of the most destructive influences that grew out of slavery is the disrespect of African American leadership. Slave narratives and historical accounts describe far too many atrocities against anyone who exemplified real leadership capability. Leaders had to be authenticated by the slave master in order to ensure that the welfare of the master was being protected (Akbar, 1996).

While I was not presenting myself as a leader, my educational background in the minds of many of the residents positioned me as different, no matter how much I articulated that the concerns of their children was a communal concern.

Such rejection of strong African American leadership is as conditioned in us as is our fear and hatred of a burning cross. It is important to realize that such efforts to undermine effective African American leadership is still an on-going part of the current society. The press, for example, fails to mention many of the outstanding accomplishments of indigenous African American leadership. On the other hand, the least important statement from a "master-appointed leader" gains front-page coverage! (Akbar, 1996, p. 10)

As I have continued to work in various venues within the African American community, I have continued to see the manifestation of these behaviors. We will trust others before we trust our own. We tend to see those of us who may be different either by virtue of education or socioeconomic status as "uppity." Do we question the origins of this behavior, or have we forgotten that we were trained as slaves to view with suspicion our natural leaders when they emerged? They were the ones branded as troublemakers, with the potential to bring trouble to the entire slave community (Akbar, 1996).

During my education process in the Cabrini community, I began to understand the issue of trust from the perspective of inner-city communities. People who live in communities like Cabrini-Green do not trust, nor do they have a reason to trust anyone. Race or ethnicity did not appear to be the issue. Anyone could potentially be an enemy. My "assistant" would caution me to never believe what I saw. He taught me to always look beyond the shadows. During my meetings with community leaders, they talked quite a bit about other Blacks who had sold out to the "system." Because we have historically lived with racism and continue to grapple with ongoing racist behaviors, we have to intentionally engage these issues within our community. I am not lightly using the terms *intentionally engage* or *intentional dialogue* as we will see in later chapters. Throughout the years I have worked in our communities, I have observed and even participated in ways in which we dance around issues when we do not want to deal with that which causes discomfort. However, to successfully evoke change, we must engage in an intentional conversation that does not allow us to hide in the shadows of superficial dialogue. To successfully evoke change requires a communal conversation among African Americans across this country.

While American society has taught us that when we open ourselves, we are potentially exposing ourselves to danger and harm (Butler, 2000), we have to work past those barriers. The concrete individual and the reality of the Black experience must be the point of departure of any phenomenological analysis of human existence (Cone, 1970). Therefore, if we open up, deeply listen to, and analyze the patterns of our language, we have a chance to break down those hidden linguistic representations that emanate from self, represent our historical baggage, and impact our internal dialogues and behaviors. In the process we will draw closer to one another—something I discovered in my interactions.

My assistant openly talked about how he had communicated to people in his community that he was helping me with my research. It was during one of our conversations that I began to focus less on who he was and understand that the relationship had changed. I had moved from a role with him where I had been the student, but in many respects still the passive observer, into the role of the participant observer. Also I began to understand that, perhaps in his mind, I had validated him as a scholarly equal, which in reality I had. He had a purpose and he walked and talked like a man with a purpose. He educated me and I, in ways, educated him. He always stayed on task with this project even during times when I did not. I heard from him at least two or three times each week even though he did not have a telephone. Perhaps it was through my lens that he began to see opportunity to evoke change.

It has been suggested that there are no neutral educational processes (Freire, 1970). Education can function in two capacities: as an instrument that is used to facilitate the integration of individuals into the logic of the present system and bring about conformity, or as the practice of freedom where men and women deal critically and creatively with reality and discover how to participate in the transformation of their world (Freire, 1970). Through the lens of my assistant I began to discover my role in transforming a world that increasingly I began to dislike due to a different interpretative schema relative to the injustices I saw. It is posited that he also began a revisioning process, based upon the images of change and hope that I brought to him through my naive desire to want to make a difference. When examining what had occurred up to this point between my relationships with the individuals that participated in my work and my assistant, words such as trust, purpose, and caring continued to enter into my vocabulary relative to assessing and understanding our interactions. These were no longer gang members to me, but people who had real purposes in life, suffered real pain, and had real needs.

When we show that we care, when our children feel the love that can only flow from us, they enter into an appreciation of an apprehended moment, which is a judgment of both value and fact (Kolb, 1984). Inherent in this new understanding of one's apprehended reality is a revisioning process that can evoke the change of one's value systems (Cooperrider & Srivastva, 1987).

When value systems change, the perceptions of one's abilities also change, and the internalized negative metaphors become critically assessed. Therefore, it is easier to deconstruct the historical context of negative behaviors that have haunted us since slavery.

We have the opportunity to focus less on the protracted post-traumatic stress (Butler, 2000) and work toward creative visioning of a new future. Unlike criticism, which is based on skepticism and doubt, appreciation is based on belief, trust, and conviction. Therefore, to appreciate apprehended reality is to embrace it (Kolb, 1984). From this affirmative embrace can flow a deeper fullness and richness of experience and the ability to critically comprehend that which is around you. One's mind becomes more open to a dialectical environment where one can critically examine that which is around. Defense mechanisms are down due to newly internalized value systems; credibility exists in the belief that I am okay (Kolb, 1984).

However, there is more to this process. When we deconstruct existing paradigms and language, we have to be able to replace the paradigms, language patterns, and metaphors with well-wrought principles due to the inherent distrust that occurs when anything becomes unsettled or dislodged (Gergen, 1994). Consequently, if within our African American community we have not, as the adults in their lives, challenged what is occurring in our educational, socioeconomic, and economic value systems, how could we begin to expect a dislodgement to have sustaining impact?

During this study, I struggled with additional questions, pondering why we allowed the school system to graduate students who cannot read. Why were these young people consistently talking about their failure to get jobs when they want to work? Why, as parents, did we not spend time with our children? Had we become so caught up in trying to make a living that we lost the value systems that are critical to the African American social order? I felt then, as I do now, that before we write off youth in gangs, and question what it is about them to value, we must become very serious about challenging the systems that may help to give rise to youth gravitating toward the gang environment.

A significant part of our ability to dislodge existing paradigms, language, and metaphors for youth in gangs is our own ability to examine the cultural context in which we engage in deficit-oriented discourse and at what levels that discourse affects youth in gangs. I found that contrary to prevailing sociological theory, all youth in gangs were not from socioeconomically deprived communities or family environments. During the course of my research, I also worked with at-risk youth living in suburbia with economically thriving

families. Yet these young people were not successful in the normal school setting and were relegated to alternative schools.

I will never forget my first experience walking into one of the alternative
schools that housed students from more economically sound communities.
When I finished interviewing the young people there, I walked out crying.
The hopelessness they articulated was of such a nature that I suddenly felt lost
for the first time during this work. I immediately went to talk with my pastor,
who counseled me that I could not give up. To this day, I will never forget
his words. You see, I wanted to cry on a sympathetic shoulder. In essence he
chastised me to become stronger because I would see far worse than this.

That experience helped me to understand the value in the concept and
context of community, the community that Rev. Dr. Howard Thurman referenced. This is very hard work, challenging systems, processes, and the status
quo. Working with young people who are angry and hurt is not an easy task,
especially when they feel vulnerable and abandoned. But, as I continue to
posit, losing this battle is not an option. The continued loss of our children is
genocide to our race. We lose our most precious resource, and we lose the gifts
God has granted us. But if we collectively work in our community, we have
the ability to support one another when the work becomes hard.

Yes, the gang environment has attracted our young people and in many
ways has developed into their alternative reality in place of an environment
where they feel locked out. The language patterns that the youth I worked
with and our youth, years later, have internalized included concepts such as
behavior disorder, which many equate to being a bad person. The culture they
have accepted is that it is socially appropriate to emerge from a high school
environment and not read at a normal grade level. Unfortunately for our
youth, as the components of deficit discourse are disseminated to the culture,
they become absorbed into the common language (Gergen, 1994), a language
that these young people have internalized. Therefore, it was understandable
why they called themselves negative deficit terms such as *demotes*. I also saw
how the term *at-risk youth* left the domain of the counseling profession and
became (and still is) conventional discourse in the domain of public discourse,
discourse that these young people are exposed to on a daily basis (Gergen,
1994).

Unfortunately, the deficit discourse and labeling of youth who gravitate
toward the gangs when depicted by the media, educational programs, public
talk shows, and the like has emerged as cultural models. The media continues
to perpetrate these cultural models, which develops a vicious circle. As our

society's actions are increasingly defined and shaped by the language of deficit discourse, the demand for intervention models also increases with those models resembling the very negative attributes they seek to change (Gergen, 1994). Filling the voids that our youth face is not complex. Over the years, I have continued to struggle with why we fail, on a large-scale effort, to effectively mentor, work with, and be there for our young African American children. There is a systemic problem that we must acknowledge because it continues to result in a vicious cycle. As African American adults who daily struggle it becomes hard to give when our spirits tend to be so depleted. When we see our children begin to spiral out of control, because we often face a lack of support in either community or family, it becomes almost impossible to garner the strength to work through the issues plaguing our children. Our spirits are depleted, as are theirs. The viciousness of the cycle continues because we allow others as well as ourselves to then describe them, their situations, as well as ours in negative discourse and then seek to bring forth change via negatively oriented interventions. It is no wonder our children turn to gangs. During my research I heard far too many youth communicate that they saw the gang providing them with respect. When we deconstructed their term *respect*, it primarily represented interaction, contact, and a hand reaching out to them, not withstanding their recognition that it was not the most pro-social hand. Yet something was better than nothing:

Interviewer:	If you were to think about the one thing that you look for the gang to do for you and sum it up in one word, what would it be? What is the important thing that you get from the gang in one word?
Informant:	Respect.
Interviewer:	Um, that is interesting. I would have thought you would have said protection. Help me understand.
Informant:	It's like they respect me more than other people, than anybody really, but my family, and they really don't respect me either, they talk to me any kind of way, put me down all the time, the gangs they don't really do that. (Easley, 1999)

· 6 ·

KEEPING IT REAL: IF IT IS GOING TO CHANGE AND OUR YOUTH ARE TO BE SAVED, WE HAVE TO DO IT

The outcomes experienced during this research set forth an expectation that positive and long-lasting change could be developed. When I summarized the critical learning I walked away with, these lessons needed to be duly noted. As a researcher, I have learned to be critical of my work as well as others'. While there were many successes experienced during this work, there were equally as many lessons learned relative to what not to do in the future.

For example, far too often we fail to understand human cognition and how existing cognitive schema lead to the formation of negative stereotypes of self and self-perpetuating attributes (Barrett & Cooperrider, 1990). Therefore, through well-intentioned intervention strategies that do not fully explain or work through the emergence of negative images of self, our youth are forced to engage in sense-making of their circumstances. As a result, they begin to see themselves as the cause of or major contributor to their circumstances. While I was able to break through those images when I engaged with them, the sustainability of that breakthrough was an unanswered question that I pondered for years.

As a result, I wanted to know—needed to know—what new strategies should be introduced to youth in gangs on a long-term basis in order to help them change their view of self and one another. How could we help our young people move beyond their current external dialogue to a point where the limits of their circumstances could change into a language of possibilities?

Through the utilization of Appreciative Inquiry, which will be methodologically deconstructed in subsequent chapters, I saw defenses break down and students open space for critical dialogue with one another. I also saw my relationship with the students shift. At first, I was an authority figure in the room whose initial value was tied to my being able to keep them out of classes for a few days. However, what I represented to them gradually changed. My insistence that they begin to look at themselves from a different perspective was antithetical to the normal interactions they had with adults. A new awareness within these young people made it easier for them to come together and begin supporting and valuing one another. A change in awareness facilitated the formation of new impressions and judgments. When this new level of awareness was promoted through an appreciative context versus a problem-solving context, the youth began to generate the positive affect for building social solidarity and a renewed capacity to collectively imagine a new and better future.

I have also learned during the course of my doctoral and subsequent research initiatives that strategies that focus on just working with youth in gangs are not enough to make a difference in the lives of our children. While we need to constantly work with youth in gangs, we also have to concurrently address change in the African American community on a macrolevel in order to sustain the change. But before we can identify strategic and systemic change, the African American community has to have critical conversations with respect to several points, which I respectfully posit are critical constructs for change.

1. To successfully change the lives of our children and the environments in which they live, we must be willing to engage in intentional dialogues that will critically work to deconstruct many issues. Over the course of a couple of years now, I have coined the term *intentional dialogue* in my work, which will be explained. There are many components to an intentional dialogue, which is grounded in the theoretical premises of discourse analysis. But the most critical component for this dialogue in the African American community is a commitment to authentically engage in a dialogical process that critically examines issues that we grapple with from a historical as well as present-day context.
2. We must reexamine and recommit to the concept of community.

3. We must critically examine our language and how we have allowed certain language patterns to manifest into a conceptual and contextual reality that is counter to who we really are.

4. In concert with the deconstruction of our language, we must develop a new pattern of language that draws upon who we really are in order to collectively move forward from a position of strength.

5. We must challenge and change our patterns of thinking. Our lives are intertwined within the complexity of a variety of systems. When we look at our situations from a silo mentality we inevitably are asking for failure. To examine life from the perspective of understanding patterns as we look beyond the immediacy of a situation is a very distinct change for us. For years, our propensity has been to be reactionary to the varying crises we face.

6. Our prevailing concept of leadership must be challenged in order to discern what constitutes effective leadership for our communities.

7. We must not shy away from collectively envisioning a new version of reality for our children and community.

8. The concepts of systems and our learning how to view our situations from a systems perspective in order to understand where change strategies must begin and should be our guiding praxis.

9. We must embrace strategy and strategic implementation. Our conversations regarding what should be done must move to patterns of language that incorporate collective action and accountability.

10. There has to be a critical mass of people committed to change and they have to be willing to stay in the process for as long as it takes.

11. When looking to evoke change, even within the overarching African American community, we must understand that cultural differences will and do influence how people perceive their world.

As African Americans, we must collectively and thoroughly embrace our history, cosmology, and connection with a higher being in order to collectively love ourselves. When we collectively begin to again love ourselves, living in community becomes a much easier initiative.

The Criticality of Community

Community is critical to African Americans. The simple fact of life is community is critical to our world. The global context of today's environment expands the concept of community beyond our previous boundaries. Yet African Americans struggle with the concept and context of community, which makes it even harder for us to wrap around this concept from a global perspective.

The concept of community has strong historical roots for African Americans. As discussed throughout this book, we come from a strong cultural and historical context of community. Cosmologically, as a people we communally lived with all and the universe. Even the results of my research and that of Sanchez-Jankowski and Padilla supported that historically, in the African American community, the relationship of the gang to its community assumed a very different context compared to today.

The behavioral competencies and skills that each of us observed, albeit their being demonstrated in an environment that was developed to be a shadow organization of mainstream society, suggested that youth in gangs possessed developed business-acumen skills, which led to entrepreneurial endeavors within the community that were designed to support the economics of the respective community. Equally important, there were strong bonds between the gang organization and the community. Many of my older subjects extensively talked about this community relationship—individuals ranging in age from 20 to 60 years, which infers a long history of community affiliation and responsibility.

The concept of community was exemplified in 1992 when the Bloods and the Crips called for a ceasefire in order to implement a $3.7 billion plan to rebuild South Central Los Angeles. The plan allotted $2 billion for general infrastructure improvement and beautification, $700 million for an education program, $1 billion for a human welfare plan designed to replace welfare payments with job creation programs, $6 million for law enforcement, and $20 million for loans to minority entrepreneurs. In return for fulfillment of these demands, the Bloods and the Crips agreed to match state funds for the creation of an AIDS awareness and research center and agreed to encourage drug lords to stop the drug traffic and invest their money in the community (Cockburn, 1992).

Community, the same term that Howard Thurman posited, was an important concept in the minds of gang members. For example, Padilla (1992) reported that youth learn to accept the neighborhood as something that is very personal, for its identity and character were believed to originate directly from all of its residents. Gang members reported that they believe neighborhood social harmony was an essential responsibility of the gang. Any element of a disturbance might make public a youngster's gang affiliation and identity, and identify the drug-dealing business. Respect for the community as a dominant theme was reported by all of Padilla's informants. Sanchez-Jankowski (1991) reported similar results. Within 31 of the 37 gangs he studied, Sanchez-Jankowski concluded that the gang and the community in which it was active had established some type of working relationship. In each of these cases, he observed situations where the gang and the community had reached a close or at least a working relationship. Sanchez-Jankowski also observed the fluidity of this relationship, which may have resulted from the psychological and social bonding that occurred between the gang and the community in addition to the process by which both parties worked to meet one another's individual needs.

Within many communities gang membership was an encouraged family tradition, and gang members were recruited at very young ages (e.g., in grammar school, where they were referred to as *shorties*). The community members intimately knew the gang members in their community and did not perceive them as a threat (Sanchez-Jankowski, 1991; Padilla, 1992). Sanchez-Jankowski also found instances where the gangs assumed a militia type role and responded to the direction given to them by the community, rather than the community responding to them.

A significant number of adults interviewed by Sanchez-Jankowski (1991) identified with the resistant component of gangs. They also identified with the desires, frustrations, and resentments that the youth experience because these individuals experienced the same feelings. He also found that gangs provided certain community services such as protection of many forms, and in many cases they were more sought after for this protection than local police.

In all of the neighborhoods that Sanchez-Jankowski (1991) studied, he found instances where gang members were extremely aware of any strangers who might be present in the neighborhood. I found similar results. In fact, I distinctly remember my doctoral director speaking to my husband regarding his concern with my being in Cabrini-Green, to which my husband responded that I was safer there than I was in the western suburbs of Chicago. You see, I could not just walk into the Cabrini neighborhood. The people that protected those buildings were informed well in advanced of my presence. My car was known, as were my movements through this community. There was never a moment that I felt fear.

Other forms of community protection, which have not been widely documented by the literature, were protecting the community from individuals outside the community. Instances in Brooklyn, Boston, and Los Angeles were reported where gangs provided their neighborhoods with occasional protection from outside commercial developers who wanted to transform their areas into high-value commercial properties (Sanchez-Jankowski, 1991).

There were also instances where social contracts between the community and the gang were broken. There appeared to be two types of situations in which ties with the community could break, the first being where the gang no longer performed the established task that the community had come to expect and, in many cases, depended upon. The second was where the community perceived members of the gang to be acting out of control or the gang membership displayed an inability to control its members (Sanchez-Jankowski, 1991).

What changed? During my research, data from younger gang members began to suggest a disintegration of the concept of community among African Americans, which led me to examine the sociological and psychological constructs of community in order to better understand it. Interestingly, I found both diverse as well as overlapping definitions as I juxtaposed the then-current definitions of community to what I was witnessing and hearing from youth during my research.

For example, Bernard (1972) suggested that community is characterized by a high degree of personal intimacy, emotional depth, moral commitment, social cohesion and continuity in time. Bender (1978) also suggested that community is best defined as a network of social relations marked by mutuality and emotional bonds where relationships are close, often intimate, and usually face-to-face. Individuals are bound together by affection or emotional ties rather than by a perception of individual self-interest. It has also been posited that the psychological sense of community is devised of elements including membership, influence, reinforcement, and emotional connection and this definition can be extended to communities at large and, in particular, the gang community (McMillan & Chavis, 1986).

Just as community could be defined in psychological terms, the concept of neighbor could also be addressed as a place and state of mind (Goldstein, 1991). Sheer proximity is the physical characteristic with interpersonal implications existing even before members would meet (Cohen, 1983). Those interpersonal implications helped to segregate people with similar personal characteristics, particularly by social class, ethnicity and lifestyle (Cohen, 1983). The sense of belonging to a neighborhood could be intense and consists of psychological factors that included a place of identification (Proshansky, Favian, & Kaminoff, 1983), a place of attachment (Rivlin, 1987), and a place where one's phenomenological sense of connection could be traced (Seaman, 1979). The local social ties, physical amenities and familiarity, individual household characteristics, and the perceived rewards of remaining versus leaving the neighborhood would lead to a positive emotional bond between individuals and their residential environment (Goldstein, 1991).

So, why did I see a sense of community deteriorating in African American neighborhoods, and why is the concept continually on the decline? How can people go about their daily lives and not even know their neighbors? Why don't gangs act protectively toward their community as they did in the past? Why, instead of protecting the young children, are they becoming more victimized by random violence between rival gangs? I heard gang members talk extensively about codes of honor they had to follow, which included taking care of the older women in the neighborhoods. What has happened in this new millennium that has caused such a disintegration of these values?

There is division of communities among African Americans that we must note and change. The processes of dividing our communities is said to have increasingly grown over years with the multitude of classifications also increasing (Akbar, 1996). So, rather than the divisions that impacted us during slavery (e.g., house versus field slave), we have fraternities, sororities, schools, churches, white-collar, blue-collar, Republican, Democrat, and a whole host of other bases for division (Akbar, 1996), which is quite contradictory to our African heritage of living in community and communality, where all people and things are interrelated (Butler, 2000).

We must have a conversation about how we currently live in community. Our overall change and the change that must be imported into the lives of our children will only manifest when we learn to truly live in community where we collectively commit to supporting one another, thereby helping to lift burdens when they become more than we can handle, as well as protecting that which is ours: our children, families, property and social well-being.

To bring forth this change calls for an authentic conversation where we come face-to-face in an intentional dialogue that addresses the many reasons why our communities have incurred relational as well as irrational breakdowns. There is nothing magical about how one goes about changing the fabric of our communities. It simply requires each of us to acknowledge those things that we, as the adults in our children's lives, remember as children: the actions of the "Ma Dears" and neighbors and neighborly actions that kept us together. Those memories are our catalysts for bringing forth a recommitment to our communities.

The Societal Impact of Language

When working toward living in community, we also have to examine how we dialogue with one another. Language is powerful. Many theorists believe that the mere act of conceptualizing and articulating our words has a distinct ability to create our reality. In other words, through language, organizational reality is apprehended, and through the significant impact of language, meaning is attributed to the dynamics of organizations (Thatchenkery, 1996) (and I add the individuals that reside in those organizational contexts, irrespective of how we describe organizations, with communities also falling into this category). Post-modern organization development theories do not contradict the concept that delinquent behavior is learned behavior. However, the real question is who or what is the teacher, considering the negative linguistic signals that gang members receive from the media, school systems, and other forms of communicative processes within our society.

Reports indicate that 90% of the family setting of children is entrenched in negative dialogue. Blame is often sought, and conversations will incorporate how bad things are (Cooperrider, 1986). Yet, during the course of my research, I brought youth together in a whole systems Appreciative Inquiry/ Search Conference process for a week. While more details regarding this week-long experience as well as the theoretical foundations that shape Appreciative Inquiry are shared in the forthcoming chapter, in summary, during that week, an Appreciative Inquiry process facilitated the students who participated (who were in an alternative school in Chicago) to critically examine their strengths and positive core. The effect of this shift was apparent early into this multiday search conference when, during day 2, the youth were asked if they wanted to set ground rules. The first day of the intervention, the students' behaviors were ensconced in obstructive measures and negative dialogue where they were quite comfortable in derogatively describing themselves.

Through structured processes, change can and does occur. The same negative behaviors they engaged in during day 1 were the behaviors that they chose not to accept toward themselves on day 2 when they worked to set ground rules. During the course of the week-long intervention, the internal and external dialogues shifted even further to the positive as their list of ground rules grew longer. Concepts such as commitment to ideals and goals entered their list. Day 2 appeared to represent the turning point where the students articulated the cognitive dissonance they were feeling due to their beginning to shift dialogue as a result of the structure of the Appreciative Inquiry intervention process.

Their discussion of personal issues within the context of a forum that did not invite a negative context suggested a tiny crack in their barriers had occurred and was widening through the dislodgment of the language and the critical analysis of their circumstances.

So, what really happened? I simply chose to utilize a process that facilitated their looking at themselves and strengths from a positive-oriented perspective. In other words, by utilizing Appreciative Inquiry, which is an organization development intervention process grounded in social construction theory that assumes a generative theoretical methodology and enriched affirming discourse-generated fresh alternatives for social action (Ludema, 1995). One of the guiding praxes of Appreciative Inquiry (AI) is that it challenges our assumptions that past history and methodologies for change are epistemologically sound. This is a critical challenge for African Americans, as well as any other culture that daily lives in a state of disempowerment.

Far too often, our epistemology is in conflict with our ontological roots. In other words, we have to learn to deconstruct our knowledge and the roots of that knowledge in order to better understand what we have become and who has orchestrated the foundation of that change. As I walked through seminary and studied African history, theology, and religious institutions, it became clearer to me day by day that who we are as a people, the nature of our being, our cosmological roots and our communal nature have been significantly skewed. In many respects, it has been a gradual process, and in other respects when we examine the history of slavery and the Middle Passage, it was quite an abrupt challenge to our psyche. Nevertheless, for African Americans in this country, the changes that impacted us were not originally made by us. Now, I am not going to say that once those foundations were laid, we did not help the mutation and growth of dysfunctional behaviors. However, as we have helped these behaviors expand, we can equally cut them off.

In order to reach the multiple blockages that youth in gangs have to face, our approaches have to have range, thereby expanding options for an examination of our knowledge and its roots as well as our social action (Ludema, 1995). These same principles would apply to interventions aimed at the African American community at large. If you consider how many years the African American community has endured negatively focused language with respect to our context and perspectives on self, relationships, and future, there can obviously be no argument with the proposition that we must consciously learn how to "flip our own script!"

During my research, the youth I worked with helped me to understand how most had bought into a historically based social order of inferiority relative to themselves and people of color in general. Over the years, as I have continued to utilize Appreciative Inquiry in African American communities. I have seen far too many circumstances where we buy into a negative deficit dialogue, internalize it, and, in some instances, wear it proudly (e.g., our use of negative language as we express "love" toward one another). Over the years, the people that have engaged with me in an Appreciative Inquiry process have had no choice but to juxtapose their dialogue to the positive dialogue that emanated from their articulating stories that highlighted collective and individual achievement and results—which clearly, as well as in many cases painfully, brought to light the negativity they had lived with for far too long.

Social construction theory also suggests that all observations are filtered through conventional stories, belief systems, and theoretical lens. However, because our actions are often predicated on the stories, ideas, beliefs, meaning, and theories embedded in negative language we have internalized, by "flipping our script," we are still free to seek transformation in conventional conduct by changing our patterns of narration internally and between one another (Cooperrider & Srivastva, 1987).

During the course of the week-long intervention, the students and I talked about their perceptions of reality. I did not make assumptions going into the intervention that these young people had been introduced to alternative ways of envisioning their existence and their options. Therefore, within the context of positive dialogue before we began our sessions, each day was introduced with excerpts that offered alternative ways for them to begin looking at their lives and options. Daily we discussed these excerpts and began to investigate what new versus old metaphors meant, how they guided their actions, and within what context could they begin to envision a different future. Inherent in the concept of introducing an alternative dialogue was my way of introducing alternative ideas. In social construction theory it is posited that human existence is an interplay of ideas that are thrust center stage in our daily existence. They often serve as the prime unit of relational exchange, which has the capacity to create new ideas (Cooperrider & Srivastva, 1987).

When we live and function in community, it is easier for us to engage in productive dialogues that serve to deconstruct, understand, and change our interplay of ideas in concert with our current as well as future relational exchanges, which I also believe impacts our internal dialogue and view of self.

As we progressed through a week-long intervention, each day of the process brought forth more questions regarding the meaning of the excerpts I introduced, which incorporated variations on the themes of positive change, shifting paradigms, and self-determination. The students were intrigued by the concept of paradigms. We talked about societal perceptions, particularly when we addressed the issues of their emerging into a job market, and how society possesses unwritten rules and regulations. Curious, they asked questions as to how they could retain their identity yet conform to the expectations of society, which was a very critical question. I can remember as a college student studying African American history we often grappled in class with the dichotomies between the concepts of accommodation versus assimilation. Consequently, it was quite interesting to me to hear years later that youth still struggle with these issues. For far too many years, the African American community has struggled with the concept of identity, accommodation, and the negativity of assimilation. Yet when I research and study issues of diversity within other cultures, you don't find these same issues as prevalent as they reside within our own community. Other people are proud to claim who they are with an attitude of defiance when it is even mildly suggested that they should accommodate to a more "mainstream" culture, if, in today's global environment there even is such a concept. Far too many African Americans still feel compelled to fit in, or if they are focused on living their "truth," it is still a much mutated version, which has gone through significant othering of who they really are.

During this process, the students were beginning to inquire in a manner that allowed them to pull their subjective selves out of what they saw around them and begin analyzing situations from a different paradigm—actions we need throughout our community. They engaged in conversations that challenged old language patterns while at the same time they began to visualize strategies for the permanent dislodgement of the behaviors associated with those language patterns and resulting linguistic representations. These actions alone made it easier for them to begin envisioning provocative choices for a different future.

While in just one week, these students were able to import the theoretical constructs of social construction theory and Appreciative Inquiry, which opened a safe space for their developing and incorporating a new worldview of self, I silently wondered how the community would work to support this change in a way that did not encourage their backtracking. You see, even then the concept of a diminishing community was at the forefront of my mind relative to our ability to continue and sustain the change I was seeing in our youth.

The space that Appreciative Inquiry helped to open facilitated these young people into being very generative when asked to envision their long- and short-term goals. Their language changed from the perspective of what they could not do to the perspective of getting started. When asked to describe their expectations of society relative to implementing their goals they were able to clearly articulate what they needed from family, school, and community. The needs the students wanted from these constituencies did not go beyond fundamental needs. They simply desired support, discipline, mentoring relationships, people who were willing to enter into their lives and serve as role models and confidants, as well as strong relationships with their families. They saw the role of the family germane to their well-being. They understood that their matriculation through life was not always going to be easy, which prompted them to simply want family members who were willing to stand by them. The dislodgement of old language also opened space for discussions centered on a critical analysis of communication breakdowns that occurred among parents, school, and themselves. They understood these relationships to be critical and were open to ways of incorporating their parents and other critical stakeholders in initiatives designed to bridge those breakdowns.

It has been suggested that face-to-face group work on a problem is the meeting ground of individual personality and society. It is within the group that personality is modified and socialized; and it is through the workings of group that society is changed and adapted to its times (Thelen, 1954). When you incorporate this praxis with the power inherent in an intentional deconstruction of language and its associated metaphors, which have the ability to gridlock our behaviors, values, and internalized self-worth, change becomes a phenomenally easier and results-oriented process.

If we are to move forward rapidly aggressively helping our youth move past the barriers they see in their lives, the change process has to become one that is a widespread collective effort designed similar to a well-oiled machine. The need for this became apparent in working with their teachers. While a number of the teachers asked to participate in one of the day's activities, they were more of an impediment to the process than help.

I had to work through their lack of understanding of how to critique their own cultural context and language when working with youth. Unfortunately, the feedback process with the teachers occurred three months after the intervention, after the data had been collected and analyzed. Consequently, during the time frame that the students began to positively dialogue about themselves, the behavior of the teachers did not change, which made it even more apparent that the first step in evoking change on a macrolevel is to engage in a cultural and historical assessment of and reconceptualization relative to our values, assumptions, paradigms, and language within the context of a whole systems approach.

Think about the negative language and imagery our youth today face when in an educational setting that is supposed to inspire them to learn. This is an issue that clearly the African American community must address when engaging in a whole systems change process. The negative environments that permeate inner-city schools in concert with lackluster facilities and challenged teachers must change in order to stop the vicious cycle of youth not effectively engaging in the learning process, becoming frustrated with the system, and opting out, which then spirals them back into negative behavior.

Change itself is a large task, which is complicated by the fact that within our society, our cultural values seem altogether too precarious and are subject to erode or ascend without any logical pattern (Gergen, 1994).

At the same time, cultural realities may not be univocal. Therefore, we tend to always have groups whose realities are scorned, who suffer unheeded, and whose visions of positive change may be muffled by the secure and sanctimonious (Gergen, 1994). However, within the context of our societal shortcomings, in order to effect change for our youth in gangs and overcome those shortcomings, we must collectively work together.

During the course of my research process, one of the first lessons I walked away with is that it was not enough for the principal of the high school where I conducted the intervention and I to be on the same page relative to what we needed to accomplish for our youth. When looking to evoke change for our youth, as well as for the African American community as a whole, the institutions that impact us must also subscribe to the process of change. They must be a part of it. Consequently, it is critical to approach the specific institutions that impact our youth and our communities at the macrolevel and propose to incorporate them into our change processes; in other words as our critical stakeholders, they have to see the need to accept the invitation to change.

If we were to simply walk into a school system and begin to "teach" the principles of Appreciative Inquiry, as soon as we leave our methodologies for change may be quickly dismissed because people tend to be uncomfortable with dislodging the paradigms they have learned or, worse yet, we could run into a similar situation previously described where the leadership is beyond adamant with respect to executing change. Within the context of change, we have to question by what processes do people collectively achieve understanding and how does failure in understanding occur? We also have to understand under what conditions are communal constructions likely to change or to resist change and how can contradictory constructions of their views be reconciled? This level of change opens a new set of questions and offers a range of resources for inquiry (Gergen, 1994). Last, we must have already in our minds a format for the design, delivery, and implementation of alternative solutions to the systems that need to be frame-expanded in order to support our youth and our African American community.

BREAKING THE CHAINS OF OUR SPIRITUAL, MENTAL AND PHYSICAL FATIGUE: THE ROLE OF APPRECIATIVE INQUIRY IN THE FIGHT TO SAVE OUR YOUTH

By design, I have intentionally addressed in a separate chapter these two constructs, which I included in the list of those I suggest are critical for change:

- In concert with the deconstruction of our language, we must develop a new pattern of language that draws upon the strength of who we are in order to collectively move forward from a position of positive strength.
- We must not shy away from collectively envisioning a new version of our reality for our children and community.

While it may sound like I am driving this point on multiple fronts (actually, I am), it is critical that we understand that for too many years the African American community has drowned in negative imagery and language that has in many ways inappropriately impacted our collective and individual voices. I strongly believe if collectively we were given the tools to understand how to alternatively view those images, language, and resulting voice, we would change. What inspired me to critically look at Appreciative Inquiry (AI) was that it provided a very simple, yet dualistically complex, way to understand all of the critical components needed to change our voice and image of self.

Over the years, my perception and understanding of these principles have also grown, which has significantly impacted how I structure change in the environments in which I work as well as utilize AI in those change processes.

In an effort to lead up to where I currently reside, theoretically and in practice relative to my vision of change and AI's role, allow me to walk through a little history relative to my initial engagement with AI, its critical theoretical framework, and how I have learned to modify how I utilize it in African American communities.

Understanding Appreciative Inquiry (AI)

Appreciative Inquiry is an organization development intervention strategy grounded in the behavioral sciences. It was first developed in 1986 by Dr. David Cooperrider, who at the time was a doctoral student at Case Western Reserve University. I first became acquainted with Appreciative Inquiry (AI) in 1996 during my doctoral program at Benedictine University. Dr. Cooperrider taught a couple of my doctoral classes as well as served on my dissertation committee. During the first class I had with David, he exhibited a high degree of passion as he described the many AI projects that had emerged since publishing his first article on AI, projects that significantly impacted social and business issues.

My interest, however, was piqued by the social issues that were addressed in the Imagine Chicago project, where youth engaged in looking at their strengths and discussing and analyzing how they could take those strengths and work toward social change. For years, young people described as at-risk youth had always been a concern of mine because I strongly then believed (as I obviously do now) that we were losing far too many youth, particularly African American youth, to gangs. As I listened to David during the first class, I began to vision how I could utilize AI as a gang deactivation intervention strategy and help redirect the lives of youth who had gravitated to gang environments, youth who were deemed by many in society to be beyond saving.

In my doctoral research, I utilized AI in concert with search conference methodology. While I will revisit both intervention strategies when I discuss a holistic approach for driving change within the African American community, for now, I want to introduce the theoretical framework of each, beginning with Appreciative Inquiry.

Cooperrider and Srivastva (1987) suggest that no matter what the durability to date, any pattern of social action can be revised because revision is inherent in the establishment of new visions of symbolizing and conceptualizing the world. While studying AI, I also investigated Dr. Frank Barrett's work on metaphors. When we critically examine our history, the many ways in which African American "reality" has been socially constructed by others becomes clear. Media, our environment, and the language others have historically used to describe us have negatively impacted our psyche in ways I believe we still have not fully analyzed. Therefore understanding the power of metaphors was just as important to my work as was my understanding how AI could work to invoke new meaning to existing metaphors.

There are many critical social constructs germane to AI, beginning with understanding the roles of metaphors and historical context. Before we attempt to change the behaviors that have developed within our communities and our youth, we must first examine the human choices we make and the foundation of those choices. The imagery to which we have been historically exposed must be studied because it represents ways we see an object as if it were something else (Barrett & Srivastva, 1991). When we look around us, the African American community is constantly bombarded with negative images. The meanings attached to those images can and often do impact how we categorize other areas of our lives, which acts as a way of organizing our perceptions (Srivastva & Barrett, 1988). Metaphors can and do work as a framework for selecting, naming, and framing characteristics of an object or experience by asserting similarity with a different, seemingly unrelated object or experience. They transfer meaning from one domain onto another and can either enrich or enhance meaning, or make sense out of something in a new and different way (Srivastva & Barrett, 1988).

Metaphors are more capable of capturing the continuing flow of experience than literal language and can transfer more meaning than that which can be said in literal translation (Srivastva & Barrett, 1988). They can be clues to the underlying paradigms of a given social system and indicators of change and development in that system's vision of reality, and they can also be seen as frame expanding: a facilitator of radically new knowledge (Srivastva & Barrett, 1988).

The African American community is wrought with metaphors, and while some are positive, far too many connote negative images via multiple streams of media, brick-and-mortar imagery (e.g., revisiting the cages of the Chicago projects), as well as subtle and not so subtle comparisons of African Americans to other cultures. I wonder how often we have a collective conversation that deconstructs those metaphors and helps us to understand where to position them in our repertoire of coping tools? Unfortunately, metaphors significantly impact how we socially construct our world, and they bring a heavy weight to our psychological baggage that is already filled to capacity. But equally damaging is how we allow the negative metaphors to overshadow the good ones that are in our midst, such as looking historically into our past and associating prior accomplishments to a future brimming with potential.

If we are to actively engage in understanding and changing how we socially construct our world and the relational interpretations of our environment that we eventually wind up internalizing, we must have a fundamental knowledge of our historical contexts and the positive social imagery that can and does reside within our past. If someone or something continues to convey a message that you are drowning in despair, and you do not have the knowledge or understanding of how you have overcome that despair in your past (or the past of your ancestors), it becomes extremely hard to even begin to conceptualize options.

I also wonder how often we even stop to think about how liberating an activity historical inquiry can be because it helps us envision a new understanding of the present and potential for a richer future (Barrett & Srivastva, 1991). Historical inquiry is critical to appreciating new possibilities because it is the recognition of the positive past that concretizes our understanding of our core strength, which is foundational to our ability to envision new alternatives that emerge from that positive core. Equally important, historical inquiry is a fundamental underpinning of Appreciative Inquiry.

Appreciative Inquiry is also an approach to organizational analysis and learning. It can and has demonstrated in the past its ability to help participants discover, understand, and foster innovations in social organizational arrangements and processes (Cooperrider & Pratt, 1995). While AI is a mode of action research that meets the criteria of science as spelled out in generative-theoretical terms, it also has as its basis a metaphysical concern that posits that social existence is a miracle that can never be fully comprehended (Quinney, 1982; Marcel, 1963; Cooperrider & Srivastva, 1987). AI has the capacity to help participants engaged in the process of framing and expressing love and support for one another, while discovering internalized strengths and goodness.

A few years ago, I consulted to a behavioral health care hospital whose primary clientele were youth. These young people had been exposed to atrocities that one never wants to imagine a child can or does witness, must less experience. The workers were experiencing significant burnout because the recidivism rate for the children was so high. This was a classic situation where interrelated dynamics of issues within the community were not addressed from a systems perspective, but the children were the ones who were suffering. It was also heartbreaking to hear about the abuses these children had experienced that led them to the hospital. So it was very understandable as to why the workers felt such a high level of burnout.

A colleague and I conducted an intervention in this setting utilizing AI. The two most critical questions we asked of the workers focused on their describing the positive attributes of the children they worked with and what each of them had done to make a difference in the life of a child for whom they had responsibility. As the AI dialogue began, you could immediately see the energy of the workers dramatically shift. We followed this facility's progress for a year. Not only did the attitude of the workers immediately change, but when we periodically checked in, the ongoing changes indicated that the positive change sustained beyond the immediacy of the intervention.

Using AI, workers and administrators began to work with the parents, which over the course of a year lowered the return rate of children to that facility. This example and others I saw over the course of time strengthened my belief that AI is indeed more than a method or technique (Cooperrider & Srivastva, 1987). As a change methodology, it begins to situate the participants in a mode of inquiry that can lead to a difference relative to how participants live and involve themselves in their various social organizations and environments. The positive focus of the inquiry helps participants locate and heighten the life-giving properties or core values of organizations (and people), which concomitantly impact the core values of the individuals participating in the AI experience (Cooperrider & Srivastva, 1987; Thatchenkery, 1996). Inherent in the AI process is a search for knowledge and intentional collective action that is designed to help evolve the normative vision and will of a group, organization, or society as a whole, a search that begins the real change processes (Cooperrider & Srivastva, 1987). In this sense, AI helps build community because people are able to envision those times where they came together despite any perceived differences.

Throughout the years, I have also utilized Appreciative Inquiry in most of my diversity work. It is a particularly powerful methodology for bridging perceptions of difference. Dialogue that focuses on strengths seems to make perceived differences very insignificant. Recently, in the French Caribbean,

I worked with a group of business leaders who believed they possessed (in some cases perceived insurmountable) differences between their workforce and themselves due to differences in culture, ethnicity, and race. In a situation where people wanted to bridge those perceived differences but did not know how to open up and engage in conversation, AI precipitated a dialogue that lasted double the time originally planned. Participants, despite the perception that in their culture they do not like to share their feelings, openly talked about experiences where in their work environment they had achieved very difficult goals because they came together working from a position of strength and common vision.

Although AI has international acclaim and utility, this was my first time utilizing it in a cultural context outside the United States. Once again, the results exceeded my expectations when it came time to begin bridging the chasms many felt with respect to community. The fact that the conversation opens with people sharing experiences when people have been at their best diminishes the need for defensiveness, thus opening space for creativity and shared vision.

In contrast to traditional action research, AI seeks to address the question of how organizations—and individuals—can engage in dialogue that is focused on the goal of seeking a common positive vision of a collectively desired future, typically manifested through storytelling and sharing of positive experiences within the organization (Barrett & Cooperrider, 1990). Appreciative Inquiry therefore seeks out the very best of "what is" to provide an impetus for imaging "what might be" (Thatchenkery, 1996). Unlike many other intervention strategies, AI starts from the initial frame of reference that "I'm okay, my organization is okay, and I have potential to impact my environment."

The hermeneutics of AI suggest that the act of asking questions of an organization or group of people influences the group by moving participants from a framework of looking at what is broken to that of one's personal mastery, strength, and personal power, which yields more confidence and comfort to journey to a future of unknown change (Cooperrider, 1986). When people can carry forward parts of their past that have been successful, there exists the suggestion of an ability to continue to be successful in new endeavors. The hermeneutics of AI are also closely tied to the ontological principles of social construction theory, for example, what we focus on and the language we use creates our reality (Gergen, 1994). In my own work, I have found that as people engage in an AI process, they become more fluid and generative in learning to see the systemic issues that will lead to better change strategies. When participants are able to move beyond defensive behaviors, required change, no matter how taxing that change can be, will become clear.

AI also incorporates the concept of heliotropic evolution. Humans, like organizations, are heliotropic in character in the sense that action has an observable and largely automatic tendency to evolve in the direction of positive imagery. We tend to move more rapidly and effectively in the direction of affirmative imagery (moving toward light) than in the opposite direction of negative imagery (Cooperrider & Pratt, 1995). Hermeneutically, AI also includes the anticipatory principle that suggests our future reality is permeable, emergent, and open to the mind's causal influence; that is, reality is conditioned, reconstructed, and often profoundly created through our anticipatory images, values, plans, intentions, beliefs, and the like (Cooperrider & Pratt, 1995). With this is the recognition that every social action somehow involves anticipation of the future, in the sense that it involves a reflexive looking-forward-to-and-backward-from activity.

Finally, embedded in the hermeneutics of AI is the principle that when engaging in an AI process that moves the participants toward action from a positive approach, the participants can develop their own provocative propositions for change that excites the members of the group, thereby simultaneously creating the anticipation of a different future.

The four basic principles that are the foundation of Appreciative Inquiry include:

1. Inquiry into the "art of the possible" in organizational life should begin with appreciation.
2. Inquiry into what's possible should be applicable.
3. Inquiry into what's possible should be provocative.
4. Inquiry into the human potential of organizational life should be collaborative (Cooperrider, 1986)

Methodologically, when working in groups, the key phases of the AI process include defining the topic choice; inquiry into the life-giving properties, which includes data collection and discovery; articulation of possibility propositions (e.g., visioning the ideal); consensual validation-agreement (through dialogue and in the case of my research the format was through search conference methodology); and co-construction of the future (the participants leave the search conference with action steps) (Williams, 1996).

If we apply the principles of AI to youth in gangs, let's begin with the first principle of AI and follow how researchers we previously discussed utilized the principles, despite not having a term such as AI associated with their propositions.

The first principle of AI assumes that every system works to some degree and, to some degree, the gang system has positive attributes. Sanchez-Jankowski (1991) noted gang leaders developing leadership, decision-making, and problem-solving skills. Both Padilla (1992) and Sanchez-Jankowski noted the entrepreneurial enterprises of gangs.

The second principle of AI assumes that inquiry into what is possible should be applicable. The third principle assumes that an organization is an open-ended, indeterminate system that is capable of becoming more than it is at any given moment while learning how to take part in guiding its own evolution (Cooperrider, 1986). Appreciative knowledge of "what is" becomes provocative to the organization inasmuch as it takes on a normative value for members. Gang members can also begin to generate new metaphors as they begin to imagine new possibilities. The last principle of AI assumes collaborative interaction and action. Historically gang members have already shown, when rallying around common principles, that as a collective unit they exhibit a very powerful and unified voice. For example, during the time I conducted my research, citizens of Cabrini-Green rallied to address the city of Chicago's plans to tear down housing in Cabrini. Key to those rallies was a coalition of People and Folks (gang nations that typically war) working together to address these issues.

While AI as a methodology can be accomplished through individual or group interviews, most people use the methodology combined with search conference in order to more effectively drive change by getting key stakeholders together in one setting. One can effectively bring together hundreds of participants and work for two to three days on planning tasks, primarily in large-group plenary sessions (Emery & Purser, 1996).

Search conference methodology is built on the premise that, if we are to create a desirable future, individuals must carefully look at the world. The complexity of today's environment suggests an explosion of information. Many intervention strategies cannot handle this explosion because they are geared toward solving complex problems, but the strategies themselves are far too simple and singularly focused. Poor planning decisions and interventions not only generate more problems but they also alienate people, thus creating an atmosphere of gloom and doom (Emery & Purser, 1996).

When you work toward getting the whole system into one place to engage in the appropriate level of diagnostics, you are able to accomplish much more work. First and foremost, you are inviting to the table a critical mass of stakeholders. I have found over the years that when people are engaged and perceiving themselves a critical component of the analysis and development of viable solutions, they tend to not work as hard toward end-running change. Simply put, people want to be a part of a process, and a methodology that affords a gathering of that critical mass is by far going to be able to generate more creative ideas than a smaller group of people.

I also respectfully posit that when you get a critical mass of people into one setting, it becomes easier to debunk the varying myths that continue to hold a race or group of people back. When we live an existence that has been forced upon us, cultural isolation and issues of separation invade our subconscious. Confronting our shadow-beast can result in a new awareness or knowledge, thus providing us with an ability to see our experiences for what they are as well as see through them, thereby enabling us to come to grips with who we really are (Anzaldúa, 2007). It is important that we examine our "stories" beyond descriptive analyses and understand them from an intrapersonal context. We must place ourselves in the center of our stories. Our issues are clearly beyond that of a struggle with duality. African Americans are forced to navigate through many polarities and contradictions, which have made many of us experts in suppressing our consciousness.

> At the crack of change between millennia, you and the rest of humanity are undergoing profound transformations and shifts in perceptions. All including the planet and every species are caught between culture and bleed-throughs among different worlds—each with their own version of reality. (Anzaldúa & Keating, 2002, p. 541)

Once we embrace our African culture and, most important, our full humanity, we concomitantly deconstruct our present reality for what it truly is, enabling us to develop appropriate strategies to change that which we no longer want to tolerate. The blending of Appreciative Inquiry and search conference is a natural blend of two powerful processes that can facilitate our collectively working through critical issues and shadow-beasts, which can be far less frightening when collectively dialoging.

> The struggle is inner: Chicano, indio, American Indian, mojado, mexicano, immigrant Latino, Anglo in power, working class Anglo, Black, Asian—our psyches resemble the bordertowns and are populated by the same people. The struggle has

always been inner, and is played out in the outer terrains. Awareness of our situation must come before inner changes, which in turn come before changes in society. Nothing happens in the "real" world unless it first happens in the images in our heads. (Anzaldúa, 2007, p. 109)

One of the key components of Appreciative Inquiry's methodology is a collaborative effort for interaction and action. Key components of search conferences include a planning and design phase and an implementation and diffusion phase (Emery & Purser, 1996). Over the years, I have also found that in order to be successful in the planning and implementation phases, there has to be additional training in strategy and implementation in concert with an understanding of systems theory. These are very important competencies for driving change in our community and are further addressed. In the years that I have engaged in change initiatives in our community, follow-through as an issue always reared its ugly head. We tend to operate in the moment. When we are in that present moment, we tend to be fully committed to keeping the commitments we make. Then reality hits. To change the vicious cycle we have and continue to be in requires our moving past a tentativeness to engage in the extensive endeavors it is going to take to successfully evoke change in our community. We have to learn how to engage in project management and to manage multiple priorities. There are basic strategies that we do not utilize that can and do help in the management of multiple-priorities processes, which is why strategic implementation as a part of our learning how to evoke effective change cannot be compromised.

There are also very basic underlying assumptions embedded in search conference methodology—assumptions about people—which suggest that people are purposeful creatures with the capacity to select and produce desirable outcomes. Ensconced in the methodology is the principle that people will take responsibility for a task they consider meaningful. Search conference methodology also includes the assumption that people can function in the ideal-seeking mode under appropriate conditions (Emery & Purser, 1996). These assumptions are compatible with those of Appreciative Inquiry. Therefore, when incorporating the principles of Appreciative Inquiry into the principles of search conference, the focus on the past becomes a look at the life-giving properties of the past in order to envision the future. The participants, as they envision a new future, engage in anticipatory learning where they work toward a social construction of the preferred future (Cooperrider, 1986). These two methodologies combined are critical to a change process within the African American community. Too often we work in isolated silos. Multiple stakeholders must collectively come to the table in order to effectively build a collective vision. It will take a very large village to drive the change that is needed in our communities and with our youth.

While the results of the interviews I conducted in my study prior to the intervention utilizing Appreciative Inquiry painted a very dark picture with our youth, the outcomes that occurred during the search conference utilizing AI provided hope. When asked to *envision* a positive approach regarding their attributes and a different future from an appreciative perspective, the youth articulated hope and very clear visions. For example, when I asked the youth to share stories or times in their life where there were real high points and they felt most alive, most proud to be them, and valued themselves most, they talked about their accomplishments in school, getting good grades, and their passing key achievement tests. In other words, their perceptions of success were no different than other children in their age brackets.

However, when reviewing the literature on the values of gang members, it is not uncommon to find the perspective that youth in gangs do not value education. For example, in a research study that investigated at-risk behavior in an emerging gang community, the researchers reported that the normal values that youth internalize toward school, such as being on time, paying attention to teachers and other staff, and getting passing grades, are not high priorities for most gang members. Yet a significant percentage of their subjects reported A's, B's, and C's in school and only 27% reported that they had below average grades or had done poorly in school (Decker & Van Winkle, 1996).

By the conclusion of the search conference, the students were able to articulate a more positive future. When asked to present their individual goals, they were very clear on chosen career paths in concert with understanding the basics of the respective career-path processes. Inclusively, when we talked about the support they would need from community and family, they were also very clear on the specifics of those needs as well.

What was interesting, however, was how much during the course of this intervention, these young people kept coming back to their need for being respected as individuals with goals. Their desire to change the dynamics between themselves and family, school personnel, and community members was articulated throughout the entire week in various forms. Unfortunately, their conversations regarding implementation steps with respect to obtaining their goals were vague, yet they understood that they needed help in this area.

Over the years as I have worked with adults in our communities, I have found many people struggle with the concepts of strategy and implementation.

People tend to immediately move into tactical steps that become disjointed because they are not tied to an overarching vision of who they want to be and the strategic implementation processes that are needed to make that vision a reality.

So, in summary, what did I see during this intervention and how was the change associated with the utilization of Appreciative Inquiry?

The Ability to Envision a New Future

When we intentionally work to build an environment that fosters one's ability to envision a different future, an environment that moves from deficit-based language to conversations of possibilities, individuals are able to see how they can move from their present condition. Youth in gangs need a purpose for living, as do we all. They also need an alternative vision for using the skills they possess such as leadership, entrepreneurship, decision making, and problem solving. When given a positive dialogical environment, our youth are capable of generating alternative ways in which they view their world, and they are equally capable of generating options for change.

Through Appreciative Inquiry, the youth in this study were challenged to examine their ideals in concert with those ideals they believed belonged to society. They learned that their ideals were not dichotomous to those of society. However, if youth are continually told that there is inadequacy in their highest ideals, and within the context of those inadequate ideals their failures are continually examined, it becomes impossible for them to develop values or achieve any semblance of self-esteem. The reason these youth described developed relationships with other gang members were in their attempts to fill voids in their lives. Arguments posit that the mind will often protect itself against anxiety by dimming awareness, a process that can typically create blind spots, blocked attention, and self-deception. If no new dialogue had occurred within a different cognitive context, there would have been every reason for these students to fight change. One's present affective state or mode will determine one's perception, learning orientation, and recall. Therefore, I can't help but reiterate that when solutions or analysis are posed in a negatively oriented framework, the responses will be similar (Barrett & Cooperrider, 1990).

While Appreciative Inquiry in both corporate and social settings has proven over the years to be a powerful *catalyst* for evoking beginning change, in youth in gangs continued processes and implementation steps involving

Appreciative Inquiry must be designed within a whole systems support, which is critical to *sustaining* the change. It is not enough to conduct front-end work despite the success of that work. Youth in gangs are affected by many external influences over and beyond their families, such as peers, their school, community constituents, and images and language they hear and see in the media. Collaborative processes that engage critical stakeholders, such as parents, teachers, and school officials, who also struggle with a deficit-oriented view of youth in gangs, are critical. Unfortunately, as I saw with the teachers of these young people, the pervasive stance toward society's discourse is pictorial and we generally accept society's accounts of their subjective states as valid information (Gergen, 1994).

All critical stakeholders have to be reeducated. We must learn to deconstruct our reality and incorporate cultural and historical recontextualization strategies. We have a phenomenal history to draw upon that enables us to reframe who we are as a result of our historical, theological, and cosmological contexts. Yet we tend to lose sight of our historical successes unless we are celebrating Black History Month. Our history and context from our African heritage should be embedded in our daily dialogues. We must move past the shadows and borderlines so adeptly described by Anzaldúa and claim our multiple birthrights for ourselves and for our children.

The Process of Valuing

At the beginning of the intervention, when asked to tell stories about the high points in their lives and share information on their strengths, most of the youth that were participating in this intervention stated that they had nothing good to say about themselves. Their behaviors were disrespectful to themselves as well as the individuals around them, yet they wanted to be respected, a theme that dominated the intervention. During the course of their disrespectful behavior, they ironically also talked about their fears, which included an early death for themselves as well as their friends.

When I individually met with them before the search conference, the language they used to describe themselves was degrading. They openly shared how they were behind in their grades, calling themselves "demotes," identifying academic deficiencies and talking about having been sent to an alternative school because of the behavioral problems they had allegedly demonstrated in their regular schools—almost as a badge of honor. Some of the youth had never been in regular high school, having moved straight from grammar school into an alternative school system, which in Chicago is a place where students have one last chance. In other words, it is an environment that daily, if not managed correctly by school administrators, could be a constant reminder of past failures. Interestingly, some social-learning theories posit that normative statements, definitions, and verbalizations increase the probability that a person will commit deviant behavior. It is also posited that the strength of deviant behavior is a direct function of the amount, frequency, and probability of its reinforcement (Sutherland, 1937; Bandura, 1969). So, what we typically see with our youth, if we accept these social learning theory propositions is a vicious circle. If the cycle of deficit-based language is never broken, it continues to function as a reinforcement that can ultimately lead to deviant behavior.

In addition to challenges within the social context for African Americans, young people have additional challenges that attack their self-esteem by virtue of being adolescents. Adolescence is a difficult period where behaviors can vacillate from the childish to adult as youth work to define their identity (Erikson, 1975). The successful matriculation of adolescents through this period can depend upon the support and relationships they have with their family members, which is why we cannot afford to allow the concept of community within the African American social context to continue to erode.

Goldstein (1991) reported that the search for an identity and self-esteem is said to involve the production of a meaningful self-concept in which the past, present, and future are linked. Unfortunately, for our youth, learning to value oneself and develop a meaningful self-concept is difficult due to the social contexts in which they live. Even in the midst of a strong parental support system, our children face multiple attacks on their self-esteem, through school, media, and their daily interactions with individuals who challenge their rights to an egalitarian society, attacks that can and will act as a negative impact upon our anticipatory reality.

When we critically examine the anticipatory realities of many of our youth, irrespective of their gang involvement, often times their anticipatory realities are not positive. Our children have hope and can articulate hope as well as a concept of their preferred future state. But the barriers they perceive to be their reality are viewed as blockages to their future. One overwhelming barrier is the reality that far too many of our youth are feared by the very society in which they reside.

As the youth who participated in the Appreciative Search conference moved through the week-long inquiry, a significant change occurred when asked to reframe the context of "me" with different language. Positive imagery can awaken the body to its own self-healing powers (Cooperrider, 1986). The shifts in behaviors and language displayed by the youth in that intervention suggested the beginning of an internal healing process. Why?

First and foremost, the way in which the students were approached was different because they were not asked to view themselves from a negative-deficient orientation. They were not asked to solve their problems. They were asked to simply talk about the goodness within them and their environment in concert with how they could personally evoke change in their world and how their gangs could evoke change. Through a positive dialogical environment where we were not going to entertain negative images, the seed was planted, and their minds began to envision new images and goals.

The topic selection of the Appreciative Inquiry process impacted their discussion of the concept of self. For five days we worked with a topic choice of valuing oneself. The youth were asked to challenge the metaphors they had internalized, those metaphors that they believed contributed to their definition of self. Consequently, the stage was set for them to begin to change how they organized their perceptions, while at the same time examining how they could attribute new meaning to their exiting metaphors, which would also enable them to transfer that meaning to new domains.

Learning to Value Others

Valuing others is interconnected with the ability to socially relate to the contexts of common goals, trust, respect, and a constructive learning environment. Valuing others is critical when building community. What I initially observed during my beginning interactions with those young people was how they defined their relationships with others and their valuing of these people in terms of social pressures. The lack of bonding with family, school, and their respective communities were consistent themes. Unfortunately, their primary role models were the older members of their respective gangs. Another consistent theme was that their relationships with other gang members were outcomes of their desire and need to fill voids in their lives.

These young people did not initially understand that their friendship values were built upon external ideals that were embedded in issues of protection, turf, and gang values. When you couple the internalization of external ide-als that do not represent a firm foundation for positive human interactions in concert with negatively purported stereotypes of self and self-perpetuating attributes, our youth have great difficulty in engaging in any level of sense making with respect to their environment and circumstances. As a result, they begin to see themselves as the cause of or a major contributor to their circumstances.

Consequently, when we begin a whole systems change in the African American community, we must have strategies for helping our youth change their views of themselves and of each other. I found that through Appreciative Inquiry, the positive approach of inquiry focused the students to systematically think about their internal and external resources and the goodness of those resources. The narrative analysis and dialogue that began on the first day of the intervention and began to exponentially increase throughout the week promoted a very different external dialogue relative to relationships and their descriptive analyses.

Through this dialogue the students began to engage in a different con-versation relative to family circumstances and their allowing others to limit their future. A noticeable changed occurred when they engaged in a dialogue regarding their ability to move outside limiting circumstances.

Relationships within their family structures also assumed a different mean-ing. The problems of a mother moved from the domain of the student and became the problem of the mother only, thus freeing space for the student to invoke a different perception of self and familial relationships. The impact of the dialogue was also evident with respect to their interpersonal relationships with one another. Their concept and context relative to trust began to shift as new social bonding occurred, despite there being different factions within the group, such as different gang factions, races, generational differences rep-resented by the student and adult populations, as well as different levels of authority. Within their prior social context, there would be no room for these factions to exist within a trusting and caring relationship.

When we communicate appreciation in another individual, we are com-municating that an individual is chosen as worthy of notice from a myriad of other objects competing for attention (Srivastva & Barrett, 1988). The new and emerging awareness within these young people made it easier for them to come together and begin supporting and valuing one another. A change in awareness facilitates the formation of new impressions and judgments. Therefore, new meanings are given to these impressions and judgment. When this new level of awareness is promoted through an appreciative context versus a problem-solving context, individuals can readily generate the positive affect for building social solidarity and a renewed capacity to collectively imagine a new and better future (Barrett & Cooperrider, 1990).

Envisioning a New Future and Recognizing the Barriers

To envision a new future, the youth that participated in this study needed to dialogue about the multiple barriers they would be required to break through. African Americans have always carried the burden of having to move through closed doors, which requires one to have a strong concept of self. This means that as a people we have to believe that we can achieve what we set out to accomplish, and we must stay motivated and focused on the prize. Unfortunately, every day when we wake up, in some form or fashion we are reminded of our barriers; but that does not stop people from articulating hope.

Not dissimilar to what our youth grapple with today, the students in this study were afraid to go to school for fear of crossing a street in rival gang territory. They openly feared death at an early age and they communicated their fears that their past mistakes would impact the rest of their lives. To an adult, to believe that the mistakes of your life (and I am not referring to criminal activities as those are obvious exclusions) at age 13 or 15 will affect your future may seem absurd. To an adult it also appears to be absurd that youth can envision their lives being over at age 15. Yet I heard these young people talk about only wanting an assurance that they would live to see the beginning of their future. Unfortunately for youth in gangs, closed pathways and minimal options were realities then as they are now. They lived with death threats on a daily basis or the fear of incarceration as do our youth now. The burden they carried and still carry is very heavy.

Our youth then and today must deal with the reality of being of color in this society while simultaneously carrying the burden and stigma of being identified as gang involved and at risk. Yet, despite these burdens, these young people articulated the concept of hope, and I believe the vast majority of African American youth can still articulate hope. When the students were asked about their dreams during the course of the intervention, their dreams were the same as those any other young person. Their involvement in a gang did not preclude their having dreams for a successful life. Their dreams included finishing school on time, going to law school, finding a good job, joining the navy, being a courtroom artist, learning computer skills, getting a scholarship, getting a nice house, majoring in electronics and marketing, as well as being a brain surgeon and a podiatrist. When searching for alternatives to help youth in gangs envision a new future, we have to move beyond the context of ordinary strategies and engage in processes that will rekindle their hopefulness.

Pathways Leading to Actions

As the intervention week came to a close, the students credited me with their ability to envision from a different paradigm. Yet it was not my victory. The victory was in their ability to unfreeze their old language and imagine new alternatives. The statements of these students were the most profound testimonies of what we learned relative to what Appreciative Inquiry can offer. AI is uniquely different in that it facilitates discovering, understanding, and fostering innovation. The students discovered a different context to their understanding of self. Through critical dialogue, they also began to understand in a different context the skills they possessed and the myths they had internalized. They also began to explore new relational meanings. When compared to other intervention strategies, which tend to be focused on suppressing the will of youth and are theoretically based in the criminal justice system, it is easy to understand what AI offered them.

So, what specifically did I learn from this intervention? Youth in gangs are capable of generating alternative ways in which they view their world, and they are equally capable of generating options for change. However, the conditions have to be right for these capabilities to fully develop and it has to be a collaborative effort in order for change to be holistically sustained. A positive dialogical environment enriched in provocative inquiry also fostered these young people to begin to build self-esteem, which is critical to forward movement. Their creative, generative, and team-oriented energies flowed as did their willingness to respond to caring in concert with demonstrating concern toward their peers. The hermeneutics of Appreciative Inquiry clearly set the stage for their attributes to emerge.

The African American community possesses the ability for both sustaining cultural institutions on one hand, and on the other hand placing them in reflexive doubt (i.e., an attitude of self-critique). Institutions that impact the lives of youth and their members should engage in reflexive doubt, which can result from shifting the dialogue. Social transformation requires new visions and vocabularies, possibilities, and practices that in their very realization begin to change alternative courses (Gergen, 1994). However, as we develop pathways for deep change, we can never forget that the strength of this type of change process is predicated upon many people engaging in a call to action with unwavering commitment.

As we begin the conversation on models for change, the utilization of an appreciative approach is going to be critical for bridging the chasms that tend to reside within our own communities. I have worked in consulting engagements within the African American community where data emerged that strongly suggested undertones of discord among the participants. Language of discord emerged that suggested hidden representations of socioeconomic as well as microcultural differences. Yet the participants were not openly conscious of their articulating verbiage that suggested racial divide.

The discourse, which was situated within the social context of the community, socioeconomic environment, African American context, and culture indigent to the location in which this work was done, had to be analyzed through an integration of both their words and context in order to obtain accurate interpretations of meanings (Fairclough, 1992; Easley, 2010). Albeit the participants all being African American, individually they were historically rooted in class and caste systems that tend to foster perceptions of superiority within the Black race, which facilitated their struggling with connectedness, clearly impairing their ability to envision change (Easley, 2010).

Positioning them in reflexive doubt helped the participants to move past an initial inability to envision change. For them, change initially meant developing a laundry list of tactical steps versus understanding that which would make deep change within their community, behaviors that appeared to emanate from historical patterns of hopelessness and disconnection.

Our ability and propensity to go in this direction suggest the need for methodologies designed to build and foster community. We have enough division from the outside forces we have to address. We cannot under any circumstances allow ourselves to develop more, particularly from an internally focused vantage.

PART THREE

A 2011 PERSPECTIVE

· 8 ·

THE ROLE OF APPRECIATIVE INQUIRY
IN THE FIGHT TO SAVE OUR YOUTH

Over the years I have learned that a good researcher always critiques his or her work. I have also learned that, as a community, we have developed many psychological defense mechanisms geared to protect us against the multitude of forces still working to challenge our sense of self. In addition to the many successes I have had with Appreciative Inquiry, I also witnessed situations where African Americans would respond to an AI process, but when engaged in a deep listening process, their verbal as well as nonverbal language often suggested a reticence toward or failure to internalize a renewed and recontextualized sense of self and possibilities.

Unlike the youth I worked with, many adults have become hardened to life. Consequently, some will view an appreciative dialogue as the act of engaging in happy talk on a temporary basis without internalizing the dialogue that is required to spiral them into action and lessen the impact of emerging from the AI process with renewed hope. I have also observed how people want to talk about change and move beyond the propensity to simply complain about how bad things are. They truly are looking for answers as to how to emerge from what seems to be a life built upon quicksand.

Understanding how to evoke change is not always an easy process, especially when we are looking to move large communities. I have often said that I do not believe it was by chance that I received a doctoral degree in organization development first and then went to seminary. Effecting change cannot simply be relegated to designing and implementing processes; we also have to learn how to move the hearts and souls of the participants.

In 2002, I began exploring the concept of discourse analysis. While Appreciative Inquiry (AI) is a form of discourse analysis, there are many other ways to analyze dialogue as well as understand how our dialogical processes shape our interactions with and between our environments. That year I also met a colleague in London with whom I have continued to research and study over the years. She had just completed a phenomenal doctoral dissertation utilizing discourse analysis as her primary methodology.

She is of Haitian ancestry and a citizen of France, where she was raised and educated, which made our work in the areas of culture, diversity, and change interesting to our academic communities due to our multicultural and global foci. Her cultural perspectives in concert with mine helped both of us grow in our understanding of challenged communities. For almost two years I worked in her community in the French Caribbean and find it interesting that, notwithstanding "differences" in issues and country context that permeate their culture, people of color that reside in the French Caribbean share many of the same issues with which we grapple.

AI resides within the general category of discourse methodologies. Throughout the years, as I have continued to have tremendous respect for AI, I have always felt the need to learn more about other theories associated with discourse. I saw a need to be less prescriptive in methodology and more open to helping those I work with to listen to their own voices while concomitantly deconstructing the real meaning behind their words, a need that is shared by many challenged communities who grapple with the negative feelings and issues that emerge when people perceive themselves to be living in a state of perpetual conflict.

> The ambivalence from the clash of voices results in mental and emotional states of perplexity. Internal strife results in insecurity and indecisiveness. The mestiza's dual or multiple personality is plagued by psychic restlessness. (Anzaldúa, 2007, p. 100)

A Required "Contradiction"

What I am going to discuss may sound antithetical to previous descriptions of and views on the power of Appreciative Inquiry. However, I have learned to feel comfortable in modifying my point of view.

I fully believe in the power of Appreciative Inquiry, but similar to African American psychologists who have worked hard to develop a different viewpoint in understanding the psychology of African Americans via the newer discipline of black psychology (Akbar, 2003), I have also learned that the methodologies that work in White communities do not always work in an African American context, or they may yield results that would not conform to an anticipated range of outcomes from "mainstream" society.

The idea that hope alone, and action undertaken in that kind of naiveté, will transform the world is an excellent route to hopelessness, pessimism, and fatalism. The attempt to do without hope in the struggle to improve the world, as if that struggle could be reduced to calculated acts alone or a purely scientific approach, is a frivolous illusion (Freire, 1997).

The foundations of our epistemologies are significantly different from our White counterparts and comprise a very broad range of experiences that give rise to how we "know." Our ontologies and epistemologies must be deconstructed by us for us in order for African Americans to feel whole and not fragmented by descriptive analyses that are not germane to the essence of our being (Akbar, 2003).

Over the course of years since I completed my doctoral work, I have also learned that when working with African American communities we must dig deep into our psychological blockages in order to evoke the change we desire. Unless those hidden representations we tend to carry within us are worked out, our ability to realize and internalize the beauty of engaging in an appreciative process will be overshadowed by the demons that still lurk in the psyche of the participants.

Black scholars in the field have understood, at least since the days of Carter G. Woodson, Anna Arnold Hedgman, Mordecai Wyatt Johnson, Benjamin Mays, and Howard Thurman, to mention only a few of the venerable ones, that the black scholar must know everything that his or White colleagues know, and then something extra that most of those colleagues will know little about and about which they probably couldn't care less. (Wilmore, 2004, p. 76)

So, while I fully support the utilization of Appreciative Inquiry in the African American community, I concomitantly "know" that there is a precursor step that oftentimes we must engage prior to being able to fully understand our uniqueness.

The Contextual Framework of a Double Loop Model

In 2003, my French colleague and I began developing an alternative change model that incorporated the theory and practice of discourse analysis and Appreciative Inquiry. Our model posited that the complementary dynamics between these two approaches via a double loop process would serve to bring forth those hidden representations at a deep discursive level while at the same time working to help participants understand, through a reconstruction process, the associated meanings that emerge. Once participants better understood the feelings and emotions they deeply buried and their associated metaphors it would be much easier to move forward in a change process (Easley & Alvarez-Pompilius, 2004).

Moving through this double loop process provides the opportunity to obtain significant information regarding the culture and microcultures of the participants, which enables researchers and change agents to have a better understanding of the environment and social context. By the time the participants engage in the second stage of *change*, where they would have exchanged (deconstructed and analyzed) on the knowledge created, they emerge better equipped to move through an appreciative process and fully internalize and appreciate their strengths and opportunities in order to evoke new visions and design associated strategic processes (Easley & Alvarez-Pompilius, 2004). As participants engage in dialogue, it is imperative that someone is charged with the responsibility to capture key points of the conversations. Once captured, those engaged in dialogue must be able to step back and critically examine the themes that emerge. The analytical process is critical and serves as a higher level of dialogue. Participants must step back and critically examine those themes as they engage in a deconstructive and analytical dialogue as to the thematic meanings that emerge. If the participants are open as well as honest with themselves and colleagues engaged in this process, a wealth of information will emerge.

African Americans identities have been shaped by the history of slavery. Following enslavement, black Americans suffered the experience of being citizens in a country that treated them as disposable goods. When African Americans look at their lives, they see unfulfilled promise of what could be if they were able to fully participate in American society. Still today, shortcomings in education, housing, wealth, and employment are exacerbated by the recognition of the marginalization of black culture and ideas from mainstream American. These realities have shaped a healing for past trauma that has led up to the present. (Mitchem, 2002, p. 103)

The application of discourse analysis serves as both a catalyst and process for helping participants deconstruct their issues in order to understand the overt as well as hidden linguistic representations of their interactions with themselves and their environment. AI serves as both a catalyst for evoking a new language based upon the praxis and principles of AI as well as a healing and reconciliation process, which allows them to move forward with a real internalization process where they accept their accomplishments and their competencies and strengths. Proponents of Appreciative Inquiry would argue that engaging in a conversation that in essence dredges up negative images and feelings is counter to the productive and positive components of Appreciative Inquiry. Yet,

As a people who have so frequently been victimized by lies—scholarly, pseudo-scientific, and otherwise—we want to be as sure as we can that we are "speaking the truth," to borrow the title of one of James H. Cone's books. But we ought to also be sure that speaking the truth depends on first seeking the truth, then knowing the truth, and finally, and indispensably, doing the truth. (Wilmore, 2004, p. 77)

When we examine the paradigms of research and change strategies, typically the models employed are selected to identify qualities pursued to the exclusion of other sets of qualities (Akbar, 2003). In our community, we cannot allow ourselves to fall victim to negating the uniqueness of our characteristics, which do not always conform to Eurocentric models of change and research. Our history, joys, and pain run deep and we have to acknowledge each aspect because these components help comprise who we are and, in many respects, constitute the foundation for our moving forward. Therefore, researchers and intervention professionals must be flexible when approaching the African American community in order to ensure that we speak our truth; for it is only through understanding how we have internalized the realities of our truth can we begin to let go and change.

That flexibility may often call for uniqueness in design in order to capture required balances with respect to perspective (Akbar, 2003) or our propensity to hide our true selves in the shadows of a psychology that may defy the parameters of normal logic. Our worldviews have to be compared and contrasted to the individuality of our experiences and not to other subjects who do not remotely share our experiences or understand how we internalize our reality.

> At some point, on our way to a new consciousness, we will have to leave the opposite bank, the split between the two mortal combatants somehow healed so that we are on both shores at once and, at once, see through serpent and eagle eyes. Or perhaps we will disengage from the dominant culture, write it off altogether as a lost cause, and cross the border into a wholly new and separate territory. Or we might go another route. The possibilities are numerous once we decide to act and not react. (Anzaldúa, 2007, p. 101)

To assume that we can consistently deconstruct our experiences within a context of appreciation while we play back in our minds the various "isms" and attacks on our psyche may be naive. The Black personality is the cumulative by-product of sustained oppression, which suggests that the only meaningful approach to the study of African Americans is from the perspective of oppression and in terms of the Black experience with Whites in America (Akbar, 2003). Therefore, to understand why I gravitated so strongly toward discourse analysis as a precursor to using Appreciative Inquiry in my work in African American communities, let us examine the hermeneutics of discourse analysis and the potential application of this methodology when looking to better understand the Black experience.

Discourse Analysis: Critical to Our Change Process?

The traditional view of discourse is that it is a form of spoken dialogue versus a more contemporary perspective that views discourse as the combination of both spoken and written texts (Oswick, Keenoy & Grant, 2000). A view of discourse that I believe is more appropriate when used in African American communities is that it is not just a linguistic device but also central to how people construct their reality (Oswick et al., 2000). There are many layers of "reality" that African Americans have internalized, and if we carefully listen, these realities do play out in our language.

More than 30 years ago Manning (1979) posited that the various ways in which language mediates between the world and perceptions of the world are the primary loci of analysis, thereby suggesting that styles of discourse be examined as they played roles in the gathering and analysis of field data. Discourse has "determining capacities" and when it is tied to social relations, identities, power, culture, and social struggle, it is believed to produce a particular version of social reality (Alvesson & Karreman, 2000; Chia, 2000). Discourses from the past can and do shape present and future behavior in the form of established societal beliefs, theories, and stories (Marshak & Grant, 2008).

Consequently, when we view discourse as central to the social construction of reality, we position ourselves to better understand how inequalities in power determine one's perceived ability to control the production, distribution, and consumption of particular language texts (Oswick et al., 2000). This perspective is quite informing and critical to behavioral scientists working to evoke change in challenged or marginalized communities and organizations (Easley, 2011).

Over the years, as I have worked in diverse communities, I have found that most of the patterns of people's lives are highly fragile and are situated within their cultural conversation, which builds the framework for how they view their world and their ability to either interact with or control their world. It is within the spaces of our words that our true meaning tends to reside (Kets de Vries & Miller, 1987; Thatchenkery, 1996; Hopkins & Reicher, 1997). When we carefully listen we will begin to understand people's perceptions of themselves and others within their communities. Unfortunately, I have heard community members on far too many occasions when engaging in conversations about rebuilding their communities utilize language that evokes separation and disparities among neighbors. Yet the participants are not even aware of their language patterns and how disparaging they sound in their descriptions of one another and their community. Language patterns that address our youth are even more negative. Consequently, it is understandable why our youth internalize these negative perceptions and either reframe or use them verbatim in their own descriptive analysis of self and life. From the time a child begins to talk he or she will repeat in one form or fashion that which he or she hears from the adults in their lives.

These language patterns structurally include central themes, root or generative metaphors, well as rhetorical strategies (Kets de Vries & Miller, 1987; Thatchenkery, 1996; Hopkins & Reicher, 1997). Therefore, it becomes very critical that we understand these root or generative metaphors and how we have given them power over our lives. If concepts and language are sufficiently reinforced, they will become internalized beliefs. If our youth are constantly hearing and seeing metaphors that reinforce negative language, why are we so surprised that it becomes their reality?

> The way that a people think and consequently how they act is a product of what they "know." (Akbar, 1996, p. 67)

When participants engage in a conversation that invites a deconstructive analysis that closely examines cultural sensitivity to language, they have the ability to evoke a comprehensive understanding of their reality; it becomes their unique education process. And if they hide behind defense mechanisms, a sound facilitation process built into the discourse analysis can begin to break down those defense mechanisms and help participants better understand their origins. Self-knowledge is critical to one's ability to evoke deep change. Building a thematic analysis of the overarching themes that emerge from our language will also provide us with informing knowledge of behavioral patterns, thereby enabling us to correct those behaviors because we see their relational values.

As previously stated, we have to always be aware that the concrete individual and the reality of the Black experience must be the point of departure of any phenomenological analysis of human existence (Cone, 1970), which means that it does not matter that others do not share our versions of our reality. It is our reality, predicated upon our perceptions, that frames our ontological perspectives of self. The uniqueness of our journey and lessons learned, if critically deconstructed and analyzed, can become the most powerful tool we have for building our future simply because the obtained knowledge helps us understand how not to repeat the past.

I strongly believe that deconstructing, thematically analyzing, and sharing information relative to our discourse is indeed the *core* of the change process. Through disclosed patterns of discourse, we can understand the relational bonds that exist between people and how structure is created, transformed, and maintained. It is also suggested that through the study of discourse as a change process we reinforce or challenge our beliefs (Barrett, Thomas, & Hocevar, 1995).

I will add another benefit to the concept of discourse analysis. When we obtain sacred space to have these critical conversations we have the privacy to dislodge the rage that has been suppressed in us for far too many years. I cannot, however, reiterate too much how important are the deconstruction and analytical processes of discourse analysis. It is not enough to engage in the dialogue. We must also closely and critically examine the themes that emerge and correlate them to the root metaphors that reinforce their existence. It is not until we engage in this level of analysis can we truly begin to diminish the power they hold over our social context.

Butler (2006) has suggested that only a thinly veiled line exists between a cry for justice and expressions of hate. Rage has a way of being uncontrollable and unstoppable, and unless its energy is redirected, the rage will consume the self. He continues that rage will develop when one's humanity is denied and an individual's or race's existence is controlled by those who attempt to objectify their existence. However, he states, there is also a duality in rage— the creative transformation which conquers circumstances and restores the soul to living a life with joy.

Therefore, once we openly acknowledge our pain, and move into an appreciative process, where we honor our historical survival as a people, our individual accomplishments, and our feelings versus repressing them, we can move past the rage and critically examine the negativity for what it is: nothing but futile attempts that we have allowed to hinder our progress.

I believe that to begin saving our youth, we have to help them move past the rage. In 1999, when I wrote my dissertation, I talked about the rage I heard from the young people I studied. Yet when they were offered a different context for looking at self, the internal as well as external rage began to dissipate. Truthfully, I was not with them long enough to help them completely dissipate all that was built up, but what I saw and understood was when safe space was offered, they were fully capable of engaging in change. I have often wondered what that tiny crack of space I offered them did in the long run and what would have happened had I been able to work with them even longer.

As a community we cannot afford to ponder these questions. We must move forward with action. It is the only way we can help our young people who gravitate to gangs change the course of their lives.

My Own Movement toward Intentional Dialogue

Over the years as I have worked in our communities as well as come face-to-face with my own personal issues and need for change, the one proposition that continues to plague me is how to move past the reticence we feel in engaging in an open and intentional dialogue. Mistrust plagues our psyches from so many angles, and understandably so. It feels that just when we think we can open up to others, betrayal will occur. So we bunker down even tighter in emotional lockdowns. Yet there is duality in bunkering down. While protecting ourselves from further emotional pain, we also prohibit our ability to realistically confront the issues that desperately need to be addressed. While this behavior that has become second nature for us, I have to question if, when we downplay our emotive states, theoretical sensitivities, and lens through which we view our lives, are we unconsciously limiting our potential (Easley, 2011)? Our mental health has to be one of the new fronts of our revolutionary struggle (hooks, 1995).

Strategies for change that align the mind, body, and spirit are very important to the African American community, and our communities have to move beyond putting Band-Aid approaches on profusely bleeding issues. We have to take society as well as ourselves to task and drive deep change. While there is personal work involved, our engagement in an intentional dialogue (the discourse analysis component of change) that can lead us to deconstruct and critically examine the hidden themes existing in our conscious as well as subconscious is vital to helping us move forward. An intentional dialogue that we collectively deconstruct and analyze is healing and helps us move toward focused change strategies that give credence to our strengths and inner beauty (invoking the Appreciative Inquiry aspect of generating a new vision and embracing our strengths as we collaboratively dream that vision).

For example, as beautiful as African American women are, we daily deal with affronts to our self-image and esteem through multiple forms of media input that challenge our internal and external beauty. Yet, when we attempt to look or act like our Caucasian counterparts, we still are ridiculed. Adding insult to injury are the accusations that we are angry, augmented by televised presentations of what constitutes "the angry Black woman."

Throughout our history, African American women have dealt with far too many issues brought on by society that would have broken the strongest backs, yet we continue to endure the struggles. However, when you hear African American women talk about these issues we seldom address the deep impact they have on our lives, and we seldom congratulate ourselves for our accomplishments. The denigration we feel impacts our lives in ways we do not talk about; yet I wonder how our suppressed feelings impact our children?

In 2010, I published an article examining the roles of leadership for women of color that discussed the need for African American women to engage in intentional dialogue. I started my propositions with a very personal experience, the sudden death of my husband and its impact upon me personally as well as professionally.

> What I quickly understood and felt were the limitations of a support system I so desperately needed. My prior successes did not diminish the fact that I was hurting deeply, my children were in severe pain, and I knew I was not always making the most rational decisions. I have no siblings and no relatives with whom I could call upon for support. (Easley, 2010, p. 221)

The critical constructs I addressed were the absence of a strong support community and my fear in admitting vulnerability due to the perceived roles and associated behaviors that went along with my title, position, and reputation. Nevertheless I clearly understood that my major responsibility, that of a parent, was being impacted on multiple fronts.

> I have close friends with whom I could dialogue, but they had their lives, and equally important, none had ever gone through the loss of a spouse. As a woman of color, I was reticent to open myself up to support groups . . . after all, I was a Black woman who had national recognition for my work evidenced by my accomplishments. How in the world could I admit vulnerability? How would I have been perceived by my colleagues if I had asked to postpone my tenure application? Would six years of my academic life go down the drain? (Easley, 2010, p. 221)

I did not seek support groups, nor did I engage in intentional dialogue. My praxis from a historical context was to not admit or allow my vulnerabilities to be seen or heard. That did not, however, diminish the fact that when I said I was dying inside, I was and I know that "death" significantly impacted my children.

> At this time in my life, I did not feel strong. I was crying inside on a daily basis, and I felt abandoned . . . by the man I had always thought I would spend the rest of my life with and by friends who were doing the best they could to support me. Against this backdrop, my responsibilities as a mother, whose children were clearly suffering just as much as I was, educator, consultant, community leader and all the other roles that externally defined me did not allow for that vulnerability to be shown. At home at night I cried, while during the day I had an image to maintain. (Easley, 2010, p. 222)

As I processed my own personal experiences, I believe had I engaged in an intentional dialogue with other women similar to me coming from similar situations, I may have been able to move more rapidly toward focused strategies. Some might counter and question the value of counseling or psychotherapy in that situation. But in our community, even those forms of intervention are often met with resistance. Just to get by on a daily basis,

I needed help with routine responsibilities that had previously been shared in my home. Community support for one another is critical. The frustrations I felt of having a child engage in afterschool sports activities with no way home while I taught business classes at night were unbearable and traumatic events to deal with.

I felt the same dissonance as my young gang members. I remember growing up with neighbors who worked together to make sure kids were safely transported home after games and other school events. So what happened? Some may argue that every African American community is not broken. While I won't debate that position, I will respectfully posit that there are too many that are, which has resulted in too many African American youth feeling that when their parents cannot handle a situation, they only have themselves to rely on. This feeling of loneliness can and does move our youth to the gang environment, which has promoted for years the concept of family. Far too many young people talked about feeling isolated and needing the protection and interaction of the gang, which is a situation we must change. Unfortunately, we do not like to talk about the breakdown of our communities. Or, if we do, it is in the sense of a complaint process devoid of solutions. It is no wonder that the youth in my study addressed the need for community support. Sadly, years later little has changed.

Authentically engaging in dialogue with one another helps us understand that we truly are not alone in our feelings, experiences, as well as perceived weaknesses A model that can result from our intentional dialogue is not designed to replace the work and healing that occurs in pastoral counseling, church ministries, or any other means of evoking change that is grounded in one's spiritual or religious realms. The purpose of proposing intentional dialoguing is to help facilitate creative transformation through systematic and strategic approaches that can be incorporated into existing religious and spiritual modalities of intervention (Easley, 2010).

New language and expressions do indeed have the power to become the core of our change processes. Through intentionally deconstructing our patterns of discourse, we can understand the relational bonds that exist between us and others and how structure is created, transformed, and maintained (Barrett, Thomas, & Hocevar, 1995). Equally important, once we understand these patterns it becomes easier for us to evoke a change in our internal as well as external dialogues, moving past the name-calling that continues to plague us as a race by us and upon us.

So, where do we begin with intentional dialogue that concomitantly incorporates the guiding praxis and principles of discourse analysis? First and foremost, we have to agree to talk. Facilitated conversations across this country are needed to begin a collective and collaborative dialogue as to why our communities and our children are in so much pain. We must agree to approach the unthinkable topics, invoking a willingness to allow the bile of our pain to rise to the top of our throats. More important, while we openly acknowledge all systems of domination—racism, class elitism, sexism, imperialism—we must acknowledge them as systems that wound the spirit (hooks, 1995). Unfortunately, damaged spirits rarely choose liberation, an issue we must overcome by using our imaginations to create self against the borders of the imposter identification forced on us by those who keep us in states of subjugation and dehumanization (hooks, 1995).

This conversation is going to be painful, but it must occur throughout the entire African American community. I strongly believe that until we have that conversation we cannot effectively heal ourselves, our children, and our lives, which will empower us to move toward a new future. I simply have found that until we face our demons, when we invoke Appreciative Inquiry, for many it becomes rhetoric. Appreciative Inquiry is so healing if we allow ourselves to open space in gratitude for all that we are. But if we either consciously or subconsciously doubt ourselves, we risk sustaining our beauty and our historical spiritual self.

· 9 ·

CRITICAL FOUNDATIONS AND CONSTRUCTS OF CHANGE

Before examining a proposed model for change in the African American community, it is important to examine the constructs that are critical for effectively designing and implementing a change model. While there is a lot of terrain I try to cover, I have learned that the absence of a full picture is a recipe for failure. Equally important, if I know there are critical components I need to ensure are incorporated into a model, it is my ethical obligation as a teacher, scholar, and organization development professional to do so.

Unfortunately everyone does not share that perspective, which is why, when looking to begin change, a critical component of our intentional dialogue is discerning as many of the variables as possible. Strategy, strategic implementation, and scenario planning are very critical concepts I explore in this chapter that work to ensure we are inclusively moving in the right direction.

I had the unfortunate experience a few years ago to witness how some colleagues will extend the dissemination of critical information for what appears to be very selfish reasons. I attended a conference in England in 2002 where the focus was primarily on discourse analysis as a driver of change. The beauty of this conference was the ability to dialogue with colleagues from many different venues and countries. I sat in a session that was presented by one of my U.S. colleagues who was describing a change process she and others had developed. The academic's institution was affiliated with a broad spectrum of governmental agencies that were available to test or implement their theories. When we possess a doctoral degree our responsibility is to bring new knowledge to our field, but I am learning that perhaps the correct terminology that should be used is *inclusive knowledge*.

As I listened to her, to the trained ear it was quite apparent that critical components were missing in their model. So I raised my hand and asked had they considered these components to which they said, "Yes—but that's next year's research." I never forgot that session. When organizations, communities, and any other entity that is working toward change relies on our production of knowledge to help them conceptualize and contextualize what needs to occur, we do not have the luxury of waiting a year to give them the complete picture, especially if we know in advance what that complete picture looks like. Self-serving needs relative to publication or grant schedules are inappropriate. We also do not have the luxury of time to "play" with the current flavor of the day. Far too many organizations have gone through that process, which yields little to no results. Unfortunately, the employees are generally the ones that suffer. Executives have golden parachutes. It is the workforce who suffers layoffs, reduction in hours, and so on.

In our case, the African American community cannot afford to play games with our change strategies because our very survival and that of our youth is at risk. While I am not presumptuous enough to say I have all the answers, I am giving you the best of what I know constitutes critical components for effective change. Concomitantly, I also suggest a constant analysis and revision process as our communities move through change because, simply put, that is how we learn what does and does not work.

Previously I identified points I respectfully suggested would be critical to our collectively working to invoke change within our communities, which concomitantly drives change for our youth who have gravitated to gangs. Those points are:

1. To successfully change the lives of our children and the environments in which they live, we must be willing to engage in intentional dialogues that will critically work to deconstruct many issues. Over the course of a couple of years now, I have used the term *intentional dialogue*, which will be explained when we move into examining the change model. There are many components to an intentional dialogue,

which is grounded in the theoretical premises of discourse analysis. But the most critical component for this dialogue in the African American community is a commitment to authentically engage in a dialogical process that will critically examine the relevant topic from a historical as well as present-day context.

2. We must reexamine and recommit to the concept of community.

3. We must critically examine our language and how we have allowed certain language patterns to manifest into a conceptual and contextual reality that is counter to who we really are.

4. In concert with the deconstruction of our language, a new pattern of language must emerge that draws upon who we really are in order to collectively move forward from a position of strength.

5. We must challenge and change our patterns of thinking. Our lives are intertwined within the complexity of a variety of systems. When we look at our situations from a silo mentality we inevitably are asking for failure. To examine life from the perspective of understanding patterns as we look beyond the immediacy of a situation is a very distinct change for us. Our propensity for years has been to be reactionary to the varying crises we face.

6. Our prevailing concept of leadership must be challenged in order to discern what constitutes effective leadership for our communities.

7. We must not shy away from collectively envisioning a new version of reality for our children and community.

8. The concepts of systems and our learning how to view our situations from a systems perspective in order to understand where change strategies must begin and end should become our guiding praxis.

9. We must embrace strategy and strategic implementation. Our conversations regarding what should be done must move to patterns of language that incorporate collective action and accountability.

10. There has to be a critical mass of people committed to change, and they have to be willing to stay in the process for as long as it takes.

12. When looking to evoke change, even within the overarching African American community, we must understand that cultural differences will and do influence how people perceive their world.

I am compelled to address the constructs of leadership, systems thinking, strategy, and strategic implement in concert with the concept of critical mass because we must have a clear understanding of what we must internalize to insure success. Failure in these initiatives is not an option, yet it does not have to even be a part of our thought process. A critical component of our driving successful change is our understanding of and preparation for a successful planning and implementation process. As I address many of these issues, I may again travel the road of not always being politically correct, particularly when I talk about leadership. So, with an advanced apology, once again I am compelled to speak my truth.

I have had the benefit of being in leadership positions over the course of my career; many were very successful endeavors and a couple with marginalized results. But if there is one thing I have learned over the more than 30 years of my career, you have to be your own analyst in order to constantly improve your game. What I hope to bring to this particular point is the accumulation of my years of knowledge and education and the benefit of those difficult lessons I have learned, which have helped make me a better leader as well as strategist.

The Criticality of Leadership in the African American Community

As we continue moving through this millennium, the dynamics and rapidity of change is forcing a reexamination of the new roles and competencies required of leaders. Bisoux (2002) suggests that today's effective leader must have the ability to deal with the complexities of change, must possess a strong sense of self, must be able to invoke group interaction, must possess sound communication skills, and must have the moral fortitude to deal with complexity. Inclusively, Kouzes and Posner (1995) believe today's leaders must have the ability to bring to the forefront the needs of people in concert with the ability to understand and better manage social capital in a world that has become very diverse. They also state that in today's context, leadership also requires an understanding that people are searching for meaning in their lives, which facilitates a movement toward a greater openness to the spiritual side of life.

This is not a new conversation. In the last 50 years, interpretative social and organizational science has abandoned the quest for a universal foundation for knowledge (Ludema, Wilmont, & Srivastva, 1997). Organization change theory is aiming to understand the heart and souls of people across many venues, which has resulted in a much different dialogue regarding hope, reconnection to basic values, and appreciation as we have seen with the expansive use of Appreciative Inquiry (Easley & Swain, 2003). The literature on leadership and transformational change is continuing to expand to include emphasis on interpersonal awareness, where questions of how to drive deep personal transformational change are examined in concert with traditional leadership theories and models (Quinn, 1996; Senge, Kleiner, Roberts, Ross, Roth, & Smith, 1999).

Throughout our history, the African American community has had very strong and powerful leaders. Yet our leadership in today's environment is fragmented, and it appears that we are not consistently engaged in those transforming conversations. I believe when we consistently engage in those conversations with the contextual backdrop of our history, theology, and cosmological heritage, our chest will spread with pride and a reemerging essence of collective purpose.

Although a phrase often misused, our world today is truly global. Consequently, those who step into leadership roles within the African American community as we embark upon change have to be persons of immense vision who can imagine what change in our community means within a global context and effectively communicate that vision to our community at large. It is also important that our youth be able to understand and visualize the global context in order to understand their role within this constantly changing world. Earlier I addressed our insularity. In fact, I have addressed it in a few contexts. I am thoroughly convinced that when we develop a broader worldview of life, visualizing change for us becomes a much easier undertaking.

Over the course of the last several years, I have taught leadership in a variety of forums: training sessions, classroom, and individualized coaching sessions. If there is one thing I have learned for sure, it is the fact that everyone who envisions themselves as leaders does not belong in a leadership role. There are constant academic debates as to whether or not leaders are born or developed. I believe that both theories are relevant. However, when developing one's leadership competencies and skills, it is critical to understand that those skills are not actualized by someone just assuming patterns of behaviors. Effective and successful leaders have to internalize the critical competencies and skills that now define effective leadership.

The context in which leadership is defined in today's world environment has already dramatically changed. Leadership competencies are required in every venue of our life. The complexity of today's world requires people daily to step into leadership roles and make decisions that impact their family, community, jobs, church, and so forth. Just because you do not lead a major corporation does not mean you do not need leadership skills. The ability to possess leadership competencies and all the subset skills that make up that competency is critical to surviving in a global world.

When we think about the work of Padilla and Sanchez-Jankowski, they saw many of the components of leadership skills in the youth they studied. Gang leaders possess some of the most complex leadership skills I have seen. However, they have not been taught to actualize those skills in a pro-social manner in venues that do not carry the threat of jail time. A couple of years ago, at a meeting that involved corporate leaders from a large stakeholder region, I was not surprised to hear the chief executive officers of large organizations talk about needing leaders with strong leadership skills at every level of their organization—including the bottom ranks.

We cannot and will not be able to keep walking away from the reality that the complexity of our world is changing at such a pace that it is hard for most to even conceptualize what change in our community means, yet we do not have a choice. We cannot rely on just one leader. We have to have a critical mass of leaders who are on the same page, selflessly leading and willing to make the difficult calls.

Our leaders have to have an ability to rapidly synthesize information and quickly react to the potential outcomes of this information from a bias toward action orientation that we often do not consistently demonstrate. We must teach others in our community to do the same. Leaders must be willing to engage in ongoing learning endeavors, as they wholeheartedly embrace the concepts of knowledge worker and knowledge management. It does not matter how many degrees a person has accumulated, the complexity and pace of change in this world means that data and content information quickly become obsolete, which is why technology increases so rapidly.

Equally critical, leaders have to be comfortable with managing large databases of information and understand the interrelatedness of information. Throughout the book I have continued to posit that our issues are not simple. In fact, I know of very few world issues that can be viewed from a silo perspective. Consequently, our paradigms with respect to how we assess and act upon information and situations must change to a point where we move beyond the limited boundaries of putting in survival mechanisms and toward understanding and identifying the appropriate change structures and systems.

Let us use the venue of education as an example. When I was growing up in the inner city of Chicago and attending an inner-city high school, graduating with a language requirement was mandatory. So we each suffered through (or at least thought we did), taking our French, German, or Spanish with benign acceptance. Unfortunately, when school systems cut resources in our communities, courses such as language requirements are the first curriculum cuts that occur. Yet allowing those types of cuts to occur within our community is suicide to our surviving within a global context, especially when our Caucasian counterparts have already moved past French and Spanish to offering Japanese, Chinese, and other languages that represent countries moving toward dominating our world economy.

When we work toward change and begin to aggressively address issues germane to rectifying the dismal conditions of many of our school systems, we have to have a clear understanding and vision of what needs to be replaced by leaders who will advocate for these replacements with unwavering urgency and an understanding of the systemic issues. Let us go back to the example of language requirements. Language requirements in today's environment are not a luxury. They are a necessity because of the global context of our world. Yet as a community we tend to allow the removal of critical resources from our educational institutions that are vital to our survival in this global world.

The workforce we complain that is replacing the U.S. workforce within our own national businesses are multilingual workers who have a worldview of this economy and socioeconomic-related systems, live outside of the United States, and are not disabled by socioeconomic problems such as a digital divide. In many countries, technology is part of their core curriculum, which means while we are playing games on computers, our international competition is learning how to do complex problem solving via technology resources that do not even reside within our school systems.

Adding insult to injury, we do not even have a handle on how many of the teachers in our communities possess the requisite training to teach these technological skills or are aware of the various resources available to help them learn. We are still in the muddy waters of a school improvement mindset where we are trying to get our students up to their appropriate grade levels with respect to basic reading and math. Clearly, when we juxtapose our current state to the current state that resides within non-African American global communities, our acceptance of this state and a one-dimensional view of its ramifications are unacceptable. As an African American community, we have not stepped out to take control of this situation and say enough is enough. We can't even get parents to consistently attend report card days.

Being as guilty as the next person, I never kept up my language skills and was even lazier as I traveled because my travel companions were multilingual.

Yes, I said lazy compared and contrasted to their being multilingual, which meant I had no excuse because I knew the terrain and understood the need to be able to speak several languages. I had equipped my son with those resources and was working on my daughter. He had immersion courses in Spanish and had been to Spain as a part of his emersion process. When my daughter asked to go to Disney World, I told her I would not send or take her there but would instead take her to Disney Paris. We went there together in 2004, when she, as a young teenager, traveled with me to France and Italy. But I did not take the time to keep up my skills, and I was always relying on others to translate critical information.

When I began teaching in the French Caribbean, I quickly learned the paradox of being linguistically limited. It did not matter that I had three degrees. I simply could not communicate with my colleagues and students and was grateful that the people who invited me to teach were willing to put translators in my classroom.

The United States is not the dominant force we once believed. Albeit English being the predominant international language, similar to diversity attitudes in our own country, when we travel outside our boundaries people do not feel compelled to accommodate us or our programs. We have to learn to work in a global context. So, as we envision change within our school systems, we have to be clear on the parameters our youth need to survive. We can no longer count on our own context to provide that information. Our leaders have to be clear on the requirements of today's environment.

We also have to understand that graduating youth who can barely read or do math in a world where even computers are being replaced by systems that compute faster than the mind could ever visualize is a kiss of death. Having instructors teach in our communities who are not up-to-date with the latest technological and pedagogical developments in their field is totally unacceptable. Their lack of knowledge hinders our youth. Equally unacceptable is the warehousing of youth in alternative school environments because we cannot accommodate learning styles or understand the appropriate strategies for reaching those who feel disengaged and disenfranchised from society. If African Americans are to globally survive, everyone coming through today's educational process has to be able to meet standards that far exceed the mediocrity we have accepted for years.

Continuing to allow our youth to matriculate through subpar systems where varying learning styles are not accommodated in concert with current curricular issues, ensures their demise in a global workforce even if they never step foot out of this country. Business leaders will continue to outsource in order to be able to produce products and services that keep their respective industries viable. That means the numbers of jobs and opportunities we so desperately need to keep stability in our communities will continue to spiral downward. It is indeed an interrelated series of issues. As we continue to downward spiral in our communities, our youth will have no other choice but to gravitate to alternative environments. If we ever thought the system was closed to us before, let's see what happens in another five years as the global economy takes another turn. We will not just be on the fringes; we won't even be close to the landscape of where the games are being played.

We need leaders in our communities who understand that we have to garner resources that provide opportunities for our youth to travel outside their boundaries. There are resources available to us. Let us briefly revisit the example I gave of the community I worked in whose leader had that community on lockdown for more than 30 years. Resources were not an issue, the people were the problem. They never questioned the paltry dollars he provided them to do community renovation projects. So, as his administration was delving out $2000 to $3000 per request, while working in the community, we uncovered millions of dollars earmarked for community development and available to us through an application process.

The people in this community never moved outside their comfort zone of oppression to understand what was available in order to evoke much needed change in their community. They never challenged their leader and took his leadership skills to task. Yet he was only one in the midst of more than 30,000 people who lived in that community—people who clearly had abdicated their personal power.

A leader with vision will understand that many people in the African American community will not have the resources to fund travel or other external endeavors our youth need to develop a comprehensive world vision. Yet a visionary leader will not allow current resources to deter the actions we need. He/she will understand that as a community we will need to come together and look for viable options within our broader stakeholder community because that leader is capable of thinking outside the box.

That leader will also understand in the deepest recesses of his or her soul the concept of risk taking. Garnering a community together to evoke change will require leaders who are comfortable with taking risk. Concomitantly, our community has to surround our leaders, especially when they take significant risks. A critical part of understanding systems thinking is that we have to know that someone else always benefits when our community suffers and when we lose our youth. As a community we can never be afraid of those "someones." The "risk" of not taking risk is far greater. We cannot continue to lose our most precious resource, our children. That clearly is not an acceptable risk we can continue to endure.

The Hermeneutics of Soulful Leadership

Throughout the years, I worked at developing a model that communicated my lens toward leadership and its relationship to organizations or, in the case of our conversation, community-based change. In 2003 I developed this model; yet outside the classroom, this book is the first public venue in which I have shared it. I believe it is most appropriate to publish it now because the understanding and internalization of its theoretical premises are critical to the success of our change strategies and impact upon our youth. The overarching premise of the model is that we each have been given by our Maker personal gifts to be used in leadership roles irrespective of the venues in which we lead. It is our choice as to whether or not and how we use our gifts.

I have often wondered how many African American youth believe they have gifts. I am not reflecting upon athletic prowess, but gifts such as the ability to connect with others, effectively communicate, write, construct stories, play music, and so on. I also think about how many children have been given negative labels in our school system, yet are very talented. There are so many doors that are intentionally closed to our young people, which is why it is difficult for them to envision their gifts. To this day, I remember my daughter coming home from school with a list of potential careers paths provided by her school counseling department. The list was both limiting and insulting to the African American community. But the worse travesty was that it was provided by an African American adult who was invoking the same barriers that we complain are provided by those who "other" us. I still remember to this day the conversation I had with the school as I demanded that the counselor develop another list that comprehensively as well as professionally represented a broader spectrum of career options to which our children could aspire, and I requested that her principal sit with her and explain the ramifications of her actions. I will always believe that we each have God-given gifts and that the foundation of those gifts serves as the underpinning for our ability to envision the best we can be. Too often we abdicate our dreams because we buy into the unwarranted restrictions others attempt to place upon us—actions to which we have the ability to say no.

I call this model "The Interactive Relational Model for Sustained Self-Empowered Leadership and Organizational Change." You may wonder why I titled this subsection soulful leadership. Today's environment requires people to lead via their hearts as well as their minds. A leader has to want to connect to a cause and lead, whether it's the Little League team or a multimillion dollar business. Effective leaders have to believe in people as well as be very principled. The ability to see and inspire a vision will require a leader to reach in the recesses of his or her soul in order to take people places they may fear going. Even though the leadership trek may be wrought with trial and error, when people feel the spirit and soul of a leader—in other words their true essence—they will follow without fear or trepidation.

During my doctoral program in concert with other contemporary theorists in the area of leadership I had the pleasure of taking a class from Dr. Robert Quinn, which truly was a blessing. During this class we were introduced to his book, *Deep Change: Discovering the Leader Within* (1996). Since first reading that book, I have either required it as a mandatory reading or highly recommended it for all of my leadership classes. I have also had the pleasure of reading his subsequent books on leadership, where he continues to take the concept of leadership to a level that most miss. Over the years I have had many students thank me for suggesting (or requiring) they read *Deep Change* and his follow-up books.

It is very difficult for people to be effective leaders unless they engage in self-exploration and confront the issues that block us from being all that we have the ability to be, competencies germane to effectively leading our organizations. We have to learn to become internally driven leaders who will not succumb to slow death (Quinn, 1996). The concept, however, of deep change for many is frightening because it requires our embracing new ways of thinking, shifting paradigms and constantly scanning the environment to see beyond the present As a result, people will often opt for slow death, where they refuse to assess or redefine their purpose in life and align their actions with that purpose and values (Quinn, 1996).

Far too many people, including our children, are examples of the walking dead in our communities. This is a critical issue for leaders in the African American community from personal and motivational perspectives. People who step up as leaders cannot be afraid to confront their own personal decay. It is not until they have dealt with their own issues that they can success-fully lead others (Quinn, 1996). How many self-proclaimed leaders have we experienced in our community who have far too much drama and give the distinct impression that their primary motivation for assuming the role of leadership is their own personal glory? These are not the people we need leading us in a change process that is going to impact our most important gift, our children. In fact, those that rise to the new ranks of leaders have to have the intestinal fortitude to bring to the forefront of our attention the deltas that exist between what we can achieve and the dismal alleged "suc-cesses" of those who have irresponsibly held the positions of leader in our communities.

We have been conditioned to address only those issues that are immediate problems for us, seldom stepping back and envisioning our rightful potential. I believe the reason we tend to take such a short-sighted approach is our failure to have an abundance of leaders who are able to take that step back: to envi-sion, self-analyze, and make necessary personal modifications in order to pro-vide the example of self-initiating change required by our communities and, equally important, by our children. We often chastise our children for their limited vision relative to success, typically making it a point to say that they ought to have a broader worldview of opportunities beyond athletes and the local drug dealers on the corner. Yet they have to have consistent examples of what this self-initiating action looks like.

While embracing and moving toward our new vision will obviously take us back to the immediacy of our situation—working through those issues are only fragments of what should be a bigger picture. Our leadership must clearly understand that while youth gravitating to gangs is obviously an immediate problem we must address, we must have a collective vision of where our youth can actualize and maximize themselves in this world. It must be a world vision where they clearly see their roles and responsibilities within a global context. Simply surviving is no longer a viable option. Our children are beautiful, talented, vivacious, and smart. But they have to see that beauty within themselves, as do we, in order to share a glowing vision of their potential to develop.

Quinn (1996) states the ability to invoke deep change requires a comfort level with risk taking in concert with a spiritual connection to oneself, where we "see," understand, and embrace our purpose. Yet how many people do we see daily that resemble the walking dead? They are afraid to rise to their purpose, and despite professing values ensconced in a strong theological belief system, far too few have really internalized an unwavering belief that our God truly wants, as well as expects, us to maximize our potential and live up to our purpose.

There is an exercise I use when I open my business communications classes. I teach my students that a significant component of successful business communication is grounded in how one sees himself or herself in the verbal as well as written communication processes. To command attention and respect when interacting with people requires self-respect. I simply ask them to observe for a week people walking down a street and note how many people have conditioned themselves to walk with their heads down toward the ground, failing to look up and at other people at eye level. I ask them to note their initial impressions of the people they see walking with their heads down. It never fails that they articulate a negative first impression. Then I ask them to note how many times they found themselves walking in the same manner, as they assess the signals they send regarding their own self-esteem.

One might wonder why this exercise is germane to the topic of leadership, but the answer is simple. To reach the potential that is our God-given right means we have to believe we are entitled to it. A love for ourselves and belief that we are entitled to being all that we can be is critical to driving change in our community. Loving ourselves is critical for the survival of our children. When you love yourself and have self-respect, you will not fear assuming the role of leader, whether it is for the Little League team or for a community-based initiative. When you love yourself and have self-respect, you will not allow others to denigrate you. When you love and have self-respect, you are willing to intelligently pursue or fight for that which is inherently yours to claim. When you daily walk around as if the world has dealt you blows to which you no longer have the strength to fight, you simply will succumb to your perceived failure. We have to collectively learn to walk tall with our eyes toward the heavens, for those heavens, however we define them, in the present are ours to claim. We have to understand that there is significant danger in seeking solutions to new problems in the same places we found the old answers, which is a tendency for people when they are afraid to step outside their box (Quinn, 1996).

People are afraid to step outside their boxes for many reasons. For some, they have been conditioned to expect that when they step outside the box, they will be punished, similar to many of the old psychological shock treatment studies. Others are reticent to step outside their comfort zone because they may not always have what they perceive to be "all the answers." I have found over the years that we will not have all the answers, but that should not stop us from stepping out on a journey grounded in faith. Each time I stepped out and began walking a path that was frightening because I could not see the end in front of me, I kept going back to the real meaning of faith and my understanding that when I learn to quiet my fears, I rest into the understanding that God simply asks us to have faith and believe.

Historically, we have been graced with being able to witness phenomenal leaders such as Rev. Dr. Martin Luther King, Malcolm X, former president of South Africa Nelson Mandela, Mahatma Gandhi, or Mother Theresa who were not afraid to step outside their box, speak their truth, and live to their purpose. But in reality, we have people with those qualities right in our own community, and they don't have to be big public figures. They could be the person that has coached the Little League team, mentoring children for years, the pastor leading the church on the corner, or the teacher that took time with children who may have lost a parent and needed someone willing to step outside their comfort zone to spend time with that child. In other words, leaders are ordinary people who aren't afraid to embark upon extraordinary journeys (Quinn, 2000).

Deep change within oneself also infers a spiritual connection where one can connect with their purpose (Quinn, 1996). But as I have respectfully suggested in earlier chapters, we need to understand our past in order to appreciate why reaching our true spiritual connection and purpose is in fact deeply rooted in our psyche. Our historical theological self, rooted in a cosmology where community and oneness with God has always been our heritage. We just have to be comfortable with allowing it to flow.

If we were to summarize some of the critical competencies we need relative to leadership, simply put, we must have people who can realize a vision, will be consistent in working from a moral system while developing and abiding by core values, are self-authorizing, not afraid to confront one's own demons, learns by doing, values complexity, and are not afraid to engage in personal rebirths (Quinn, 1996).

If we take these concepts and apply them to my leadership model, one must concurrently look at the model from the vertical as well as horizontal perspectives. Those theorists who have historically posited that you cannot lead your organization (or in this case community) toward a vision until you have a vision of who you are and "whose" you are in line with your calling are clearly on target. How many organizations have we witnessed hit rock bottom because their leadership did not possess one-third of the competencies suggested by Quinn? The failure to personally align before one remotely attempts to step into a venue of leadership is clearly asking for either death by stagnation or death by incompetence. One only has to cite the Enrons, World Coms and other similar organizations in our world to understand the potential magnitude of outcome. It will take years for our economy and the people who worked for those and similarly situated organizations to recover from the ineptness of the individuals who led those organizations.

People are always poised and ready to take you off your path. It's their "job" in life. But if you are grounded in your own personal power of who you are spiritually as well as understanding your own individual grounding and strengths, you will not move to anyone else's music but that of your calling. That same grounding is what you provide for your organization by virtue of living your truth, which is why, in the absence of that personal power, it is unrealistic to assume that you can help your organization become empowered.

Our children need to understand personal power. During the course of my research it became very clear that our children do not understand what it means to stand in their own personal power, which is understandable. They are young. I often would chuckle at how my son would confirm with me if he was right about something as he "stood" in his personal power. From a verbal stance, he would be unwavering in the articulation of his position. But he would always have the look that silently said, "Mom, am I right?" I learned over the years how to validate his positions in concert with delivering the appropriate lessons in a manner that did not thwart his desire to continue standing in his personal power. I have also learned over the years that no matter how strong our children emerge, inevitably they need our guidance and validations of their truths. We cannot validate their truths if we are living lies.

The concepts of organizational power and personal power also need to be discussed from a very different perspective. Power as a concept is very complex. There are many power games played in our communities by people who have absolutely no vested interest in the outcomes relative to our lives and the lives of our children. We become pawns in their own games. Yet far too many times we are enamored by these people because of their ability to exert charismatic power. Far too often, we do not take the time to discern who the power brokers are and their real motives. When our change processes begin, we have to put on the lens of discernment in order to avoid their blocking efforts. Power strategies, in any venue, always have been and always will be dualistic. In many ways, power strategies can help drive change at a rapid pace because the right brokers are in place. However, on the flip side, if not understood and equally managed, power strategies in the wrong hands can derail a noble cause.

I have taught power strategies as a class for more than 10 years. One of the first exercises I ask students to do is to identify the organizational chart of their particular business context. On that chart, I ask them to identify those people who are allegedly in power by virtue of title and position. Next, I ask them to identify who the real power brokers are in their organizations and to develop a shadow organizational chart. Over the past 10 plus years I have conducted this exercise, inevitably 80% of the students always see that the organizational chart that theoretically represents who is in power is antithetical to the "real" organizational chart that identifies where the true power lies in the organization.

As we begin to invoke true change within our communities, understanding the dynamics of power and its intersection with and relationship to systems are critical concepts for us to deconstruct. Far too often, what we see in front of us is not real. Generally, it is within the shadows where the real issues, as well as those with whom we must interact, lie.

As we reexamine the concept of power in my model, personal power in concert with understanding the dualities of the perceptions of power are critical concepts in the execution of that model. Even if a leader is capable of standing in his or her personal power, the failure to understand the power dynamics in the contextual setting in which they work will derail many and most efforts.

Finally, if an individual is successful in achieving personal change via alignment with his or her vision and personal power, there is no doubt that they will be able to successfully do the same within their own organizational context.

The Complexities of Culture and Context

When looking to understand people and their respective actions, we must understand that difference will lie even within the same race or ethnicity. Unfortunately, in this country we are not traditionally trained to recognize microcultural differences and understand how they impact behavior.

Microcultures represent distinctive cultural characteristics that reside within the context of a broader culture. For example, when my colleague from France and I walk into a venue in the United States the initial assumption (until she speaks) is that two Black women are walking into a room, with little to no thought that microcultural differences exist. Yet the differences between us are huge. For example, the existence of 18 years in age difference signifies that we view the world from different contexts. I am a baby boomer and she represents Generation X. She grew up in Europe and I grew up in the United States; consequently her view of diversity and culture is very different from mine. We have differences in religion, language, and country context. For her, she is French first and then a woman of color. For me, I am a woman of color and then an American citizen, which speaks volumes as to how we culturally locate ourselves.

While my illustration of our differences point to the existence of microcultures from a broader context, the same principles apply to African Americans living in the United States. Regional differences (growing up in the South versus the North), socioeconomic status, education, political agenda and family backgrounds will impact how we view life (Boje & Rosile, 1994). While it is not imperative in a change process that we identify every microcultural difference, we must clearly understand that they do exist and understand why they can and will emerge when we engage in an intentional dialogue. When we recognize microcultures, we better understand the need to engage in a continued exploration of context in order to be inclusive of everyone's voice when we work toward change.

I had to learn this lesson the hard way. I entered into a consulting engagement in an African American community in the South, blindly assuming that because I, too, was African American I would better understand the culture and racial issues that my people in this part of the country faced. I was very wrong in that assumption. People live within interpretative communities, or discourse communities, that provide a horizon of understanding that often serves as the foundation of their facts (Fish, 1989; Barrett, Thomas, & Hocevar, 1995).

Growing up in the North, I had not been exposed to the Creole culture and its proclivities within the broader African American context. I assumed understanding due to my being African American, which emerged as only one factor in the clients' layers of culture, and I did not consider or even question my ability to understand or know their situation (Easley, 2010). I assumed knowledge by virtue of the common denominator of race. However, I quickly learned that I was limited by the fact that I had never lived in the South, did not understand southern culture, particularly African American southern culture, and was completely unfamiliar with the Creole culture (Easley, 2010).While the complexity of the situations that occurred during this intervention forced the participants to move back and forth from their perspectives relative to history, culture, race, and the perception of racism (reflective-reflexive actions) to the intervention, making it possible to produce more intelligible interpretations of observations (Strauss & Corbin, 1990), there should have been more theoretical sensitivity on my part, as the researcher, toward understanding the possible depth as well as range of the perceptions and plausible interpretive schemas *before* I entered the organization (Easley, 2010). Consequently, when I now enter communities that I have not had an extensive exposure to, one of my first steps is to engage the participants in a dialogue that will help them deconstruct their microcultures and their plausible impact upon their desired outcomes, actions that are quite enlightening for the participants.

The Dance of Effective Implementation

Earlier I identified competencies I believe are critical for African Americans to internalize in order to effectively drive change in our communities. While each competency and their respective skills are critical, there are two with which we often struggle that I want to address. They are our ability to:

- Embrace strategy and strategic implementation. Our conversations regarding what should be done must move to patterns of language that incorporate collective action and accountability.
- Develop a critical mass of people committed to change who are willing to stay in the process for as long as it takes.

Strategic implementation is problematic for many, including major corporations, largely because it is very process oriented. However, one of the first prerequisites to strategic implementation is a commitment to get the job done. When evoking change, everyone is not going to be on the same page, or have the same level of commitment. What is necessary is a critical mass of stakeholders who want to make a change for our communities and youth and are not afraid of accountability. Effecting consistent communication patterns for those who are involved with strategic implementation as well as those who are on the fringes is very important. People fear what they don't understand or cannot see in front of them. Consequently, transparently keeping people abreast of processes and outcomes is important to minimizing attempts to derail the initiatives. As we saw in the 2008 presidential election and prior campaign strategies, advances in technology make it much easier to ensure that the "truth" is communicated versus allowing others to import their own interpretations.

So, what exactly is strategic implementation? Once an overarching vision has been developed with an associated mission, specific goals are set. In essence the strategy is the plan of action broken into tactical steps that are disseminated into individualized operating units. Strategic implementation requires effective feedback processes and a constant scan that there is goal congruency among all units. Effective leaders have to make sure that the people who comprise the critical masses and are committed to working the plan are coached and counseled on an ongoing basis to ensure their comfort level and success with the implementation processes.

Leaders also have to ensure that there is congruency among goals, which means we have to ensure that the agreed-upon goals must have specific foci with linkages among efforts and tactical steps where we can see where one tactic is supportive of another, ultimately leading to completion of strategic goals. People who are willing to drive the strategy must possess the core competencies needed and be willing to actively engage in learning, which concomitantly provides key opportunities for our youth to take their innate skills and put them into action. As the adults in their lives, we can help them refine their competencies and skills while embracing their fresh ideas and approach to change as they become more involved in our change processes. The commitment to teaching and the willingness to learn also helps bridge communication gaps that are typically brought on by generational differences. Community-based change that focuses on driving a new life for our youth also becomes a bridge-building process.

Goals and objectives must be verifiable, which in essence means real-istic and able to be brought about in a timely manner. The reason this is so important is that people can and do lose hope when initiatives drag out. The leadership of a change effort must also make sure that performance outcomes are consistently viewed and measured, and, when required, cor-rective action to appropriately stay on course is taken without people fight-ing back because they are tied to methods that are either not working or too outdated.

Oftentimes as I have worked in communities, particularly in African American religious communities, I have seen well-meaning church folk dig in their heels and attempt to thwart a specific action because it meant that the strategies they were tied to for years would no longer be implemented. Folk would cave in simply because they did not want to hurt the feelings of the older members.

However, if for years you have been doing fish fries and not teaching a community how to fish for itself, clearly it is time to stop the fish fries, no mat-ter how many Ms. Sally's and Mr. Charles's have chaired those fish fry com-mittees over the years. The psychological contracts that tie people to these metaphorical fish fries are strong, which means leaders have to also be aware of the psychological contracts that prevail in a given system. Psychological contracts are simply unspoken agreements that everyone believes others have bought in to, when in reality there is no consensus relative to these unspo-ken agreements. Those contracts or unspoken beliefs that have marginally worked in our community must change. The jettison of old values and beliefs in a strategic implementation process also means people involved in change must be willing to step outside their prevailing paradigms, their currency, and deconstruct prevailing psychological contracts, while being willing to embrace new paradigms and perspectives, actions that will definitely make many people very uncomfortable.

Over the years, I have also learned that leaders must help those that they lead anticipate the unexpected. Early in my doctoral program, we began to study scenario planning, which involves scanning the environment for indi-cators of change that may or may not be visible to the naked eye. We have to carefully examine the political, economic, social, cultural, and global contexts to understand what the possibilities of an immediate shift to our environment could be and how we would have to incorporate potential change into our strategic-planning processes. Understanding and planning for those shifts is similar to playing chess. When you anticipate various moves, you learn to lay multiple options. If we remain insular to our context and global environment, we will be clueless as to the potential dangers we can and may encounter.

Understanding and factoring in scenario planning is important for another critical reason. If the environment shifts and there is an impact to resources, the African American community must be prepared to protect the accomplishments obtained via our change processes. Unfortunately, the basic nature of humanity suggests people protect their own turf if unexpected change occurs. Consequently, we have to be prepared to protect our communities and their resources—human capital as well as material resources. Over the years we have witnessed many shifts to the environment that have negatively impacted our communities. Because we lack power, we inevitably become victims of the shifts.

You might ask, what does a real scene relative to scenario planning look like? Let's take one we typically take for granted: education. Not too long ago, if a person matriculated through an undergraduate program, they had sufficient education to progress through their chosen professions. However, as time has passed, the educational requirements in most careers have continued to morph to new levels. Where a few years ago a bachelor's degree was sufficient for entry-level positions, now a master's degree has become the prerequisite for either entry or career movement. Unless people have closely watched the trends, we miss them and are caught off guard, thus requiring additional time to return to school to catch up.

As an administrator in higher education, I saw another example that clearly could have been avoided. Far too many colleges and universities failed to anticipate the change in the demographic profile of the entry-level college student. Administrators were comfortable in their belief that traditional age students (18–22) would forever embark upon our doorsteps. Suddenly, higher educational administrators saw and felt the reality and resulting implications from the fact that baby boomers had fewer children than their parents. College recruiting numbers were significantly impacted. Ironically, while the 18–22-year-old student population declined, more adults were returning to school.

Unfortunately, far too many college professors were not trained to educate adult learners who require a very different type of classroom experience. As a result, many universities lost ground until they were able to make the necessary adjustments in their recruiting strategies, admissions policies, and pedagogical platforms. The travesty, however, was that the scrambling actions that had to occur could have been avoided. Most institutions have research departments that simply could have incorporated into their research agendas scenario-planning strategies for student profiles and demographic shifts. Consequently, the issue was never our capability to see the shifts coming. The majority of educational institutions unfortunately who teach strategy and scenario planning never incorporated these processes into their own strategies.

The need to anticipate environmental shifts is a reality for people from a personal perspective. For example, as an educator and a consultant, I have to be very careful to ensure that I am managing my currency relative to the competencies and skills college professors and consultants should possess as the global environment shifts. Arming oneself to understand environmental shifts requires basic skills that are not always standard-operating procedures in our communities. First and foremost, we have to travel to understand the world, which brings me back to an earlier point that is critical for our youth and our community at large. On a whole, the United States is far too insular. The African American community takes the concept of insularity to a new level. Even if financial resources are issues for us, we must find ways to obtain resources in order to expose ourselves and our youth to the world beyond our individual doors.

Equally important how we think—our prevailing paradigms—must begin to shift in order to understand the linkages that serve as the quiet indicators of change. Oftentimes those indicators are not dramatic but nevertheless are in our face. We simply have to learn to view the world and think about the realities in front of us from a system's perspective. For example, as I have continued to talk about our youth being left behind because of the subpar educational systems we continue to tolerate in our communities, I am not just looking at these issues from a local perspective.

As I have traveled, I see the dichotomies relative to the educational training our youth receive compared to our international colleagues. I see the impact relative to adults as well. Let us revisit my colleague from France. Despite our having similar research interests and our being successful in our collaborations, there are marked differences in our training that would have significantly placed me in an inferior educational position to her had I not had other advantages. Her educational training far outpaced mine simply because of the structure of the French educational system—clearly not an indictment of my institutions or programs. Inclusively, she has taught in more international environments than I have simply because, in Europe, to teach in a different culture may mean driving 150 miles versus an 8-hour plane trip. Equally critical is her language competency—which we won't address because

I have already admitted my deficiencies in that area, which is not acceptable in today's environment.

She is also 18 years younger than me, which means technologically she has advantages. My advantage, which I had to learn to work, is my 20 plus years of experience in the corporate sector and 17 years of experience in institutions of higher education in both administrative and teaching positions, which arms me with the ability to apply knowledge in ways that she has not experienced. We have to understand our advantages and how to work them. If I did not have those advantages and understand how to make them work for me, she and I would not be on an equal playing field in a global environment where we compete for the same jobs.

As a community, we must learn to better leverage ourselves and teach our youth these same competencies. Our world is changing and continues to change. We have to understand change from a macro- and microperspective. To keep our heads buried in the sand will be suicide for the African American community on many levels.

Our youth, irrespective of whether or not they are in gangs, need to understand strategy as well as scenario planning. Far too many young people I worked with during the course of my research had limited perspective with regard to their future. For many, the future was not even a possibility since they had witnessed so many of their friends dying before they reached 21. Yet part of importing hope to our youth who have gravitated to gangs is their understanding that they do have a future and it is their choice to change paths.

Understanding personal power and personal choice aligned to strategy and scenario planning are interrelated concepts that the adults as well as young people in our community need to incorporate into their paradigms. Each of us must decide whether we confront our internal decay, which brings about deep change, or opt for slow death (Quinn, 1996). The reason, however, I believe making that choice is difficult for many is because we often do not have a handle on how to devise our own personal strategy and garner critical stakeholders and resources, which is why collectively working to improve this competency within our community is critical.

Collectively, we also have to improve our skills in strategy implementation. The downfall of strategic implementation is that it typically will become an event, even for corporations. I still have memories of my days in the corporate-business sector where leaders would gather every 4–5 years and devise a strategy that often wound upon on one of the executive's bookshelves. They had done their periodic duty, and it was now time to go back to business as usual. Unfortunately, I saw the same in higher education.

Even if the frequency of the strategic-planning process increased, staying on target for many organizations is difficult. The simplicity of project-management strategies tends to allude many. However, in the African American community, we cannot allow strategy implementation to fail. As I have continued to posit, there is far too much resting on the success of our invoking change in our community—our youth.

Our implementation processes have to be well thought out and designed, incorporating options that result from our engaging in critical scenario planning, with well-developed goals and tactical steps that incorporate appropriate feedback loops and communication processes. The metrics we use to define our success must be agreed to by all involved in the process of change, and they have to be obtainable metrics that allow us to visualize and actually see results. The actualization of results keeps the hope factor alive—we cannot afford to lose either.

We have to change our paradigms relative to outcomes and become highly skilled in the areas of visualizing and invoking results. Over the past 12 years a significant portion of the student population I have taught were adults returning to school, in fact more than 70% have been age 30 or older. At the beginning of each class I would ask them why they returned to school. While many had noble reasons, few could articulate, when asked, how the education process drove their strategy and if they even had a personal strategy where they had identified key goals and tactical steps. Many were even shocked by the question.

Strategy for African Americans has to be a layered process in concert with strategic implementation. We each must visualize our personal strategy, which incorporates visualizing our personal vision of who we are and where we want to go in our lives. Similar to implementing a collective strategy, every activity we engage in must support our personal strategy. Yet that concept is often in conflict with the walking dead that Quinn describes, aimlessly moving about life without living to one's purpose. Once again I must respectfully posit that when we understand our historical, theological, and cosmological roots, it is easier to understand that each of us has a purpose in life. It may not be to lead a major *Fortune* 500 corporation; it may simply be to work hard to make a difference in people's lives through the everyday interactions we are capable of having with one another. Nevertheless, we should each focus on meditating in order to identify the calling we have and work to put that vision and mission into a goal-oriented strategy that we daily work to implement.

When our youth see the adults in their lives working toward their purpose, it becomes easier for them to understand and visualize that they too have a purpose in life to which they must develop their own personal strategy. Equally important, I have learned that it must be something they want to do with their life. As parents, many times we get frustrated because we want things for our children that are totally antithetical to their personal desires. But, if they are rooted in a strong foundation, they will find their way. I use to chuckle when my son said before he embarked upon his college career that he would never major in business like Mom. Yet at graduation tears were in my eyes as he walked across the stage with his diploma in International Business, which was his choice! Our children will not stray far from their roots if their foundation is strong. Consequently, it is up to us to ensure that they rest on a strong foundation. I do not believe that it is too late for our youth who have gravitated to gangs to shore up. But their ability to rise above their hopelessness is definitely going to be predicated upon how we help them shift their paradigm regarding their options in life. It is not going to occur by our engaging in rhetoric. They have to see results, the results of our designing and implementing a strategy that will evoke critical change in the African American community.

· 1 0 ·

THE MODEL FOR CHANGE

Throughout this book I have worked to set the context relative to the issues regarding our youth gravitating to gang environments juxtaposed against the overarching issues that reside in the African American community. I have also introduced a different type of framework for how we should be viewing the interrelatedness of these issues, strongly suggesting that until we address the systemic problems that frame our social context, it will be very difficult to address the reasons why our youth gravitate to gangs.

I have also introduced competencies that are critical for driving change in our communities, in concert with identifying the linkages of those competencies to one another as well as to strategic change outcomes. In other words, I have set the stage for introducing a change model.

You might wonder why a model is important. This model is a roadmap, not necessarily set in stone, but designed to posit a starting point and the varying steps that are critical when executing change. Equally important, a model for change sets the stage where people can collectively gather around a critical topic in which they believe while simultaneously evoking a time for healing.

Far too often, I become frustrated as I read books that only reiterate our situation. I believe our time for talk is over because what we continue to lose is too valuable. We cannot continue to lose our children to gang violence, nor should we continue to tolerate the inequities that plague us. However, we also cannot continue to rely on others to do the work for which we are accountable.

I am going to step out on a limb and say that this book represents a call to action, with an action strategy identified, albeit one that can and will undergo modifications. I do not expect that everyone will rise to this call. But everyone is not needed. A critical mass committed to change is what we need to begin the process.

The Venue for Beginning

Change is hard under normal circumstances. The situations we must address in the African American community represent problems that have psychologically, emotionally, and physically drained us for years. Consequently, we must fortify our strength and work from a venue that can constantly replenish our spirits. While the tasks in front of us are daunting, they are attainable, particularly if we understand in the beginning what needs to be in place for us to start, work, and end in celebration.

To be successful, we must draw upon the foundations of our strength: our cosmology and theology, which is why I place the headquarters for our change processes in the Black church. We need a place where we can come just to "be" and sit with one another as well as have sacred space to engage in intentional dialogue and reenergize. We need the skills of our theologians in helping us respond to the difficult questions of "why?" in contrast and comparison to our religious beliefs.

I can't begin to describe how healing it is when you have a venue of that nature to which you can go. I often share with others how my seminary has always been a place of healing for me. Although I was accepted to seminary right before the death of my husband, I did not begin my walk until the following year. Consequently, coming to seminary was situated in a space and time that represented my asking some of the most difficult questions I had asked in my life. But there is not a day that I felt intimidated in asking the hard questions and having people of faith who were struggling just like me, either engage in the debate I needed to have in order to answer my questions, or were willing to just "sit" in my pain—which is just as healing.

One day in a class where we were doing a form of exegesis, one of my academic colleagues had written a scenario that exactly described the scene

I experienced the night my husband died. I had suppressed many of these moments because they were too painful for me to remember. When she began reading her paper, I began to cry uncontrollably, something no one in that room had ever seen me do or probably thought me capable of doing. I had become very good at playing the role of the strong Black woman with all the titles and other descriptors associated with being me. As I sat in my seat and cried for at least 15 to 20 minutes, my fellow students and faculty just sat with me, not trying to console or say it would be better. They simply sat. Throughout the years I had attended seminary, God had allowed them to see me, not my titles, degrees, or other points of reference. I was in pain and the hurt was so deep that I felt like I was choking. I did not need consoling. I simply needed to "be." They understood that. And after my cry, I simply said, "Thank you."

There are so many burdens we carry in life that we need a place to "be." When we embark upon change that will challenge us, we simply need a place to "be." I have always believed that our asking the tough questions will not challenge or shut down our belief systems. As we ask those tough questions— such as "Why are so many of our children dying senseless deaths?"—God will quietly answer us because we have chosen to still be in conversation with Him.

Collegiality is important to change. My seminary faculty pushed me to academic levels I have not been previously pushed despite my having a doctorate degree because they could see my soul at levels that others won't try to see. A support system where people understand the issues as well as the experiences is critical. Yet people who support one another must also be committed to ensuring that we each are actualizing to our purpose.

It has been suggested that African American religion, often simply called "the Black church," is intimately tied to our spirituality. While not the same, Mitchem (2002) believes they are very connected because of the historical roots the Black church has played in the African American community. Black people across the Diaspora will frequently seek healings from the internal divisions we experience when our lived experiences and practices do not match those of the majority culture, which drives a need to rediscover a sense of self and community identity ensconced in a search for religious meaning (Mitchem, 2002).

> The black church has an actual and meta actual form. It inhabits the imagination of its people in ways that far exceed its reach. Although it is no longer a truly invisible institution, it will always be invisible to some extent because it embodies a spiritual idea . . . The black church is in a sense "virtual" space created by the worship practices of the congregation. (Holmes, 2004, pp. 5–6)

As a people rooted in a strong theological and cosmological history, we have allowed many of those roots to erode, critical roots that kept our ancestors strong during the worst time in our history—slavery. Even in today's environment, many people still theologically and spiritually struggle with a connectedness to something bigger than themselves that has the ability to strengthen as we move through life's challenges.

> An examined faith is a critical way of seeing that shows things in a belief system that are life-threatening and life-taking. An examined faith inspires people to discard beliefs, images, and symbols that have the potential to support scapegoating and destruction . . . An examined faith discards any religion and any God who commands Black people to sit idly contemplating love of their oppressors while they (Black people) are threatened and destroyed by those who hate them. (Williams, 1997, pp. 99–100)

Will the Manner in Which the Black Church Operates Need to Change?

When we examine the historical context of the Black church, it has a unique history of acting as a strategic and systemic change agent. Yet throughout the years, there have been and continue to be from the ranks of both lay as well as the religious community critiques regarding the effectiveness of the Black church in today's environment. There are reasons that our church is being criticized, and to move forward we have to critically examine those reasons and vow to evoke immediate change. The need for the Black church to serve as a venue in our change process is far too critical to allow it to episodically operate within that process of change.

Historically, the independent church movement among Blacks, during and following the Revolutionary War, can be regarded as the prime expression of resistance to slavery and represents, in every sense of the word, the first black freedom movement (Wilmore, 1998). If we fast-forward to the 1960s, the Black church underwent critique, particularly by the Nation of Islam, who accused Black preachers as being instruments of White oppression (Wilmore). Juxtaposed against the movement of the Nation of Islam and critique of the Black church was the emergence of leaders such as Rev. Dr. Martin Luther King Jr., who understood the ability of the Black church to galvanize African Americans, and the growth of Black theology, which emerged and grew out of the Black church (Terrell, 2005).

Although there have been lulls in the record of the Black church relative to social activism, there is a historical context where the Black church took an open and expressed stance against the injustices incurred by its people. We need the leaders of our Black churches to again assume this stance.

We can no longer afford to have questions emerge as to why our critical religious institutions continue to be perceived, in a postmodern context, ineffective in social activism. Strategic change in the African American community calls for helping people better understand our dilemmas in order to invoke ways to **heal** our hearts and souls and **change** the dynamics of our socioeconomic condition. People who are entrenched in despair, poverty, and subjugation need to have a strong reinforcement that God loves them. The issues and travesties that continue in this era of postmodernity call for the resurrection of the Black church to again take its rightful place as a significant change agent and leader in our community.

The Interplay between Scholars-Practitioners: The Critical Role of Black Theologians and Pastors

When the remembered promises press for the liberation of people and for the humanizing of their relationships, the reverse of this thesis is true: everything depends upon interpreting these transformations critically. The way of political hermeneutics cannot go one-sidedly from reflection to action. That would be pure idealism. The resulting action would become blind. Instead, this hermeneutic must bind reflection and action together thus requiring reflection in the action as well as action in the reflection. The hermeneutical method to which this leads is called in the "ecumenical discussion" the action-reflection method. (Moltmann, 2006, p. 44)

As I walked through seminary, I struggled with many questions that tend to delve deep into one's faith. However, I have always posited the venue of seminary allows the mind to wonder to depths and dimensions we might not normally experience.

In the midst of my questioning and exploring liberation theology, I have read key theologians who engage in a discourse on political theology. I struggle because I have yet to find a roadmap with that resonates and helps me understand how to bring the commonalities of liberation theology, Black theology, womanist theology, political theology, feminist theology, and all other various forms of theological commentary and dissent against social injustice into one common strategic and systematized methodology of protest and action-oriented strategies. I have also continued to be frustrated by my own question as to how marginalized people, especially our youth, who feel totally left out, sustain a hopeful consciousness and belief system when faced with the intensity of oppression.

In far too many venues, when working in marginalized communities, I have witnessed little hope even in the face of people spending significant hours in church. People continue to question as to whether or not they are truly entitled to God's mercy. To theologically struggle with the concept of entitlement to God's mercy is antithetical to that which we are theologically taught, which may mean for some the intensity of the pain begins to erode the belief system.

To begin forming a framework for my own answers I began to give considerable thought to merging strategic change with liberation theology irrespective of the audience, that is, a combining of methods that would force the reflection-action relationship posited by Dr. Moltmann as well as force those difficult connections to the forefront of our conversations.

While there are theoretical underpinnings and methodologies in organization development that open space for the reflection-reflexive modeling posited by Moltmann, who is considered to be a leading thinker in systematic theology, I believe the context for change must also include an ecumenical conversation within the venue of church. This conversation should address the cultural dynamics of the community juxtaposed to our theology, therefore provoking and evoking a detailed examination of issues, the environments, and internalized beliefs. We need this reflection-action to better examine how we understand the psychodynamics of our interpreting our theology and views on theodicy.

As I have continued to posit, an intentional dialogue allows for the engagement, discussion, and sense-making deconstruction of issues emanating from socioeconomic status, history, internalized social norms and myths, as well as work toward understanding how one's oral traditions, literatures, ethical norms, and culturally sensitive folklore impact behaviors. I also believe that when you ensconce these reflective conversations against biblical context, there is a real opportunity to simultaneously begin a healing process. To heal, there must be discussion that begins to deconstruct the hidden representations of behavior that emanate from self before there can be a concerted effort to change a worldview and its resulting actions. Change must occur internally first before one can change their external circumstances. However, as previously suggested, there must also be a regenerative component, which may correlate to Moltmann's propositions on action. As we reflect, we have an ability to refine the actions.

Visioning without strategic implementation depletes the spirit. Driving change requires multilevels of planning, a concept not often included in the typical theological conversation. Yet there are many lessons we can learn regarding planning from the Bible. I also believe that when we engage in a reflective-action ecumenical conversation we address many issues that open space for better understanding a God that does indeed understand our human frailties.

Within the overarching confines of the African American religious community lie two critical entities, pastors and theologians, who can help us engage in our critical conversations. Each has a very important role to play in a change process. When we critically assess what each of them brings to the table, it is clear as to why a collective effort must be in place with both working side by side.

Cone (2001) says the Black theologian is critical of faith and will apply contextual-dialectical methods when looking to evoke understanding of divine revelation and truth. The role of Black theologians is critical when helping African Americans search for alternative ways of helping our people engage in effective "knowing." Cone goes on to suggest that no people in America need to learn how to love themselves more than African Americans. Historically, we have struggled with wondering if God really loves us. If we layer those questions with other "isms" that mark our dualities, then the questions as to our position with God becomes more intense.

Per Cone (2001), the violence we engage in against one another is a poignant expression of a need to understand the perspectives brought forth by our black theologians. He further believes that theologians, in concert with the pastoral community via intentional actions, can help us better develop a theology that will speak to the problem of Black self-hate and thereby create a religious value system that encourages us to love ourselves passionately and without compromise. This theology must be consistently preached from the pulpit, which speaks to the critical role of African American pastors.

> A man's conviction that he is God's child automatically tends to shift the basis of his relationship with all his fellows. He recognizes at once that to fear a man, whatever may be that man's power over him, is a basic denial of the integrity of his very life. It lifts that mere man to a place of pre-eminence that belongs to God and to God alone. (Thurman, 1976, p. 51)

The Black theologian questions the validity of existing Christological constructs in determining what constitutes both saving knowledge and a saving praxis for Black people in America (Terrell, 2005). According to Terrell, Eurocentric biblical interpretations have to be challenged if we are to rise above the internal struggle we have with issues of theodicy and our inherited right to live in an egalitarian environment. This level of deconstruction is very important as we work hard to ensure that African Americans who come from many different spaces and places are not left out of the change process.

As I have written more aggressively over these past few years with respect to issues within my community, I have become increasingly more conscious of the many layers African Americans have to work through to heal. Through my walk in seminary, I have become far more sensitized to issues of sexuality and its intersection with theodicy and theology. My seminary and church denomination was one of the first to embrace the lesbian, gay, bisexual, and transgender communities. I chose my seminary because of its stance on social justice. I had no idea when I chose this seminary, I would also learn about tolerance and inclusion from a very different perspective.

As a heterosexual woman, I was a minority in this community, which meant I had to work through understanding how bias from a heterosexual perspective is just as marginalizing, especially when society posits a voice of righteousness and dominance with respect to sexual preference. I learned about the additional layers that one experiences when you make a conscious choice to stand in your truth regarding sexual preference. I also learned about a different type of pain that people feel, that of rejection within one's own community. I learned how people who are perceived to be "different" via mainstream society's (and often I question is there such a thing in today's environment as "mainstream") definitions question if God really loves them. But equally important, I learned about the dualities of oppression and repression that hurts our community.

I first briefly wrote about this issue in 2010 when I addressed the topic of leadership for women of color. One of the editors asked that in my contributing article I include in the dialogue issues of sexuality. While at first I was taken aback by the request, I realized that if I were to give equal voice to African American women and our feelings regarding the oppression we daily feel, I had to be inclusive, albeit my thinking I initially was inclusive. Change without unity can be challenging. Yet, when I began researching issues of African American women and moving beyond the domains of race and gender, I found that women who have chosen to live as lesbians and bisexual individuals have faced a triple threat of oppression; they were forced to work through the landscape of oppression relative to issues of race, gender, and sexual orientation at levels that defy most people's understanding.

While it has been posited that living the life of a lesbian is a life that draws its strength, support, and direction from women, recent studies suggest that marginalization within the African American community is sometimes higher than that within White communities, with Black women who regularly attend church displaying higher instances of homophobia than their male counterparts (Reynolds & Powell, 1981; Negy & Eisenman, 2005; Redmond, 2006).

I understand what it is to be African American and a woman in a society that privileges men and white skin. But until I walked alongside my LGBT brothers and sisters I never understood those additional layers of rejection, oppression, and feelings of disempowerment, particularly from our own community, where we need to be supportive of one another despite our perceived differences. Disempowerment, irrespective of its origins, is counterproductive to living a healthy life. People of all orientations, faiths, race, ethnicities, and color must come together to make a difference in this world.

Flexible thinking for many is uncharted waters. Yet in today's challenging environment we cannot hold on to concepts or boundaries that reflect rigidity, which when compared to bias is equably debilitating (Anzaldúa, 2007). Our youth also need to learn what it means to shed their rigid stances and understand that there really should not be perceived differences because you belong to a different gang or live in a different community. For far too many of our youth, rigidity has meant death. Children fear walking home from school because they cross into different territories. Same principle, same type of "ism" being practiced, same type of discrimination—unfortunately it gets people killed versus ostracized.

Rigidity means death. (Anzaldúa, 2007, p. 101)

Only by remaining flexible are we able to stretch our psyche horizontally and vertically in order to move from convergent thinking–analytical reasoning that tends to use rationality to move toward a single goal (via a Eurocentric perspective) to divergent thinking characterized by movement away from set patterns and goals and toward a whole perspective that includes instead of excludes (Anzaldúa, 2007).

It can never be determined just what a man (woman) will fashion. Two men (women) may be born of the same parents, grow up in the same environment, be steeped in the same culture and inspired by the same faith. Close or even cursory observation may reveal that each has fashioned a life working paper so unique that they take to different roads, each day bringing them further apart. Or it may be that they move along precisely parallel lines that never meet. (Thurman, 1976, p. 111)

We cannot afford disharmony at any level. Fortunately, contemporary theologians of color are not afraid to address these issues. They understand the need for reflection and critical analyses. In the African American theological community there sometimes is a debate between which perspective holds preference when looking to evoke change, the needs of the individual or the needs of community. Proponents of new methods of pastoral theology continue to posit that communal needs for survival and liberation begins with the experience of the culture versus objectifications and abstractions about the culture, allows for the significance of communality versus individuality, and expands the operations of ministry (Watkins Ali, 1999).

So, what does it really mean to expand the operations of ministry? From my lens, observations, and reflections as a student of theology, I concur that:

> It is the task of the Christian theologian to do theology, in light of the concreteness of human oppression as expressed in color, and to interpret for the oppressed the meaning of God's liberation in their community. (Cone, 1986, pp. vii–viii)

We also need the reflections of our theology brought to the pulpit on Sunday mornings, which drives the need for both theologians and the African American clergy to come together as the initial drivers of our change process. When you combine that which they each bring to the table, their critical role in a change process helps to erase our fears, grab on to our cosmological heritage, and embrace all that is ours by right. Or, as Dr. James Cone respectfully posited as he began to address issues relative to liberation theology,

> Black power means black freedom, black self-determination, wherein black people no longer view themselves as without human dignity but as . . . human beings with the ability to carve out their own destiny. (1969, p. 6)

Our youth equally important need to reexamine and reframe their praxis regarding their relationship to God and self. There is no reason for a child to assume that he or she will not live to see their 18th birthday because of violence.

> To the child of God, a scale of values becomes available by which men are measured and their true significance determined. Even the threat of violence, with the possibility of death that it carries is recognized for what it is—merely the threat of violence with a death potential. (Thurman, 1976, p. 51)

How then do we begin?

A Call to Action

Step 1: The Gathering Part 1—In the Venue of the Black Church

African American Pastors and Theologian Community Outcomes
- A revised agenda for the Black church
- Curriculum and pedagogical strategies for teaching African American history, theology, and cosmology
- Strategies for how the Black church will support the change process
- Communication strategies between the religious community as well as from the pulpit to the people
- Itinerary for supporting the change process—the how to's
- Strategies for evoking paradigmatic shifts within the Black church from the "fish fry" mentality to evoking true change
- Defining and developing metrics to assessing the progress of the religious leaders
- Select the five pilot states and their respective cities
- Crafting and implementing the call to action for leaders
- Selection of a facilitator team

Step 2: The Gathering Part 2—The Call for and Development of the Leadership Team

- Understanding and accepting the parameters of the call to action
- insuring that there are appropriate representatives from all walks of life in the African American community
- Step 1 of the Leaders' Meeting: Engaging in a learning process: Our history, cosmology, and theology
- Step 2 of the Leaders' Meeting: Leadership Development
- Step 3 of the Leaders' Meeting: Strategy Development, Design, and Implementation
- Step 4 of the Leaders' Meeting: Engaging in an Intentional Dialogue
- Step 5 of the Leaders' Meeting: The Appreciative Inquiry Process
- Step 6 of the Leaders' Meeting: Movement toward Design and Destiny

**The Appreciative Inquiry Process: Recommended Inclusions as
We Co-Construct the Future**

Ensure in the Co-Constructed Future, Design, and Delivery Phases

- Very specific dreams for the new future that do not speak in abstract language but have very specific goals and targets
- Strategies for taking those dreams into their communities and building consensus and coalitions of support
- Strategies for leading those coalitions
- Strategies for developing training institutions that will shore up those coalitions to the skill levels of the leader
- Metrics for success
- Performance standards
- Strategies for garnering financial resources
- Specific definitions as to what constitutes manageable steps and processes (e.g., year 1 select one to three goals with stipulated and monitored metrics)
- Extensive strategic and technologically sophisticated communication strategies to keep the African American community informed
- Strategies for building additional teams and team-building training and development
- Strategies for communicating and sharing with our global communities who face similar challenges as well as opportunities
- Strategies for flipping the script of our language so that an appreciative language becomes the norm and not the exception
- Strategies to ensure that our youth are committed and connected to change processes and have a clear understanding that "it's about them."
- Strategies for staying connected to our nexus, the Black church. In fact this is an extremely important point to incorporate into the process, because the Black church should remain that place of safe space where people engaged in this process go to for reflection, prayer, and reinforcement of next steps.
- Strategies for ensuring ongoing review and revamping of processes where we assume a total quality mindset for implementation and improvement

Stage 1 of the Model: The Call for Action

The Church is the only hope for the children because the schools want to see them fail.[1]

To evoke deep strategic change that focuses on our youth and our community, there must be a call across denominations to gather together pastors and theologians. Not every denomination, church leader, or theologian will choose to or is needed to be involved. Let me be very clear: only those who are interested in evoking change for the betterment of our youth and the African American community are needed. It will take only one or two people in the theological community (pastoral and theologian) to call for the first gathering. Yet, in the call for this gathering, through their centralized offices, church leaders will need clearance from their respective denominations to engage in this process.

I have had the pleasure of working with church leaders in the past designing strategic change processes, and in far too many cases I have found the politics within many churches to be quite intense. This sometimes means many pastors will temper their "truth" for fear of being attacked or ostracized by ill-informed church leaders who fear change but have huge spears of influence.

Yet the nexus of our change has to be within the Black church. When we face doubt and fear, our spirits can and will be revived within the walls of our sanctuaries. Trained pastors and theologians have studied the Black condition as well as the historical, religious, and cosmological contexts of our ancestry. This information must be shared within our community. The knowledge can and will ignite our spirits.

At this first gathering, with deep and spiritual facilitation, ministers and theologians must engage in an authentic conversation that includes only them, regarding issues plaguing the Black community and the Black church. Those conversations must be multitiered, yet initially centered on how and why the Black church is perceived as failing to effectively address the deeply rooted and systemic issues that prevail within the African American community. These individuals must also identify the specific change strategies that must occur with the Black church and the metrics to ensure those goals are accomplished.

The Black church has always led the point of attack when others have wanted to spiritually drain the African American community. Consequently, our pastoral and theological leaders must be on point with a well-defined agenda and collectively determined to ward off those who will work to deplete the spirits and resources of a change effort. They must also understand how to gauge the effectiveness of change. In other words, as we collectively move through a change process, the Black church must effectively support efforts, utilizing its power and influence, where individually we may not yield results, and people continually are given the appropriate messages to keep them abreast of priorities and, equally important, progress. As the pastoral and theologian community identifies the "new" role for the Black church, there must be accountability and visibility in identifying progress, which must also be real and measurable progress.

Unfortunately, the recent change and influence record of the Black church has been questioned on multiple fronts. In 2008 in one of the larger United Church of Christ churches, the senior pastor posited the question within the contextual framework of the Book of Acts as to whether or not, in the midst of our chaos, are we a "fired up church or a church that has fizzled out?" (Smith, 2008). In a 2001 study that addressed the role of African American churches in urban school reform, the author concluded that, at least in theory, African American church leaders did recognize the challenges facing our students who attended urban schools, and they recognized the potential they possessed for exercising political power in education politics. However, during that time, the overall effect of the African American church on urban school reform ranged from minimal effect on policy development to the limited activity of building supportive programs within individual churches. Church leaders reported implementing internal initiatives such as tutorial programs, mentoring programs, and history awareness programs and worked together in crisis. However, once the crisis was over, they retreated to their own turf and viewed their individual ministries as their primary goal (Middleton, 2001).

Similar views and reports occurred during a study that examined potential roles of Black churches in HIV/AIDS prevention. Issues relative to trust among Black churches and community-based organizations were also reported, despite the overwhelming percentages of African Americans afflicted by this disease. In a study by McNeal and Perkins (2007), pastors also reported concerns with their comfort level in addressing these issues with their respective congregations. Concerns were raised that the primary role of the church is to save souls and that other organizations would be far more effective in providing help on this issue. McNeal and Perkins also found that the church was viewed as having the primary role of dealing with the body and keeping unclean spirits from it.

Our pastoral and theologian communities must engage in an authentic conversation as to how Black people see themselves *entitled* to change and the role of the Black church in addressing these theological questions. I will never forget my work in New Orleans where we broached the topic of entitlement and found African Americans pushing back on that concept. Yet who suffered the most during Hurricane Katrina? To this day, I believe that the failure of many in New Orleans to have internalized their rights to an egalitarian environment partly contributed to the travesties the African American community suffered in New Orleans and is still suffering during its reconstruction process.

Therefore, this group of initial leaders must be willing to have the liberation, womanist, and Black theology conversations in concert with perspectives brought forth by Black psychology in order to understand the foundational messages they must communicate through the pulpit as a critical part of our healing processes. This must be a conversation that authentically addresses our perceptions and the underlying antecedents we have learned from our varying experiences that have grown to become our internalized truths. In other words, we must have an *intentional* dialogue.

These conversations will serve as the beginning deconstructive dialogue that the African American community needs in order to understand how to break down these truths. Far too many of us have forgotten our cosmological and theological foundations, and most of our youth have never been exposed to either. It is within the Black church that I respectfully posit we can and will rediscover the beauty we hold within ourselves.

The change that is needed to spiritually, mentally, and physically liberate African Americans is not for the lighthearted. In fact the change that is needed to liberate all marginalized people is very challenging. Cornel West called the contemporary African American church "one of the few institutions within a shattered Black civil society that could attempt to project some kind of hope and some kind of meaning" in the face of present and more pervasive "walking nihilism" (cited in Hawkins, 1993, p. 15)

The outcomes of these meetings are simple and include the following:

- An identified agenda for those Black churches that choose to participate in a change process, which addresses the new and supporting role the Black church will assume.
- The curriculum and pedagogical methods for teaching leaders and participants in a change process our history, cosmology, and theological roots before we begin *any* initiatives. We must be armed with a context of our history and roots in order to understand the myths we have internalized.
- Strategies for supporting a change process that are designed to replete our spirits when we get tired.
- Communication processes between church and theologian communities.

- Schedules and itineraries for future meetings and forward movement.
- Strategies for challenging and moving past the "fish fry" mentality and how to evoke that paradigm change throughout their pastoral communities.
- Metrics to determine progress.
- Selection of the pilot states and their respective cities.
- Crafting and implementing the call to action for leaders.
- Selection of a facilitator team.

The design and development of a change strategy have to be effectively managed, which calls for the selection of pilot states and cities within those states. Therefore, one of the last roles and responsibilities for the gathering of pastors and theologians at their initial meeting should be to identify and determine which states should serve as initiators of the change process.

I strongly advocate that we begin with no more than three to five states, with fewer being better, and within each of those states no more than one major city. Critical criteria for selection of the respective cities should be locations where youth are suffering the most from gang involvement and the overarching issues plaguing the African American community are the most intense.

After this group of theologians and pastors identify the respective cities and states, a central location must be selected for the initial meeting and a Call to Action for leaders strategically disseminated throughout the African American community. There are many ways to disseminate this call to action. The Black church can serve as a focal point for the dissemination process, but we also do not want to delimit participation by making it an exclusive communication strategy for the call for leaders. Consequently, as this call is crafted, there will need to be strategies in place to ensure that it is appropriately and widely disseminated. However, with the vast Internet and social networks available to us, ensuring that there is breadth and depth to the call to action should not be an issue.

Finally, it is recommended that this group also select and gather a team of experts in organization development who are capable of designing the processes for the leaders. While gathering large numbers of people together to work toward change is not a difficult process for those who have been trained to do so, to not have this step of the model implemented can impact the productiveness of both the sessions as well as of the outcomes.

There are many resources for people of color who are trained in whole systems change processes. However, I encourage a detailed examination of their credentials. Everyone who professes to be an expert in this field is not. They may have limited experience or academic training. To design and facilitate a gathering of this size and critical impact calls for both extensive experience in concert with, at minimum, a doctorate in the field, thereby guaranteeing that the individuals are highly trained and educated to know when to deviate from the set agendas, which over the years I have found to be, more often than not, a likely scenario simply because we are working with people.

Stage 2 of the Model: The Gathering of Leaders

Over the years, I have witnessed many ways to invite and select people to step into leadership roles when change is being designed. Invariably, many fall by the wayside when they realize the intense commitment, despite their having gone through intricate application and screening processes. Therefore, I do not advocate screening processes, applications, or any other levels of preferential treatment designed to get people to the table and assume a leadership role in this process. I believe once a call to action is placed, we should open our hearts to those that decide to step forward and embrace them for their courage.

I also advocate a cross section of people from all walks of life in the African American community participating as the core leadership team. We need our youth, gang members, gang leaders, local community members, social justice advocates, other ministers, politicians, teachers, change agents, neighbors, and other assorted arrays of people. This will be an engagement that impacts everyone, including our youth. The participation is not just for the elite and those who have previously held leadership positions. Quite frankly, they have had their turn, which means that it is respectfully posited that they step aside and allow others to work.

I also do not want to suggest that people from other ethnicities or races who support change in our communities are not invited to accept the call. There are far too many people who have walked side by side African Americans for us to say you cannot join us. And, if the momentum is large enough, perhaps some of our global neighbors may want to join in the initial launch in order to provide input on the change processes. Inclusion is good, but we must always remain focused as to who the real beneficiaries are of these actions: our youth and the African American community.

Those who come will need to understand, as articulated in the call for leaders, that a desire to make a difference in the lives of their community and youth is the primary qualification for selection. They will also need to understand that they will undergo training and development as well as be held accountable for outcomes. If these criteria are succinctly presented in a nationwide call, I sincerely believe those who truly want to make a difference will be the ones who rise to the occasion. Once at the venue for leaders, the next level of intense work begins.

Step 1 of the Leaders' Meeting: Our Historical, Cosmological, and Theological Lessons

As pastors and theologians gather, their processes include developing the curriculum and pedagogical strategies for teaching our history, cosmology, and theology. These lessons, however, must be taught at the beginning of the leaders' gathering. People who are willing to embark upon change must have an appropriate context to understand how far we have deviated from our roots and the significance and impact of that deviation. For example, within the context of really understanding and delving into the theology that kept us alive during slavery, we need to have an authentic and critical conversation on how we have internalized others' versions of suffering and how those versions conflict with our cosmology.

I strongly believe that when we begin to deconstruct our understanding of these issues in the context of an authentic curriculum on our cosmology we will understand why many African Americans have trouble with the concept of entitlement. There are many scholars who have critically examined our cosmological roots. As I have read the works of Dr. Mbiti and others, I am appalled that so few African Americans have been taught these truths. Albeit my possessing three degrees, it was not until I entered seminary and studied courses in African and African American religions that I began to really understand my history.

I truly believe when our leaders critically internalize the dichotomies that exist in our prior teachings, they will be armed with a different level of determination and strength needed to embark upon this journey. They must, however, also understand their role in ensuring that with every step of the journey they pass on this learning.

Step 2 of the Leaders' Meeting: Leadership Development

Those that choose to embark upon and continue in the leadership role for driving change in the African American community will be responsible for ensuring that people are delivering outcomes and effectively navigating through waters where resistance rises similar to high tides. These leaders must be internally fortified, which means they need to clearly understand and be comfortable with their personal vision, power, and desire to personally change in order to evoke community-based vision, power, and changed as suggested by my leadership model.

Consequently, these leaders must go through intensive leadership development training and interventions designed to help them better understand and reframe self. The training also has to be designed to challenge their existing worldview in order to emerge with a new one, which will help empower them as leaders in a changing environment (Quinn, 1996).

Additionally, the following constructs should be included in order to provide them with a holistic development process. These constructs address the following propositions:

1. Leadership development is self-development (Kouzes & Posner, 1995).
2. Leadership is a relationship (Kouzes & Posner, 1995).
3. Leaders must shift their orientation from a control model to a connect model (Easley, McMaster, & Tate, 2003).
4. Leaders must have a systemic worldview and understand their organization as a system (Senge, 1990).
5. Leaders must develop an appreciation for chaos and an orientation that allows them to promote change rather than to manage it (Wheatley, 1999).
6. Inherent in a systems view of their organization, leaders must understand and learn how to diagnose behaviors as well as learn effective system intervention strategies for driving organizational change (Easley, McMaster, & Tate, 2003).

With these assumptions imbedded into a curriculum that helps the leader take a critical look internally, I do believe we can and will emerge with a strong and fortified group of committed people leading this journey.

Step 3 of the Leaders' Meeting: Strategy Development, Design, and Implementation

Those who decide to embark upon this journey must also be able to critically differentiate between irrelevant strategies and goals in concert with what constitutes penetrating and sustaining change. Consequently, during this stage of the change process, it will be critical for leaders to obtain intense training on important competencies and skills. The training should be dualistically designed. First and foremost, content knowledge of the competencies and skills will be vital. However, methodologies that allow simulation of application will be equally relevant to ensure that the leaders are comfortable that they are armed with sufficient knowledge.

Far too often when teaching or training, we don't do a good job of aligning theory to praxis, which leaves the learner with serious voids. As we embark upon our change process it will be necessary for our leaders to have the theory, understand how to apply it, and be comfortable in transferring their knowledge. Therefore, those competencies and skills are as follows:

- Visioning
- The concept of paradigms and paradigm shifts
- Mission development
- Systems thinking
- Strategy design and development
- Scenario planning
- Metric design and development
- Feedback loops
- Communication strategies
- Accountability reporting
- How cultural difference will impact visioning, and the design and roll-out of the other aforementioned competencies
- Setting performance standards
- Facilitation processes
- How, in the process of moving forward, we loop back to the venue of the church for reinforcement

- How to provide an orientation and training on the competencies and skills to others

Sustaining an educated population of leaders and other change agents will require ongoing orientation and training. Therefore, at this stage of the change process, it may be prudent for this initial group of leaders to discuss the plausibility of a training institute as a support arm for this initiative.

Step 4 of the Leaders' Meeting: Engaging in an Intentional Dialogue

At this stage of development, our leaders have been introduced to a historical, cosmological, and theological context many may not have known before, and they are armed with the critical competencies and skills to get started on a process that ensures they are engaged in a focused and outcomes-oriented process. Consequently, the next step is to begin their engagement in an intentional dialogue, utilizing discourse analysis.

You might ask if all the training places the cart before the horse, and my reply to that is no. As I have taught throughout the years, I have always had a strong propensity toward utilizing a discrepancy analysis in my teaching strategy. Simply put, when you have the foundational knowledge in place that evokes what one could connote as the "appropriate knowledge base for change," it becomes easier to understand the deltas that have existed in your prior knowledge and strategies previously used to evoke change.

Consequently, when our leaders become trained on required core competencies and skills it becomes much easier for them to understand where we have previously failed to evoke sustaining change processes, while concomitantly understanding the new strategies that must be deployed. I will never suggest that the list identified above is inclusive of everything. It clearly is a start that serves as the beginning praxis for forward movement.

The engagement in an intentional dialogue should be designed as a search conference where individuals are grouped to work through critical issues during a multiday process. Frequent feedback during this process among and within the groups is vital. Each group will not have all the answers, but as the process is designed in stages, at the conclusion of each stage, the participants will hear what others have contributed to their dialogical process.

I will never try to be prescriptive as to what critical questions should emerge in this intentional dialogue. However, there are some perspectives and points I suggest should be considered as a beginning list. These include:

- What are the participants' perceptions of the state of the African American community?
- What are the etiologies of these issues?
- How do they cause us pain?
- Describe how we love ourselves and if we can't describe that love, what is impeding it?
- Has the pain numbed us and if so can we awaken?
- What are the more obvious as well as salient issues that reside within our communities?
- If needed to relegate our issues to a top 10 list to start change, what would be on that list and why?
- What are the issues impacting our youth gravitating to gangs?
- What is the gang environment in its present-day context and its relationship to the African American community?
- What, if anything, has changed over the years and why have those changes occurred?
- What are the older gang members' perceptions of youth violence and their role in delimiting or ameliorating that violence?
- What critical support systems to our youth's progress are breaking down?
- What are the systemically related issues between those support systems and how do we help others understand their relationships?
- How do we identify and address all the connections of our systemic issues?
- How has the African American community allowed this breakdown to occur?
- How and where do we count on others and can this state of affairs change?
- What are the metaphors we have internalized that impact our progress?
- How do these metaphors compare and contrast to the learning that the leaders studied?
- How do these metaphors and their internalizations impact our ability to evoke change in our communities?

- How do we break down these metaphors?
- How do we spread the breaking down of these metaphors?
- How do these metaphors negatively impact our psyche?
- How do these metaphors negatively impact our children?
- What is the state of affairs for our youth?
- What is the state of affairs for community?
- How can we regain feelings of community and responsibility that bring African Americans closer to and supportive of one another?
- How can we begin to evoke change in our communities?
- What are the major paradigm shifts we have to engage?
- How do we begin to engage in those paradigm shifts?
- What are the visions and outcomes we desire for our future?
- How can we collectively bring about the results of those visions and outcomes?

This is a beginning list, which can be broken down and distributed to different groups, or if time during the search conference allows for it, participants can engage in dialogue regarding each issue in their respective groups.

My personal preference is to allow each group to address the issues. I believe it is critical to our own understanding to allow many perspectives on the same issue to flow. I also believe, through a collective thematic process (which can be more appropriately determined by the individuals designing the intervention), it is important to allow people to group the issues into the major themes they see plaguing our communities.

The conversations have to flow freely because many of these issues have never been constructively discussed in a collective environment and engagement structured for action. Most times when we engage in these discussions they are vehicles that allow people to vent. Participants in this process must understand that the inevitable outcome of these conversations will be strategic action plans designed to remove the identified blockages.

As people engage in the intentional dialogue, it is important that professionals facilitate the groups in order to capture the thematic data resulting from these conversations. It is often difficult to get one's arms around an abundance of feedback and data. However, if the focus on the process is to relegate the information to a thematic analysis, a higher level of feedback will emerge that will help guide others toward the specifics of a change process.

Toward the conclusion of this intentional dialogue, critical events must occur. First and foremost, as previously stated, sufficient time must be allowed for ongoing feedback among the groups. To a large extent, this is the reflection-action process previously described that helps facilitate a broader understanding of how African Americans truly feel. Inclusively, there needs to be time to invite people to speak not only to their intellectualizing of the process of intentional dialogue but also how they feel in the very marrow of their bones regarding their engagement and what they heard. I truly believe change really begins at this visceral level and we need to allow that sacred space for it to emerge.

At the conclusion of these sessions before moving on to next steps, there needs to be a healing and reconciliation process led by our theological community. We need to pray because the information, if people really speak their truth, will hit us at a gut level that will be difficult for many to process. The potential shutdown of participants due to overwhelming pain is a major reason why the theological and pastoral community has to stay engaged at every level of this process. When people hurt at gut levels, the propensity to run is high. Yet, the only way we will evoke the deep-seated change that is needed is to hear our issues, feel our issues, and pray our way through that healing process in order to emerge with a determination that defies anyone attempting to break through. We must emerge with a determination to no longer live a life of disempowerment that is causing our very seeds—our children—to concomitantly live in despair.

The outcomes that need to occur from this process relative to data collection are combined lists of thematic issues from each group. Assuming there will be a substantive number of leaders in attendance, there will also need to be groups of people assigned to design and facilitate this process and to engage in a real-time thematic analysis. Following the search conference, these individuals will need to convene in order to combine their various thematic breakdowns into the next level of analysis. I highly recommend African Americans who are trained in qualitative research methods be the individuals who engage in all levels of analysis of the data. Their listening as well as facilitation skills must be strong in order to hear the dialogue at very deep discursive levels.

Step 5 of the Leaders' Meeting: The Appreciative Inquiry Process

At this point, those who have agreed to work as leaders in the change process have been extensively oriented and trained in multiple dynamics of change management. Equally important, they have collectively discussed and identi-fied critical issues facing the African American community. This information has been analyzed and major themes have emerged.

Each of these leaders should be going through major paradigm shifts. They have been exposed to critical constructs for driving change and are armed with a deeper understanding of the African American community and youth contexts. Consequently, what is now needed is a better understanding of how to turn these issues around.

At this point, an Appreciative Inquiry (AI) process is appropriate to help these leaders begin to conceptualize the rebuilding processes needed for our youth and communities compared and contrasted to the decay in which we have allowed ourselves to mentally and physically live.

One may ask at this stage, are these leaders going through all of this work and training in one period? There is a tremendous amount of information they will have to internalize and process. Consequently an initial role for them, as leaders, will be to develop the project management components relative to setting the schedule for their gathering and follow-up steps. Feedback loops must be developed in order to ensure that all participants are aware of next steps, time, locations, and so forth. A small group of leaders will need to vol-unteer to handles these logistics.

People will need time in between sessions to internalize what they have covered. They need the time to allow the reflective-action processes to appro-priately emerge and develop. It will be healthy for them to return to their respective communities and juxtapose that which they see to that which they have learned. Time in between will allow them discussion opportunities with friends and colleagues, which will also help gather momentum. But we must be careful to not allow too much time to pass. When too much time passes in between sessions or critical components of a strategy, people tend to lose momentum and focus.

When they come back together will be the time for them to engage in an Appreciative Inquiry process. Similar to the design of the search confer-ence where they engaged in intentional dialogues, they should be broken into smaller groups where they have the opportunity to engage in deep discursive discussions.

The AI process is generally broken into stages, which includes partici-pants discovering when they have been their best by sharing stories of their peak experiences. This stage is very important because it is at this point that we tend to see the language change. It is generally the participants' ah-ha moment where they are able to actually see and understand by the sharing of their positive stories the core strength they have as individuals and communities.

The next stage encourages them to dream of that ideal state. What is it that our people really want out of our lives, experiences, and environments? The power in this stage of the process lies in the fact that the leaders already have discussed their ability to evoke positive change. Consequently, the mind can move in a much more generative direction when it comes to co-constructing a new future that holds so much promise for our youth and communities.

Many of my more traditionally focused AI colleagues might suggest that having first engaged in intentional dialogue, the participants might in fact be limited in their abilities to dream because of the negativity associated with that dialogue. I would agree to this proposition when working with people who have not suffered severe psychological, physical, and spiritual abuses.

However, I continue to respectfully posit that it is absolutely critical for African Americans, and any other group of people who have experienced severe disempowerment and disenfranchisement, to engage in a process that helps them develop a healthy cognitive dissonance as to what those experiences really are. One might respectfully ask how an engagement in this dialogue can result in a healthy cognitive dissonance. The intentional dialogue is handled in a facilitated group process that allows for the members of that group to support and encourage one another. Throughout the years I have utilized this process, I have seen a healthy type of bonding and awareness develop among and within people. I also respectfully posit that to fully appreciate our beauty, we have to move past the negative internalizations that many have due to the varying levels of abuse we have experienced. We must conclude that these issues were never about us. Therefore, by virtue of having moved through processes that begin and encourage a dislodgement of internalized "isms," we begin to fully appreciate our accomplishments, which results in a much more powerful and generative experience.

The next stage of the 4–D process is the design stage where there is a more fine-tuned process for co-constructing the future. Emphasis is on designing strategy and implementation steps. The learning that the leaders have gleaned from the prior training will be germane at this stage. They will better understand the differences among strategic goals, tactical steps, and project-management strategies for staying on target.

The final stage of AI is on setting forth a destiny where change is sustained. This stage and resulting dialogue is very critical for African Americans. It is at this point that we must fully embrace our global context and set forth strategies that will continually keep us developing with a global mindset.

Again, while I do not want to be prescriptive in my recommendations relative to the design of the Appreciative Inquiry questions, I do suggest that the initial Appreciative Inquiry questions thoroughly investigate the positive accomplishments of youth when they have interacted or worked in their community, in school, and with their families, the strengths of our working in community, the strengths we show as a race, the strengths we show when gathered in prayer, the historical change processes we have successfully implemented and those times where gangs have made positive change within the African American community.

Our acceptance of "othering" has to stop. We do not have to walk borderlines. It is now time for a healthier appreciation of all that we do and all that we are.

Step 6 of the Leaders' Meeting: Movement toward Design and Destiny

In a lecture at Benedictine University in April 2005, Dr. David Cooperrider spoke of his interview with Dr. Peter Drucker where Drucker said to him, "The task of leadership is to create an alignment of strengths, making our weaknesses irrelevant." It is at this stage of the model that I will stop. I believe the foundation provided for those that answer the call for leadership will provide them with the tools to identify the strategy and next steps. I also believe that if I were to go further into detail, I would not be giving my brothers and sisters the respect they need in their newly defined role of leader.

However, as they matriculate through the AI process, I will make one more prescriptive point and recommend that in their design stages they will need to ensure that their co-construction of a future incorporates the following:

- Very specific dreams for that new future that do not bespeak of abstract language but have very specific goals and targets
- Strategies for taking those dreams into their communities and building consensus and coalitions of support
- Strategies for leading those coalitions

- Strategies for developing training institutions that will shore up those coalitions to the skill levels of the leader
- Metrics for success
- Performance standards
- Strategies for garnering financial resources
- Specific definitions as to what constitutes manageable steps and processes (e.g., year 1 select 1 to 3 goals with stipulated and monitored metrics)
- Extensive, strategic, and technologically sophisticated communication strategies to keep the African American community informed
- Strategies for building additional teams and team-building training and development
- Strategies for communicating and sharing with our global communities who face similar challenges as well as opportunities
- Strategies for flipping the script of our language so that an appreciative language becomes the norm and not the exception
- Strategies to ensure that our youth are committed and connected to the change processes and have a clear understanding that "it's about them"
- Strategies for staying connected to our nexus, the Black church. In fact this is an extremely important point to incorporate into the process, because the Black church should remain that place of safe space where people engaged in this process go to for reflection, prayer, and reinforcement of next steps.
- Strategies for ensuring ongoing review and revamping of processes where we assume a total quality mindset for implementation and improvement

While the many components of this model may appear overwhelming to those who have not worked similar processes, the one thing we have to remember is that nothing is beyond our ability to conceive as well as implement. We also have to remember that these issues were not developed overnight and a complete eradication of the issues that plague us will not occur overnight. However, we have to start somewhere. I am convinced that armed with a well-defined strategy where people are trained and understand their roles and responsibilities, the African American community will achieve our desired results. Change for our youth and our communities are within our reach. It is up to us, however, to commit to working the process of change.

PART FOUR

FINAL THOUGHTS

· 1 1 ·

CELEBRATING OUR SUCCESS: APPRECIATING OUR EFFORTS, YOUTH, AND FUTURE

Taking time to appreciate ourselves and results should never be something we do just at the end of a victory. To keep our spirits uplifted, we should daily celebrate our individuality, accomplishments, and future goals. Sometimes just the thought of engaging in change can be overwhelming. Far less cognitive dissonance occurs when we remain in a familiar state, irrespective of how bad we may believe that state to be. What we must remember is that making a difference can be the results of many ripples in a pond. There are many venues in which the African American community can share knowledge, results, and hope in order to encourage new ripples. However, we have to be intentional and strategic with our processes for encouraging others. In other words, we have to take time for that intentional appreciative dialogue to celebrate all that we are.

A few years ago, I worked with a group of leaders from a hospital with which I have a close relationship. I sat on the board of this hospital for nine years, and both my children were born there. My doctor is on the staff of the hospital, and I have never been hospitalized anywhere else but in this hospital. Consequently, I have seen the tireless service they provide to the African American community from many angles. When the leadership team began to speak of the need to do something to uplift themselves, I suggested they engage in an Appreciative Inquiry process to not only facilitate their strategic movement but also, more important, to help lift their sagging spirits.

Caregiving in any form can be tiring. It does not matter if you provide healthcare, are a mom or dad, a caregiver to family members, a teacher, or an activist in your community or church. Because we are emotionally involved, the expended energy can be quite draining, especially when situations become complicated. Exacerbating this situation is people's propensity to inadequately take care of themselves spiritually, physically, and mentally. We all know the basics of living daily in a spiritual context: proper exercise, diet, water, and rest. But far too many of us fail to execute a regime that keeps us balanced. Consequently, when we fail to add our taking time to celebrate "us," we only increase how fast and intense we become depleted.

Similar to the previously described example with the behavioral healthcare providers (when I first introduced AI), I had this group engage in an appreciative conversation that addressed all that they do: the lives they save on a daily basis, the people they help become physically and emotionally better, the families they nurture, and the list goes on. When they looked at this list and really understood all that they do, you could see an immediate shift in their energy. They left that intervention vowing to take time weekly to share with one another an intentional appreciative dialogue where they focused on sharing their accomplishments, irrespective of how small they may have felt them to be.

Appreciating ourselves, our accomplishments, and our life is something we must do daily. Far too often we fail to acknowledge the goodness God has given us and our situations. Simply taking a moment to acknowledge all that we have and are given helps recharge our spirits and our souls.

We must also take the time to honor one another at a personal level far more than we normally do. Reconnecting with family and friends is very spiritually uplifting. I am not a telephone person, so I have often hid behind the busyness of my schedule as my excuse for not calling. But a few years ago, when I was introduced to social media, I became an avid fan of Facebook. I have been able to stay in contact with family, friends, and former students on a daily basis. In many cases, it is my Facebook friends who will offer the daily encouragement I need just to get through the challenge of a day. I, as well as others, write uplifting quotes on our Facebook walls. I always begin my day with selecting a quote or Bible verse to which I feel spiritually connected to at that moment. However, I never understood the utility of that action for others until I was out of the country for a couple of weeks engaged in a schedule that did not allow those extra minutes to post. Upon my return, my Facebook friends commented how they missed the quotes. We also share with one another when a particular post has been spiritually uplifting. I have seen the number of people engaging in this type of inspiration grow at exponential rates for the past three years.

Just knowing you have made a difference in a life that day speaks volumes for the need to stay connected as a human race, and the beauty of this type of process is how easy it is to stay connected to friends, family, and colleagues that live in different countries. Sharing with our global community is clearly the wave of our present and future. The act of global sharing is something positive we must introduce to our youth as well. The walls we once envisioned separating us as a global community clearly no longer exist.

As the African American community embarks upon change, we must intentionally focus on taking time for sharing our appreciation for all we have done and all that we will do via any and all available venues. We must intentionally focus on uplifting one another, and equally important, we must intentionally focus on uplifting our youth. I also believe when and where possible, as we begin a task, we ground ourselves in prayer. I am very cognizant that everyone does not share the same religious traditions. Prayer, however, tends to be universal. It does not matter what your religious constructs are, prayer solidly grounds us in an understanding that someone or something greater than ourselves is in charge. The connection to that greatness is a lifeline we can never afford to disregard.

· 1 2 ·

THE GLOBAL APPLICATION
OF THIS MODEL

While the context of my model is that of the African American community, the application of it is global. Earlier in the book, I made the point that real democracy in a global world appears to be another unresolved problem of modernity (Hardt & Negri, 2005). Far too many people continue to view issues and, equally important, outcomes of poverty, power, and domination through lens and interpretative schemas that have not changed for years. For the most part, it is a selfish lens that is grounded in a historical context that condones and perpetrates a wide divide between those that have and those that have not.

Adding insult to injury, in the United States, we continue to witness an erosion of the middle class that points to a continued denigration of people's ability to simply make it in this world. When you add issues of class, race, ethnicity, gender, and religious discriminatory practices to the fundamental economic imbalances, the landscape looks grim. It has also been suggested that nihilism is not just confined to Black America. Psychic depression, personal worthlessness, and social despair are widespread in America (West, 2004). I will take this concept one step further and suggest that the depression resides on a global level.

> The oppressive effect of the prevailing market moralities leads to a form of sleepwalking from womb to tomb, with the majority of citizens content to focus on private careers and be distracted with stimulating amusements. (West, 2004, p. 27)

So, how do we begin to wake up the global masses? At what point does the pain become so profound that we can no longer take it? How do we move beyond the artistic expression of discontent to a well-developed strategy that engages multiple forums of stakeholders?

> Freedom is the creative passion for the possible. Freedom is not just turned towards things as they are, as it is in domination. Nor is it directed only to the community of people as they are, as it is in solidarity. It reaches out to the future, for the future is the unknown realm of possibilities, whereas present and past represent the familiar sphere of realities. (Moltmann, 1999, p. 159)

As we reach to the future, we must also understand our history and respect the fact that each group of disenfranchised people has their individualized histories. Globally, theologically, as well as systemically we must move beyond our own context to understand and identify historically repeated behaviors that continue to disenfranchise masses of people around the world. As I have traveled and studied other communities, I think it is safe to say, albeit cultural differences, the strategies used for domination and disenfranchisement are similarly situated across the globe. Cultural proclivities will impact how individual communities respond. Yet, to be effective in driving global collective change, we also have to actively look at the similarity of our contexts, histories, and experiences in order to understand the widespread implications of the proposed model.

Our understanding our history is critical to ensuring we do not repeat our past, irrespective of which continent we are working to address change. For example, if we look at the African American historical context, one can and should ask what did the Middle Passages and the evacuation and post-evacuation stages of Hurricane Katrina in New Orleans in 2005 have in common? Arguably, one can posit that each represented very deliberate oppressive actions. As the dungeons and Middle Passage represent social and relational vulnerability for Africans, so were the evacuation processes in New Orleans. History repeated itself. The theological questions did not change. The people hardest hit by Katrina represented the city's poorest in socioeconomics and they were African Americans. Many had little money, resources for evacuating, or transportation. They totally had to rely on either the goodness of friends or the efforts of their city—another representation of social and relational vulnerability that divides people and impacts one's freedom, vulnerabilities that exist across our global communities.

When you look at the particulars of the Middle Passage, it has been suggested that nowhere in history has a people experienced such a long and traumatic ordeal as Africans during the Atlantic slave trade, yet as I have stud-ied Jewish theologians, many have suggested that the atrocities at Auschwitz were beyond being traumatic.

While a debate as to which systematic dehumanization process might be worse, in the end it is perspective. To understand the travesties occurring in today's environment, we have to move beyond the "which is worse" conver-sation toward a deconstruction of how these travesties continue to manifest themselves in a post-modern-day context.

God has granted me opportunities to travel, and I have seen poverty and oppression in varying degrees. While I am continuously drawn to ask how African Americans can look at these issues through a different lens, I also have asked the same of communities which I have visited. People who are subjected to poverty and other issues of "isms" across the world must learn to examine and alter their psychological perspectives relative to evoking their own change. Consequently, the contextual framework of an intentional dialogue, in concert with the strength building capacity of Appreciative Inquiry, systemic and stra-tegic change processes, and all the other nuances I have described in this book are not just relegated to the African American community. The model can and will work in multiple contexts because it privileges the individuality of the communities that would be applying its constructs and steps. A new movement is long past due that awakens the global masses of people who live in abject poverty. We must learn to envision options for changing the conditions of our lives no matter what continent we live on. These are global issues, and they affect far more people than we even want to imagine.

In December 2010, I spent a few short hours in Haiti. I was on my way to the French Caribbean and had to be rerouted for what appeared to be ridiculous reasons. Yet I have learned that very little happens by chance. It was ordained that I step foot on Haitian soil even if it were for a few short hours. I saw poverty after the earthquake at levels I had not seen before. However, it was not just the physicality of poverty via demolished structures. I looked into the eyes of my Haitian brothers and sisters and I saw a level of hopelessness that I had never thought I would see. Intuitively, I believe this hopelessness did not just appear to emanate from the aftermath of an earth-quake. I saw the spirits of too many people crushed, and I intuitively felt that they had been crushed for many years. Immediately I began reflecting upon an assignment I had students do in one of my graduate organizational behav-ior classes. They had to examine ethical dilemmas on a global context, the etiology of these dilemmas in concert with recommending change strategies.

In the class where the students made their presentation everyone was numbed by the description and root cause analysis of the ethical atrocities that impacts people across the globe. While I am not naive relative to how corporations take advantage of the poor, the massive subjugation of people living in both third-world and industrialized countries as researched and described by my students was sickening. People continue to be exposed to living and working conditions that go beyond evil, often at the hands of profiteering corporations and, in many cases, governments who allow the profiteers to come into their respective countries because they need the income.

Yet, these situations were in many respects no different from the city I spoke of that had a mayor subjugating them for more than 30 years. We cannot assess these situations from a one-dimensional analysis that will only yield results that never work to sustain change. If we are to look at travesties that plague far too many communities—dumping that has long-lasting health impact, little to no viable wages paid for inordinately long hours, the continued abuse of child labor in communities who have no power to fight these travesties, and the list goes on—one can again say it is strictly perspective as to which situation is worse.

I strongly believe that as a global community, we have to step outside the box of our individual struggle and examine in deeper discursive levels our struggles as humanity and address the constructs as they emerge relative to our failures as a human species. Whether the poverty and disempowerment is in the African American community, communities in India, the Philippines, Cambodia, Brazil, the barrios of California, Haiti, or across Europe does not matter. Subjugation is subjugation, which has a sustaining negative impact on our youth as well. Unfortunately, as previously stated, we have to continue to remember that this negative impact did not just begin today. There is not an inhabited continent where gang violence is not exponentially impacting our youth, who are running from the complexities of life that appear to offer no hope for change.

As the adults in their lives, we must commit to our youth efforts toward evoking change that is deep, collective, and multidimensional and concomitantly factors in the varying aspects of our subcultural points of reference. There is also a need for urgency. We cannot afford to continue waiting for others to bring forth change. While far too many of our environmental issues are dire, there is no motivation to change the economic imbalances of power and domination. The people who face subjugation have to feel the need for change.

· 1 3 ·

REFLECTIONS AND CONCLUDING COMMENTS

The Insertion versus Removal of Self

As I wrote this book, I continued to reflect upon the time I wrote my doctoral dissertation. As I reread the dissertation document, I remembered feeling as if the Spirit had channeled messages through me. You see, there were many pages written in that document that I did not remember writing.

Yet years later, I now understand that the messages I conveyed in the dissertation were just the beginning of a journey I would experience that has led to this book. The doctoral dissertation served as the foundation for my own reflection-action activities. However, as I wrote this time, I consciously asked God to remove any agenda I might possess. As I began writing this book, I also began to understand that my personal journey with this work is not over. In fact, as the book goes to press, it is just the beginning for a new phase in my life. I feel the Spirit is calling me and others to step out on faith and actively work the model with a focus on refining it as well as assessing new dimensions of possibilities for our youth and communities.

While I don't know how many people over time will read this manuscript, or what the ultimate societal impact will be, I do know that the last few years of my life have been a fundamental journey of change. There have been times where my experiences have felt like a lifetime of compressed spiritual, book, and visceral knowledge sometimes coming at me at such a pace that it was very hard to process everything all at once. Each new opportunity to learn impacted my soul. Consequently, as I wrote this book, I strongly felt that now was the time I needed to share that which I have learned, as well as my lingering and emerging questions.

My soul cries for justice, yet I realize my own limitations. But I have never felt that the journey of one cannot make a difference. Indulge me as I provide one more example.

In August 2009, I deeply felt the pain of people who were losing jobs or watching businesses close as a result of a troubled global economy. I grappled with how many people did not know how to effectively reemerge in a job market that had dramatically changed; yet there were no public announcements that the rules for what constitutes a productive workforce had also changed. Newspaper articles routinely featured stories as to how a layoff status was negatively impacting a person's success in the recruitment processes of many organizations. Business leaders and human resource professionals were suggesting that because a person had been laid off, they lacked the competencies and skills now required by organizations having to navigate through new economic foci. Having taught business courses for many years as well as still serving as a consultant to businesses, I knew that people did possess these competencies and skills, yet typically did not know how to effectively represent themselves.

To do my part, in August 2009, I had my Web master add a blog to my consulting Web site. This blog has and continues to serve as a free public site for information on the fundamentals of marketing and branding oneself as well as understanding the new, yet unspoken rules of work. Definitions for critical competencies and skills are provided as well as methods for professional development. In 2011, we began a dialogue on entrepreneurship as an option to navigating through tough economic waters.

Initially, I struggled with getting this information to people. While I had mailing lists and utilized social-networking sites, I also reached out to more than 500 radio stations across the country and asked that they simply make the announcement of this public service and give people the Web address. While a few did, I was astounded by the number of people who replied that they were not going to help me "market" my consulting practice. What we were doing had absolutely nothing to do the consulting practice. Needless to say, I was amazed at the short-sightedness of people, but I never gave up because I knew people needed this information. Most important, I knew God will always be in the mix when your heart is in the right place.

Today, this blog is read by people in more than 40 countries and the readership has exponentially grown to the point that it is difficult to keep up with the comments. Just over the course of two months, close to 18,000 people wrote comments regarding their desire to see more frequent updates, and they voiced their appreciation for our efforts. Many also wrote that they were amazed that this information was provided at no cost and subsequently linked the site to their Web pages, which means that more than the 18,000 over the course of two months actually read the blog.

Now many of you might ask, what on earth does this example have to do with what is presented in this book? The lessons I gleaned from this experience reinforced my understanding that life will always place people in our path who oppose change. However, we have to learn to not give away our power and allow the naysayers to park on our doorsteps. Persistence is important as is faith in that which you are doing. We always have to be open to understanding that there is always an opportunity to refine that which we do. I have a list of recommendations from our readers as to how we can improve the blog. Consequently when we take it to the next level, which will be very soon, I am going to incorporate their recommendations into the change processes.

There will always be times when we ask, "What can I do since I am only one?" We each can make a very positive difference in this world that evokes fundamental change if we simply use our talents. During my years teaching, there have been many times, as we were studying change management, my students would become extremely frustrated with what appeared to be hopeless situations in today's world. They clamored to know what they, as one, could do. My guiding praxis for them has always been simple.

Each individual has the capacity to make a difference. I always use the analogy of one pebble at a time in water. That one pebble will make a small ripple. Several pebbles in the water will make a small wave and when you have small waves, they build into larger waves. In other words, if we each throw our individual pebbles into the water, we ultimately will make much larger waves of change.

Many people have thus far benefited from the blog. It has been our small pebble in the water, which due to others linking and making their own individual ripples, has turned into much larger waves, which continues to provide additional opportunities for making a difference in someone's life. The same fundamental principles must hold true as we begin our systemic and focused work in the African American community designed to make a difference in the lives of our children as well as our own lives. If our accomplishments initially are only a few, we cannot become discouraged. The ripples will grow and ultimately many people will benefit. However, we have to start the process.

More Musings

Some of us have never seen a prison in our lives but were born into bondage . . . Freedom is defined by reality and not how we perceive it, but it's absolute.

Absolute reality should not always be interpreted as what we can see, touch, taste, feel, or smell. Freedom is the ability to exist absent of bondage and many of our minds are still enslaved . . . Come into the light . . .[1]

Throughout this journey I have continued to grapple with issues plaguing our youth who are disconnecting from society. And I had my own experiences of loss to deal with at the same time. Yet I do know if we stay grounded in our beliefs that God never lets go of us, we find the inner strength to work through insurmountable challenges. I see our youth in their own way working through their challenges and attempting to articulate their issues and truth (albeit the influences of the media who continue to work toward taking the hip-hop discourse into another whole arena). So it did not surprise me that as I walked through this leg of my journey, I continued to ponder if there is a different role for ministry to more effectively partner with our young people and move the dialogue into a more pro-socially appropriate course of protest action and movement toward change?

What happened to the partnering that occurred during the protest movements of the 1960s and 1970s where individuals from all walks of life collectively stood for change? How can we reemerge as a supportive community for our children as well as for ourselves? And where have we failed to support our youth in the manifestation of their goals for a better life? How can we effectively communicate to them that their life experiences thus far are indeed their personal journeys that do not end with the experience, but serves as the foundation for emerging as stronger individuals?

During the years I have worked as a consultant with African American Catholic churches, one of the principle issues we dealt with was the loss of youth in the church as well as in viable ministries. We continued to deal with the problem through meaningless programmatic measures, never getting to the heart of matters relative to why our youth are engaging in mindless vacations from society. So, at what point do our actions move from convenient programmatic measures to more systemic and strategically oriented change, issues that are critical and germane to our cultural development?

I have also pondered what is the role of the African American academy in addressing issues of disenfranchisement of youth and the African American community? How do we as faculty of color move into a more constructive *results-oriented* discourse that culminates in pro-social action? Are we as wounded as our other brothers and sisters in our community? Are we continuing to "speak" as we write only to a limited audience? I do not believe as faculty of color we can remove ourselves from these processes and engage in rhetorical debates.

As I researched issues plaguing African Americans in the academy in 2010 for a book published in 2011 that addressed the same topic—and I intentionally point out the dates to show that the situation has not changed—I was amazed at the consensus of African American academics and scholars regarding disempowerment, disenfranchisement, and other "isms" that continue to reside and plague them in institutions of higher education. So what does this mean? The sickening reality of this is example is that discrimination, disenfranchisement, lost dreams and hope are impacting people throughout the African American community, from our youth to individuals who have worked to obtain the highest levels of education afforded in this country. In other words, the nonsense will not stop until we say enough!

There is a deeply rooted sickness in the world that must be called out for what it is and eradicated. I have also pondered how, from a global perspective, do we bring people together who have commonalities relative to disenfranchisement? Far too many people across the globe are living in marginalized situations and environments. We must remember what I said earlier: There is not an inhabited continent on Earth that does not have a gang problem impacting youth.

There truly is power in numbers. But to eradicate these issues calls for an intentional global conversation and people willing to work toward change. This is why I had to incorporate into this book a beginning model. And I want to be clear, it is a beginning. My ego will not suffer if the model is improved by others. We cannot continue to live a life where we simply hope things will change and not collectively work to evoke that change.

Albeit rhetorically asking the question earlier, we have to constantly keep in the back of our minds the reality that if the work that addressed gang violence more than 80 years ago did not successfully address the problem, are we naive enough to think change is coming? If the conditions in the African

American community only continue to worsen, are we naive enough to think that they will suddenly get better? Our paradigmatic thought processes, attitudes toward entitlement, and strategies for evoking and continuing the change process have to be different.

These are just a few of the tough questions I have asked as I have traveled my journey. We all ask "why" of God, ourselves, and of our society. We also understand that the youth of today, particularly our youth of color, are disconnecting from society, yet, in their own way still attempt to articulate their issues via venues they understand. They need guidance as to how to envision change and understand the power of their inner guidance system.

Because these issues are globally situated, there is a need for global partnering as we work to address issues plaguing youth and our local and global societies. The paradigm shift has to incorporate movement from just dialogue to pro-socially appropriate courses of action and focused results; similar to the movements of the 1960s and 1970s where individuals from all walks of life, race, and ethnicities worked side by side for change.

We need a healing across the world. I hope and pray for global communication in an Appreciative Inquiry modality where communities of people who choose to utilize this model and embark upon change decide to set up a global communication forum for exchange, uplifting and sharing an extensive outreach to other communities that will encourage them to collaboratively work to evoke their own change. The sharing of success stories and appreciation of our efforts as well as gently engaging in constructive feedback designed to improve that which we do will be critical to a worldwide movement. Most important, our youth need to see, hear, internalize, and participate in a global conversation that allows them to share with their peers. When people engage in conversation that helps them realize that within their social context, they are not alone, that conversation will spread hope. Hope with action can and will change our world.

Despite the depth and breadth of my questions, through it all, I know answers are going to be provided, which is why, as I wrote, I prayed for the insertion of my lessons but the removal of my agenda, even if I thought I did not have one. If this book helps but a few, it would have made writing it worth the time and effort spent.

So, I conclude by asking any and all that read this book to walk with me as we work toward change. Pray with me as we continue to ask for strength and most important believe with me.

Never give up on a child!

NOTES

Introduction

1. Caitlin A. Easley. Unpublished poem "A Child that Fights." This poem was written in 2005, approximately a year after Caitlin's father passed, and reflects her thoughts regarding her internal struggle with loss.

1. My Lens, Perspectives, and Context: Yet a Collective Set of Challenges

1. While there are specific citations relative to the concept and context associated with Appreciative Inquiry, I want to note that credit must be given to Dr. David Cooperrider, who was the originator of Appreciative Inquiry in 1986 via his doctoral dissertation at Case Western Reserve University.

10. The Model for Change

1. Rev. Dr. O. Smith, unpublished sermon, February 28, 2010, Covenant United Church of Christ.

13. Reflections and Concluding Comments

1. J. Easley, 2011. Unpublished prose. It has been my pleasure to add the reflections and poetry of both my children, each who have a phenomenal talent as writers. My son, at age six, won the Gwendolyn Brooks Poet Laureate contest, and my daughter has been writing music, prose, and poetry since she was in grammar school. Our children across the globe have so much talent; we just have to encourage them to bring it to the forefront of their lives.

BIBLIOGRAPHY

African American women and where they stand. (2007). *NBC Nightly News*. Retrieved February 15, 2008, from http://dailynightly.msnbc.msn.com/archive/2007/11/20/476352.aspx

Akbar, N. (1996). *Breaking the chains of psychological slavery*. Tallahassee, FL: Mind Productions & Associates

Akbar, N. (2003). *Akbar papers in African psychology*. Tallahassee, FL: Mind Productions & Associates.

Allen, D., & Hardin, P. (2001). Discourse analysis and the epidemiology of meaning. *Nursing Philosophy, 2*, 163–176.

Alvesson, M., & Karreman, D. (2000). Varieties of discourse: On the study of organizations through discourse analysis. *Human Relations, 53*(9), 1125–1149.

Ander, R., Cook, P., Ludwig, J., & Pollack, H. (2009). *Gun violence among school-age youth in Chicago*. December 1, 2010 from http://crimelab.uchicago.edu/gun_violence/report.shtml

Anzaldúa, G. (2007). *Borderlands/La Frontera, the New Mestiza* (3rd ed.). San Francisco: Aunt Lute Books.

Anzaldúa, G., & Keating, A. (Eds.). (2002). *This bridge we call home, radical visions for transformation*. New York: Routledge.

Ashby, H. (2003). *Our home is over Jordan*. St. Louis, MO: Chalice Press.

Bandura, A. (1969). *Principles of behavior modification*. New York: Holt, Rinehart & Winston.

Barrett, F., & Cooperrider, D. (1990). Generative metaphor intervention: A new approach for working with systems divided by conflict and caught in defensive perception. *Journal of Applied Behavioral Science, 26* (2), 222–224.

Barrett, F., & Srivastva, S. (1991). History as a mode of inquiry in organizational life: A role for human cosmogony. *Human Relations, 44*, 236–244.

Barrett, F., Thomas, G., & Hocevar, S. (1995). The central role of discourse in large-scale change: A social construction perspective. *Journal of Applied Behavioral Science, 31*(3), 352–372.

Beating death of Derrien Albert, 16, caught on video. *Huffington Post.* Retrieved September 22, 2010, from http://www.huffingtonpost.com/2009/09/27/beating-death-of-derrien_n_301319.html

Bell, E., & Nkoma, S. (2001). *Our separate ways.* Boston: Harvard Business School Press.

Bender, T. (1978). *Community and social change in America.* New Brunswick, NJ: Rutgers University Press.

Bernard, J. S. (1972). *The sociology of community.* Glenview, IL: Scott, Foresman.

Bisoux, T. (2002). The mind of a leader. *Biz Ed,* September–October 2002.

Boje, D., & Rosile, G. (1994). Diversities, differences and authors' voices. *Journal of Organizational Change Management, 7*(6), 8–17.

Bolitho, W. (1930). The psychosis of the gang. *Survey,* February, 1930, 501–506.

Botsford, F. (2001). Spanish police hit Basque youth wing. BBC News. Retrieved February 11, 2002 from http://news.bbc.co.uk/2/hi/1205478.stm

Butler, L. H. (2000). *A loving home.* Cleveland, OH: Pilgrim Press.

Butler, L. H. (2006). *Liberating our dignity, saving our souls.* St. Louis, MO: Chalice Press.

California Department of Justice, Division of Law Enforcement, Bureau of Investigation. (1993, March). *Gangs 2000: A call to action. The Attorney General's report on the impact of criminal street gangs on crime and violence in California by the year 2000.* Retrieved October 28, 1996, https://www.ncjrs.gov/App/Publications/abstract.aspx?ID=149300

Cathcart, R. (2007). Los Angeles combating gangs gone international. *New York Times.* December 26, 2007. Retrieved February 19, 2010 from http://www.nytimes.com/2007/12/26/us/26gangs.html?_r=1

Chia, R. (2000). Discourse analysis as organizational analysis. *Organization, 7*(3), 513–518.

Cobb, P. (1994). Where is the mind? Constructivist and sociocultural perspectives on mathematical development. *Educational Researcher, 23*(7), 13–20.

Cockburn, A. (1992). Beat the devil. *The Nation, 254,* 738–739.

Cohen, J. (1983). The relationship between friendship selection and peer influence. In J. L. Epstein & N. Karweit (Eds.), *Friends in school.* New York: Academic.

Cone, J. (1969). *Black theology and black power.* New York: Seabury Press.

Cone, J. (1970). *A black theology of liberation.* New York: J. B. Lippincott Co.

Cone, J. (1986). *A black theology of liberation* (2nd ed.). New York: Orbis Books.

Cone, J. (2001, Fall-Winter). The content and method of black theology. *Journal of Religious Thought, 32*(2), 90.

Cooperrider, D. (1986). *Appreciative Inquiry: Toward a methodology for understanding and enhancing organizational innovation.* Unpublished dissertation, Case Western Reserve University, Cleveland, OH.

Cooperrider, D. (2005, April). Unpublished lecture notes at Benedictine University.

Cooperrider, D., & Pratt, C. (1995). *Appreciative inquiry, relational realities and constructionist approaches to organizational development.* Paper presented at Case Western Reserve University, Cleveland, OH.

Cooperrider, D., & Srivastva, S. (1987). Appreciative inquiry in organizational life. In W. Pasmore & R. Woodman (Eds.), *Research in Organizational Change and Development,* Vol. 1, pp. 129–169. Greenwich, CT: JAI Press.

Davies, B. (1991). The concept of agency: A feminist post-structuralist analysis. *Social Analysis*, 30, 42–53.

Decker, S., & Van Winkle, B. (1996). *Life in the gang, family friends and violence*. New York: Cambridge University Press.

Domash, S. (2010). America's Most Dangerous Gang. Retrieved October 2, 2010, from http://www.apfn.org/apfn/ms-13.htm

Easley, C. A. (1999). *The role of Appreciative Inquiry in the fight to save our youth*. Unpublished dissertation, Benedictine University, Lisle, IL.

Easley, C. A. (2010). Easing the path for African American women in leadership: The spiritual, cultural and healing aspects of African American women dialoguing. In R. G. Johnson III & G. L. A. Harris (Eds.), *Women of color: Taking their rightful place in leadership*. San Diego, CA: Birkdale Publishers.

Easley, C. A. (2010, March). Expanding a conversation: Is how we live as a culturally diverse society congruent with our underlying assumptions, methodologies and theories regarding change? *Journal of Applied Behavioral Science*, 46(1), 55–72.

Easley, C. A. (2011). Developing my higher self: My life as an African American woman in the academy. In S. Jackson & R. G. Johnson III (Eds.), *The Black professoriate, negotiating a habitable space in the academy*. Peter Lang: New York.

Easley, C. A., & Alvarez-Pompilius, F. (2004). A new paradigm for qualitative investigations: Towards an integrative model for evoking change. *Organization Development Journal*, 22(3), 42–59.

Easley, C. A., McMaster, M., & Tate, C. L. (2003). *Charting new territory and exploring new frontiers: Examining an interdisciplinary approach to teaching leadership through the integration of communications, organizational behavior, organization development and psychology*. Proceedings of the Midwest Academy of Management.

Easley, C. A., & Swain, J. W. (2003) "Niccolo Machiavelli: Moving through the future as we learn from the past." *International Journal of Organization Theory and Behavior*, Issue 1, Volume 6 (Spring 2003).

Egerton, R. (1988). Foreword. In J. D. Vigil, *Barrio gangs: Street life and identity in Southern California*. Austin: University of Texas Press.

Emery, F., & Purser, R. (1996). *The search conference*. San Francisco: Jossey-Bass.

Erikson, E. H. (1975). The problem of ego identity. In A. Esman (Ed.), *The psychology of adolescence*. New York: International Universities Press.

Fairclough, N. (1992). Discourse and text: Linguistic and intertextual analysis within discourse analysis. *Discourse and Society*, 3, 193–217.

Fish, S. (1989). *Doing what comes naturally*. Durham, NC: Duke University Press.

Freire, P. (1970). *Pedagogy of the oppressed*. New York: Continuum Publishing Co.

Freire, P. (1997). *Pedagogy of hope*. New York: Continuum Publishing Co.

Freire, P. (2006). *Pedagogy of the oppressed*. (30th anniversary ed.) New York: Continuum Publishing Co.

Garcia, M. (1981). *Teacher perceptions and actual performance levels of junior high school Latino gang and non-gang affiliated students on a variety of school-related variables*. Unpublished doctoral dissertation, University of Southern California, Los Angeles.

Gergen, K. (1994). *Realities and relationships, soundings in social construction*. Cambridge, MA: Harvard University Press.

Goldstein, A. P. (1991). *Delinquent gangs, a psychological perspective.* Champaign, IL: Research Press.

Gouldner, A. W. (1970). *The coming crisis of Western sociology.* London: Heinemann.

The Governor's Commission on Gangs Final Report. (1998). Gang Crime Prevention Center in the Office of Illinois Attorney General Jim Ryan. Retrieved March 17, 1998, from http://www.acsp.uic.edu/~ag/gcpc

Graff, P. (2002). Moscow braces for skinheads on Hitler's birthday, India-Reuters. Retrieved April 15, 2002, http://story.news.yahoo.com/news?tmpl=story&u=/nm/20020415/wl_india_nm/india_69137_1

Grant, D., Kennoy, T., & Oswick, C. (Eds.). (1998). *Discourse and organization.* Thousand Oaks, CA: Sage Publications.

Green, B. (1999, April 4). The greatest enemy that children have. *Chicago Tribune.*

Hagedorn, J., with Macon, P. (1988). *People and folks, gangs, crime and the underclass in a rustbelt city.* Chicago: Lake View Press.

Hardt, M., & Negri, A. (2005). *Multitude: War and democracy in the age of empire.* New York: Penguin Books.

Hardwick, L. (1995). *The relationship of youth gang membership to academic achievement: A comparative analysis.* Unpublished doctoral dissertation, University of Akron, Akron, OH.

Hardy, C., Phillips, N., & Clegg, S. (2001, May). Reflexivity in organization and management theory: A study of the production of the research "subject." *Human Relations, 54*(5), 531.

Hawkins, D. B. (1993). Academics, politics and the pulpit: Power to influence elections strongly vested in the Black church. *Black Issues in Higher Education, 10*(22), 14–16.

Holmes, B. A. (2004). *Joy unspeakable: Contemplative practices of the Black church.* Minneapolis: Fortress Press.

hooks, b. (1995). Feminism: Crying for our souls. *Women & Therapy, 17*(1–2), 265–275.

Hopkins, D. N. (2005). *Black theology of liberation.* New York: Orbis Books.

Hopkins, N., & Reicher, S. (1997). Social movement rhetoric and the social psychology of collective action: A case study of anti-abortion mobilization. *Human Relations, 50,* 261–286.

Isett, S. (1994, December). From killing fields to mean street. *World Press Review, 41,* 34–35.

Itano, N. (2001, August 17). Curbing gangs in Cape Flats. *Christian Science Monitor.*

Jacinto, N. (2009). Survey shows rise in youth gang problems. *WireTap Magazine.* Retrieved February 25, 2010 from http://www.wiretapmag.org/blogs/race/44147/

Jeffery, P. (1993, January). Targeted for death: Brazil's street children. *Christian Century, 110,* 52–55.

Jeffries, S. (2001, February 4, Sunday), Teen gangs terrorise chic Paris. *Observer,* Guardian Newspapers Limited.

Kets de Vries, M., & Miller, D. (1987). Interpreting organizational texts. *Journal of Management Studies, 12,* 251–273.

Kolb, D. (1984). *Experiential learning.* Englewood Cliffs, NJ: Prentice Hall.

Kouzes, J. M., & Posner, B. Z. (1995). *The leadership challenge: How to keep getting extraordinary things done in organizations.* San Francisco: Jossey-Bass.

Landesco, J. (1932). Crime and the failure of institutions in Chicago's immigrant areas. *Journal of Criminal Law and Criminology, 23,* 238–248.

Lockwood, A. (1993). The professor of gangs. *Focus in Change, 10,* 10–14.

Ludema, J. D. (1995). *Narrative inquiry: Collective storytelling as a source of hope, knowledge and action in organizational life.* Unpublished doctoral dissertation, Case Western Reserve University, Cleveland, OH.

Ludema, J., Wilmont, T., & Srivastva, S. (1997). Organizational hope, reaffirming the constructive task of social and organizational inquiry. *Human relations, 50*(8), 1015–1052.

Macko, S. (1996). *Street gangs come to the South Pacific* . . . Emergency Net News Service. February 10, 2002 from http://www.emergency.com/nz-gangs.htm

MacWilliams, B. (2002, May 10). Many foreign students in Russia fear for their lives. *Chronicle of Higher Education.* Retrieved May 10, 2002 from http://chronicle.com/weekly/v48/i35/35a04601.htm

Main, F. (2010). Gang leaders rap Chicago police anti-violence plan. Retrieved Sept. 3, 2010, from http://www.southtownstar.com/news/2669022,090310gangs.article

Manning, P. K. (1979, December). Metaphors of the field: Varieties of organizational discourse. *Administrative Science Quarterly, 24,* 660–671.

Marcel, G. (1963). *The existential background of human dignity.* Cambridge, MA: Harvard University Press.

Marshak, R., & Grant, D. (2008). Transforming talk: The interplay of discourse, power and change. *Organization Development Journal, 26,* 33–41.

Mbiti, J. (1990). *African religions and philosophy.* Oxford: Heinemann Publishers.

McMillan, D. W., & Chavis, D. M. (1986). Sense of community: A definition and theory. *Journal of Community Psychology, 14,* 6–23.

McNeal, C., & Perkins, I. (2007). Potential roles of Black churches in HIV/AIDS prevention. *Journal of Human Behavior in the Social Environment, 15*(2/3), 219–232.

Middleton, J. A. (2001, May) A role for the African American church in urban school reform. *Urban Education,* vol. 36, no. 3, 426–437.

Miller, W. B. (2001). *The growth of youth gang problems in the United States, 1970–98.* Office of Juvenile Justice and Delinquency Prevention, United States Department of Justice, Office of Justice Programs.

Mitchem, S. (2002). *Womanist theology.* New York: Orbis Books.

Moltmann, J. (1999). *God for a secular society, The public relevance of theology.* Minneapolis: Fortress Press.

Moltmann, J. (2006). *The politics of discipleship and discipleship in politics.* Eugene, OR: Wipf & Stock.

Moore, J. W. (1978). *Homeboys, gangs, drugs and prison in the barrios of Los Angeles.* Philadelphia: Temple Press.

National Guard may be called in to curtail Chicago gang violence. Retrieved September 22, 2010, from http://hiphopwired.com/2010/04/27/national-guard-may-be-called-in-to-curtail-chicago-gang-violence-video/

Negy, C., & Eisenman, R. (2005). A comparison of African American and White college students' affective and attitudinal reactions to lesbians, gay, and bisexual individuals: An exploratory study. *Journal of Sex Research, 42*(4), 291–298.

Oswick, C., Keenoy, T., & Grant, D. (2000). Discourse, organizations and organizing: Concepts, objects and subjects. *Human Relations, 53*(9), 1115–1120.

Other. *Wikipedia.* Retrieved February 10, 2011, from http://en.wikipedia.org/wiki/Other

Packer, J., & Goicoechea, J. (2000). Sociocultural and constructivist theories of learning: Ontology, not just epistemology. *Educational Psychologist, 35*(4), 227–241.

Padilla, F. M. (1992). *The gang as an American enterprise.* New Brunswick, NJ: Rutgers University Press.

Pettigrew, A. M. (1979, December). On studying organizational cultures. *Administrative Science Quarterly, 24*, 570–581.

Piaget, J. (1972). *The principles of genetic epistemology* (Wolfe Mays, Trans.). New York: Basic Books. (Original work published 1970).

Plea for gang violence crackdown. (2007, February). *BBC News.* Retrieved October 2, 2010, from http://news.bbc.co.uk/2/hi/americas/6338609.stm

Proshansky, H. M., Favian, A. K., & Kaminoff, R. (1983). Place-identity: Physical world socialization of the self. *Journal of Environmental Psychology, 3*, 57–83.

Quinn, R. E. (1996). *Deep change: Discovering the leader within.* San Francisco: Jossey-Bass.

Quinn, R. E. (2000). *Change the world: How ordinary people can accomplish extraordinary results.* San Francisco: Jossey-Bass.

Quinney, R. (1982). *Social existence: Metaphysics, Marxism, and the social sciences.* Beverly Hills, CA: Sage Publications.

Race/Ethnicity. (1999, July). 1996 National Youth Gang Survey. Retrieved October, 11, 2010, from http://www.ojjdp.gov.pubs/96natyouthgangsrvy/surv_6c.html

Redmond, D. (2006). *The influence of knowledge of homosexuality and religious importance to homophobia among African American students at a historically Black college.* Unpublished doctoral dissertation, Texas Southern University, 2006.

Reynolds, L., & Powell, L. (1981, October 31). Black lesbian bibliography. *Off Our Backs, 11*(9), 9, 17.

Ricoeur, P. (1992). *Oneself as another.* Chicago: University of Chicago Press.

Rivlin, L. G. (1987). *The inner world of the Black juvenile delinquent.* Mahwah, NJ: Erlbaum.

Rosas, A. (2009, January 17). 2008 saw increased violence in Chicago, statistics show. *Chicago Tribune.*

Rosenthal, R., & Jacobson, L. (1968). *Pygmalion in the classroom.* New York: Holt, Rinehart & Winston.

Sanchez-Jankowski, M. (1991). *Islands in the street, gangs and American urban society.* Berkeley: University of California Press.

Save the Children. (1988). *Ebony,* 33–41.

Seaman, D. (1979). *A geography of the lifeworld: Movement, rest, and encounter.* New York: St. Martin's Press.

Senge, P. M. (1990). *The fifth discipline: The art and practice of the learning organization.* New York: Currency Doubleday.

Senge, P., Kleiner, A., Roberts, C., Ross, R., Roth, G., & Smith, B. (1999). *The dance of change: The challenges of sustaining momentum in learning organizations.* New York: Doubleday/Currency.

Shaw, C. R., & Mckay, H. D. (1942). *Juvenile delinquency and urban areas: A study of rates of delinquency in relation to differential characteristics of local communities in American cities.* Chicago: University of Chicago Press.

Sivaraman, S. (1998, August). Development-Cambodia: Violent Crime Thrives in Wounded Society. *World News.* Retrieved February 10, 2002 from http://www.oneworld.org/ips2/aug98/04_04_007.html

Smith, Rev. Dr. O. (2008, May 11). Unpublished sermon, Covenant United Church of Christ.

Smith, Rev. Dr. O. (2010, February 28). Unpublished sermon, Covenant United Church of Christ.

Srivastva, S., & Barrett, F. (1988). The transforming nature of metaphors in group development: A study in group theory. *Human Relations, 41*(1), 31–64.

Steffe, L. P., & Gale, J. (Eds.). (1995). *Constructivism in education*. Hillsdale, NJ: Lawrence Erlbaum Associates.

Strauss, A., & Corbin J. (1990). *Basics of qualitative research. Grounded theory procedures and techniques*. Newbury Park, CA: Sage Publication.

Sutherland, E. H. (1937). *Principles of criminology*. Philadelphia: Lippincott Press.

Tannenbaum, F. (1938). *Crime and the community*. Boston: Ginn.

Taylor, E. (1986). In Chicago: Raising children in a battle zone. *Time, 128*, 14.

Tenkasi, R., Thatchenkery, T., Barrett, F., & Manning, M. (1994). The impact of schemas and inquiry on consultants' constructions of expectations about the client system. *CEO Publications* (G 94–13) (256), 1–29.

Terhune, C. P. (2005–2006). Biculturalism, code-switching, and shifting: The experiences of Black women in a predominately White environment. *International Journal of the Diversity, 5*(6), 9–15.

Terrell, J. (2005). *Power in the blood? The cross in the African American experience*. Eugene, OR: Wipf & Stock.

Thatchenkery, T. (1996). Affirmation as facilitation. A postmodernist paradigm in change management. *OD Practitioner, 28*(1 & 2), 12–22.

Thelen, H. (1954). *Dynamics of groups at work*. Chicago: University of Chicago Press.

Thrasher, F. (1927). *The gang*. Chicago: University of Chicago Press.

Thurman, H. (1963). *Disciplines of the spirit*. Richmond, VA: Friends United Press.

Thurman, H. (1976). *Jesus and the disinherited*. Boston: Beacon Press.

Tobin, K. (Ed.). (1993). *The practice of constructivism in science education*. Mahwah, NJ: Lawrence Erlbaum Associates.

Townes, E. (Ed.). (2005). *A troubling in my soul: Womanist perspectives on evil and suffering*. New York: Orbis Books.

Virtanen, T. (Ed.). (2001). *Youth, racist violence and anti-racist responses in the Nordic countries*. Finnish Youth Research Society. Retrieved February 3, 2002 from http://www.alli.fi/nourisotutkimus/julkaisut/virtanen/html

Von Glasersfeld, E. (1993). Questions and answers about radical constructivism. In K. Tobin (Ed.), *The practice of constructivism in science education* (pp. 223–238). Mahwah, NJ: Lawrence Erlbaum Associates.

Watkins, A. C. (1999). *Survival and liberation*. St. Louis, MO: Chalice Press.

Wattenberg, W. W., & Balistrieri, J. J. (1950). Gang membership and juvenile misconduct. *American Sociological Review, 15*, 181–186.

Weisbord, M. R. (1992). *Discovering common ground*. San Francisco: Berrett-Koehler Publishers.

West, C. (1993). *Race matters*. New York: Vintage Press.

West, C. (1999). *The Cornel West reader*. New York: Basic Civitas Books.

West, C. (2004). *Democracy matters*. New York: Penguin Group.

Wheatley, M. J. (1999). *Leadership and the new science: Discovering order in a chaotic world* (2nd ed.). San Francisco: Berrett-Koehler.

When death squads meet street children. (1993, July). *Economist*, 39.

White, R., Santina, P., Carmel, G., Rosario, L. (1999). Ethnic youth gangs in Australia: Do they exist? *Australian Multicultural Foundation*. Retrieved Downloaded February 10, 2002 from www:amf.net.au/projects/ethnic

Williams, D. (1997). Straight talk, plain talk: Womanist words about salvation in a social context. In E. M. Townes (Ed.), *Embracing the spirit: Womanist perspectives on hope, salvation, and transformation* (pp. 97–121). New York: Orbis Books.

Williams, R. (1996). Survey guided Appreciative Inquiry: A case study. *OD Practitioner, 28*(1 & 2), 43–51.

Wilmore, G. (1998). *Back religion and Black radicalism: An interpretation of religious history of African Americans*. Maryknoll, NY: Orbis Books.

Wilmore, G. (2004). *Pragmatic spirituality*. New York: New York University Press.

Wink, W. (1992). *Engaging the Powers: Discernment and Resistance in a World of Domination*. Minneapolis: Fortress Press.

INDEX

academy
  African Americans in, 205
  racism in, 20–21
accommodation, 97
accomplishments, appreciating, 194–95
accountability
  need for, 12, 19
  views on, 1
action, 167, 169, 173–79
ADD, 62
adolescence, 114
adults, working with, 123
advantages, learning to work, 159
African Americans
  in academy, 205
  community (See community, African
    American)
  deterioration in conditions of, 38
  held responsible for gang phenomenon,
    36
  macrocultural differences, 153–54
  men (See men, African American)
  psyche of, 69

psychology of, 125
self-hate of, 169
social stratification of, 23, 29, 79
strategy for, 160–61
suffering of, 28
uniqueness of, 126, 127–28, 130
women (See women, African American)
worldviews of, formation of, 52–53, 61
AIDS, 42, 90, 176
Akbar, Na'im, 29–30, 69
Albert, Derrien, 17
anger, 25, 27, 131, 132
anticipation, 156
Anzaldúa, Gloria, 24, 25, 113
Appreciative Inquiry
  application of to youth in gangs, 108
    (See also intervention, Appreciative
    Inquiry)
  as change methodology, 105
  combined with discourse analysis, 126
  combined with search conference meth-
    odology, 108–10
  development of, 102

in diversity work, 105–6
evocation of new language in, 127
focus on positive in, 95, 96, 105, 111, 115
global application of, 199, 206
with healthcare providers, 194
heliotropic evolution in, 107
hermeneutics of, 106
historical inquiry in, 104
intervention using (*See* intervention,
       Appreciative Inquiry)
during leaders meeting, 186–89
in model for change, 174
and need for understanding of systems
       theory, 110
phases of, 108
principles of, 107, 108
stages of, 187–88
use of, 108
See also discourse analysis
assimilation, 97
assumptions, challenging, 60–61, 78, 95
Auschwitz, 199
Australia, 34
awareness, change in, 88

Barrettt, Frank, 103
barriers, 51, 114, 117–18, 146
behavior, disrespectful, 113–14
behavior, gang, 53–56
being, 165
belief system, challenging, 2, 18–19
Bell, E, 43, 44
Bender, T., 92
Bernard, J. S., 92
Bible, 169
Bisoux, T., 140
blog, 202–3
Bloods, 90
bonding, lack of, 45, 115
borders, 24, 25
boundaries, 145, 150
Brazil, 34
Breaking the Chains of Psychological Slavery
       (Akbar), 29–30
Butler, L. H., 131

Cabrini-Green, 78–81, 91, 108
Call to Action, 173–79
Cambodia, 34
careers
    educational requirements for, 157
    suggested to African American students,
       146
caregiving, 194
Caribbean, French, 124
change
    actions and, 3
    beginning, 51
    and challenging belief system, 2
    commitment to, 89
    critical components for, 138–39
    entitlement to, 176–77
    Eurocentric psychologies in, 59
    global context of, 49–50
    and leadership, 48–49, 50
       (*See also* leadership)
    made by single person, 203–4
    and ministry, 26
    model for, 12–13
       (*See also* model for change)
    and need for conscious decision, 12
    and need for engagement, 15
    need for institutions to incorporate, 99
    need for support for, 112–13
    need to address in African American
       community, 88
    and need to understand reality, 13–14, 16
    reluctance to envision, 23–24
    resistance to, 49–50
    and self-knowledge, 130
    strategies for, choosing, 21
    time for, 3
    vision for, 11
    See also reform
change, macrolevel, 15
change, strategic, 14
change, systemic, 14
change, whole systems, 116
change management, 26
Chicago
    alternative schools in, 114

Cabrini-Green housing project, 78–81, 91, 108
gangs in, 20, 37
homicide in, 71
violence in, 17, 35
children
death toll, 11
and indifference, 76
lack of support for, 45, 46
loss of, 5, 7
need for constructive emotional dialogue, 77
search for security, 71–72
support for, 62–63
See also youth
choice, personal, 159
church, Black
critique of, 166–67
divisions within, 29
historical role of, 165–67
leadership in, 166
loss of youth in, 204
in model for change, 16, 164, 173, 174–77
politics within, 175
recent role of, 176
as source of strength, 164
view of, 176
cognition, human, 87
collegiality, 165
comfort zone, 145, 150
commitment, 155
communication, 155
communication, business, 149
community
building, 105
concept of, 139
definition of, 20, 92
gang's relationship to, 90–92, 93
global concept of, 90
need for, 7
need to recommit to, 88, 93
and survival, 30–31
Thurman's concept of, 30
views on, 1

community, African American
complexity of issues facing, 15
considered broken, 134
criticality of, 89–90
disengagement of with youth, 14–15
disintegration of concept of, 92, 93
historical roots of, 90
insularity of, 158
issues in, 5
need for accountability in, 12
need for engagement of, 16
responsibility for, 12
sense of, need to recapture, 31
strengths of, 164
Cone, J., 127, 169, 172
consciousness, African, 2, 20
context, of gangs, 37, 46, 47
contracts, psychological, 156
control, 26, 48
Cooperrider, David, 75, 102, 103, 189
corporations, 200
cosmology, 15–16, 30, 164, 177, 180–81
credentials
Easley's, 19–20
of organizational development experts, 179
Creole, 154
crime, Black-on-Black, 42, 44
crime, organized, 34
Crips, 90
critical mass, 139, 154
culture
differences within, 153–54
othering, 24, 146, 189
culture, Creole, 154

death
causes of, 42
of child, effects of, 4
fear of, 113, 117, 172
death, spiritual, 6, 70
death rates, 44, 71
Deep Change (Quinn), 147
democracy, 23
"demotes," 84, 113

depression, 197
despair, 26
destiny, 48
dialogue, constructive emotional, 77
dialogue, intentional, 132, 138–39, 177
   beginning of, 135
   benefits of, 168
   facilitation of, 185, 186, 188
   feedback, 185, 186
   global application of, 199
   in leaders meeting, 183–86
   and need to acknowledge
      microculture, 153
   need to engage in, 88, 132–33
   negativity associated with, 188
   purpose of, 134
dialogue, internal, 51–52, 59, 63
   See also metaphors
dialogue, negative, 63, 94, 95, 96, 101
differences
   within race, 153–54
   See also othering
discourse, deficit, 83, 84–85, 114
discourse analysis, 124, 126, 127, 130–31
discourse and construction of reality,
   128, 129
disempowerment, 41
disenfranchisement, 41
disengagement, 1, 14–15
dissertation, 13, 201
dissonance, cognitive, 28, 29–30, 43, 193
distrust, 81, 131
domination, acceptance of, 68
doubt, reflexive, 118–19
dreams, 189
Drucker, Peter, 189
duality, 27–28, 67

earthquake, Haitian, 199–200
Easley, C. A.
   blog, 202–3
   credentials, education, 19–20
   dissertation, 13, 201
Ebony, 39
Economist, 39

education
   alternative schools, 79, 114, 144
   college students, 157–58
   European systems, 158
   expectations in, 63–64
   failure of, 46
   foreign language requirement, 142–43
   functions of, 82
   in global context, 143
   labeling in, 61–62
   lack of success in, 83–84
   lack of support for, 63
   learning styles, 144
   need for scenario planning in, 157
   negative dialogues in, 63
   school reform, 176
   standards, 144
   teachers, 98–99, 144
   technology in, 143
   value of, 111
   views of, 76–77
Egerton, R., 38
El Salvador, 35
employment, 39, 42, 46
engagement, need for, 16
entitlement, 176–77, 180, 206
entrepreneurship, by gangs, 54–56, 108
epistemology, 95, 125
ETA, 34
evolution, heliotropic, 107
expectations, 57, 63–64, 76, 97

Facebook, 194–95
failure, programming for, 52
family, African American
   destruction of, 69
   deterioration of, 42, 44
   relationships within, 116
   role of women in, 43
family, in gang environment, 134
father
   absence of, 45
   effects of racism on, 45
   loss of, 5–6
feedback, 185, 186

Finland, 34
flexibility, 24, 171
Folks, 108
foundation, 161
France, 34
freedom, 198
French Caribbean, 124
future
    co-construction of, 108, 174, 188, 189–90
    envisioning, 112, 117–18
    vision of, by youth in gangs, 76–77
    vision of, lack of, 42
future, positive, 111

gang intervention. *See* intervention,
    Appreciative Inquiry; intervention,
    gang
gang members
    internal dialogues of, 52
    values of, 111
    youth (*See* youth in gangs)
The Gang (Thrasher), 37
gangs
    African Americans held responsible for,
      36
    behavior of, 53–56
    in Chicago, 20
    and city populations, 33, 35
    context of, 37, 46, 47
    entrepreneurial enterprises of, 54–56, 108
    gravitation to, understanding, 21–22
    historical existence of, 46
    international prevalence of, 33–36, 47
    involvement in, 41
    leadership of, 142
    migration patterns of, 33
    need for new ways of addressing, 205–6
    organizational traits of, 54–56
    origins of, 12
    population of, 33, 36
    positive attributes of, 108
    positive changes made by, 189
    reemergence of, 38
    relationship to community, 90–92, 93
    studies of, historical, 37–40

    youth in (*See* gangs, youth; youth in
      gangs)
gangs, Caucasian, 33
gangs, Hispanic, 33
gangs, youth
    international rise of, 33–36
    prevalence of, 2, 4, 5
    roots of, 13
gifts, 146–47
global context, 143
goals
    need for congruency among, 155
    verifiable, 156
    working toward, 160–61
God, 30, 68–69
Goldstein, A. P., 114
group work, 98
groupthink, 37
Guatemala, 35

Hagedorn, J., 54, 57
Haika, 34
Haiti, 199
hate, 131
health, 42, 44
heritage, need to recover values of, 31
history
    African American, 113, 126–27
    need to understand, 17, 27, 50, 104,
      180–81, 198
HIV/AIDS, 42, 176
Holocaust, 199
homicide rates, 39, 71
    See also death
homophobia, 171
homosexuality, 25, 170–71
Honduras, 35
hope, 111, 114, 117
hopelessness, 23, 58, 84, 161, 199
housing projects, 78–81, 91, 108
Huffington Post, 17
hybridity, 24

ideals, 112
identity formation, African American, 29

ignorance, 24
imagery, negative, 101, 103, 107
  See also metaphors
imagery, positive, 104, 107, 115
Imagine Chicago, 102
implementation, 111–12, 154–61, 169, 188
  See also model for change
incarceration, 39
indifference, 76
information, explosion of, 108
inquiry, historical, 104
institutions, breakdown of, 39
insurance, health, 42
intervention, Appreciative Inquiry
  changes in language during, 98
  discussion of perceptions of reality, 96–97
  ground rules, 94
  lessons from, 118
  and teachers, 98–99
  topic selection, 115
intervention, gang, 17–18, 37, 39,
    46–47, 205
  See also intervention, Appreciative
    Inquiry

jail, 39
job market, 39, 46
justice, 131

Katrina, Hurricane, 20, 23, 176–77, 198
knowledge, construction of, 56
knowledge, inclusive, 138
Kouzes, J. M., 140

labeling, 25, 61–62
Landesco, J., 38
language, 94, 129–30
  See also dialogue
language, foreign, 142–44
language, negative, 84, 101, 129
  See also discourse, deficit
language patterns, 89, 97, 139
layoff status, 202
leadership
  in Black church, 166

and change, 48–49, 50
competencies of, 141–42, 147–48, 182–83
development of, 181–82
Drucker on, 189
effective, 16–17, 140, 141, 155
of gangs, 142
and intentional dialogue, 183–86
model for, 147–53
in model for change, 173, 177, 179–90
need to challenge concept of, 89
paradigm shifts, 187
qualities of, 145
selection of, 179
and vision, 148–49, 151
leadership, African American, 79–81
leadership, soulful, 147
learning styles, 144
lens, for African Americans, 2
lesbians, 25, 170–71
liberation, 61, 135
life, appreciating, 194–95
loneliness, 134
Los Angeles, 35, 90

Manning, P. K., 128
Mara Salvatrucha 13, 35–36
marriage rates, 44
matriarchy, 43
Mbiti, J., 180
McKay, H. D., 38
McNeal, C., 176
men, African American, 5–6, 44–45
mentor, 60–61
Mestiza, 24
metaphors, 52–53, 96, 103–4, 115
metaphors, generative, 129–30
Mexico, 35
middle class, erosion of, 197
Middle Passage, 198
  See also slavery
Mitchem, S., 165
model for change
  Appreciative Inquiry in, 174
  call for action, 173–79
  global application of, 197–205

importance of, 163–64
initial meetings, 177
leadership in, 173, 177, 179–90
need for experts in organizational development, 178–79
role of Black church in, 16, 174–77
Stage 1, 173–79
Stage 2, 179–90
Moltmann, J., 168, 169
Moore, J. W., 58
mortality rates, 44, 71
murder rates, 39, 71
myths, debunking, 109

Nation of Islam, 166
National Youth Gang Center (NYGC), 35
neighbor, concept of, 92–93
  See also community
New Orleans, 20, 23, 176–77, 198
New Zealand, 34
nihilism, 39, 197
Nkoma, S., 43, 44
Norway, 34

Office of Juvenile Justice and Delinquency
  Prevention (OJJDP), 35
ontology, 95, 125
oppression, 49, 50, 67, 170–71, 198
organization and language, 94
organization change theory, 140
othering, 24, 146, 189
others, valuing, 115–17

Padilla, Felix, 54, 55, 58, 90–91, 108, 142
paradigm shift, 160, 206
paradigms, prevailing, 158
parents
  bond with child, 45
  effects of loss of child on, 4
  loss of, 5–6
  need for support of community, 5
Paris, 34
past. See history
pastors, African American, 169
  See also church, Black

People, 108
Perkins, I., 176
persistence, 203
picture, complete, 137–38
planning, 169
  See also implementation
policy wheels, 56
political correctness, 19
poor, working, 46
positive, focus on, 112
  See also Appreciative Inquiry
Posner, B. Z., 140
possibilities, 104
post-traumatic stress syndrome, 69
potential, 149
poverty, 22, 23, 46, 68, 199–200
power, organizational, 152
power, personal, 151–52, 159
praxes, challenging, 27
prayer, 15–16, 195
prison, 39
process, double loop, 126
protection, 91–92, 93, 115
psychology, black, 125
purpose, 160–61
Pygmalion Effect, 57

questions, asking, 165
Quinn, Robert, 147, 149

racism
  in academy, 20–21, 205
  effects of, 45
  experience of, 20
  need to intentionally engage, 81
  prevalence of, 22
rage, 131
reality
  construction of, 128, 129
  and language, 94
  perceptions of, 76, 96–97
  understanding, 13–14, 16
reality, anticipatory, 114
reality, apprehended, 82–83
reality, present, 70–71, 72, 109

recreation, wholesome, 37
reform
    resistance to, 36
    See also change
reform, school, 176
religion, African American
    relationship with African American spiri-
        tuality, 165
    See also church, Black
religion *vs.* theology, 12
research
    Eurocentric psychologies in, 59
    focus in, 57
    in media, 58
researcher
    perspective of, 78
    role of, 53–59
respect, 85, 111, 113
rigidity, 171
risk taking, 145–46
role models
    lack of, 42, 47
    need for, 11
    older gang members as, 115
*The Role of Appreciative Inquiry in the Fight to
    Save Our Youth* (Easley), 13, 201
Russia, 34

Sanchez-Jankowski, Martin, 53–56, 58, 90,
        91, 142
scenario planning, 156–58
schools, alternative, 79, 114, 144
search conference methodology, 108–10
security, search for, 71–72
self-concept, 113–15
self-critique, 118–19
self-esteem, 30, 42, 63, 112, 114
self-hate, Black, 169
self-knowledge, 130
self-respect, 149
seminary, 26, 164–65
sexism, prevalence of, 22
sexuality, 170–71
sharing, global, 195
Shaw, C. R., 38

slavery
    and African American leadership, 79
    effects of, 69, 72, 198–99
    similarities with Hurricane Katrina, 198
    surviving, 15–16, 30–31, 68, 166
    women's experience of, 44
social causation, 38
social construction theory, 96, 106
social media, 194–95, 202–3
social service, 26
social work, 26
society, expectations of, 97
Spain, 34
spirit, 135
spirituality
    and change, 26–27
    need for understanding of, 70
    relationship with religion, 165
Srivastva, S., 103
standards, 144
strangers, 91
strategy, 111–12, 154, 160–61, 188
    See also model for change
students, relationship with, 88
subjugation, massive, 200
success
    appreciating, 194–95
    perceptions of, 111
support
    during adolescence, 114
    and change, 112–13
    for children, 62–63
    desire for, 98
    lack of for African American children,
        45, 46
    lack of from community, 134
    need for, 111
    parents' need for, 5
    and self-esteem, 114
Sweden, 34
systems theory, 19, 110

talents, 146–47
Tannenbaum, F., 38
Taylor, E., 79

teachers, 98–99, 144
technology, 143, 155
Terrell, J., 170
theodicy, 170
theologians, African American, 169
   See also church, Black
theology, 164, 170, 172, 177
   loss of grounding in, 70
   loss of power of, 15–16
   need to understand, 180–81
   vs. religion, 12
   See also spirituality
theology, liberation, 24, 168, 172
theology, pastoral, 172
thinking, flexible, 171
thinking, patterns of, 89, 139
Thrasher, Frederic M., 37
Thurman, Howard, 27, 30, 70, 84, 90
travel, 158–59
triads, Asian, 34
Truth, Sojourner, 27
Tubman, Harriet, 27

ultimatums, 17
underemployment, 46
unemployment, 42
United States
   erosion of middle class in, 197
   insularity of, 158
   view of, 49

values
   changing, 82–83
   of gang members, 111
Villaraigosa, Antonio, 35
violence
   in Chicago, 17, 35
   levels of, 1, 5
   and love of self, 169
   need for new ways of addressing, 205–6
   prevalence of, 22
violence, racial, 34
violence, redemptive, 22–23
vision, 148–49, 151
vulnerabilities, reluctance to admit, 133

Weis, Jody, 17, 35, 39
welfare system, 45
West, Cornel, 177
will, power of, 51
women, 22, 43
women, African American
   angry, 27, 132
   experience of slavery, 44
   internalized cognitive dissonance
      in, 43
   issues relative to, 23
   marriage rates of, 44
   need to engage in intentional dialogue,
      132–33
   relationships with men, 44–45
   role of in family structure, 43
   spiritual autobiographies of, 27
   strength of, 45
   struggles of, 132
   subculture of, 43
   in workplace, 43, 44
workforce, 143, 202
workplace, African American women in,
   43, 44
worldviews, formation of, 52–53, 61

youth
   language patterns regarding, 129
   need for analysis of current
      situation, 31
   See also children
youth, at-risk, 84
youth in gangs
   attitude toward gang environments,
      76, 77
   desire for attention, 77
   interventions with (*See* intervention,
      Appreciative Inquiry)
   justification of studying, 75
   lack of success in schools, 83–84
   language patterns of, 84
   perceptions of reality by, 76
   use of Appreciative Inquiry with, 108
   views of self, 113–14
   visions of future, 76–77

ROCHELLE BROCK &
RICHARD GREGGORY JOHNSON III,
Executive Editors

Black Studies and Critical Thinking is an interdisciplinary series which examines the intellectual traditions of and cultural contributions made by people of African descent throughout the world. Whether it is in literature, art, music, science, or academics, these contributions are vast and far-reaching. As we work to stretch the boundaries of knowledge and understanding of issues critical to the Black experience, this series offers a unique opportunity to study the social, economic, and political forces that have shaped the historic experience of Black America, and that continue to determine our future. Black Studies and Critical Thinking is positioned at the forefront of research on the Black experience, and is the source for dynamic, innovative, and creative exploration of the most vital issues facing African Americans. The series invites contributions from all disciplines but is specially suited for cultural studies, anthropology, history, sociology, literature, art, and music.

Subjects of interest include (but are not limited to):

- EDUCATION
- SOCIOLOGY
- HISTORY
- MEDIA/COMMUNICATION
- RELIGION/THEOLOGY
- WOMEN'S STUDIES

- POLICY STUDIES
- ADVERTISING
- AFRICAN AMERICAN STUDIES
- POLITICAL SCIENCE
- LGBT STUDIES

For additional information about this series or for the submission of manuscripts, please contact Dr. Brock (Indiana University Northwest) at brock2@iun.edu or Dr. Johnson (University of San Francisco) at rgjohnsoniii@usfca.edu.

To order other books in this series, please contact our Customer Service Department:

(800) 770-LANG (within the U.S.)
(212) 647-7706 (outside the U.S.)
(212) 647-7707 FAX

Or browse online by series at www.peterlang.com.